P9-AGO-732

Social Causes of
Psychological Distress

SOCIAL INSTITUTIONS
AND SOCIAL CHANGE

An Aldine de Gruyter Series of Texts and Monographs

EDITED BY

Peter H. Rossi
Michael Useem
James D. Wright

Bernard C. Rosen, **The Industrial Connection: Achievement and the Family in Developing Societies**

Paul Diesing, **Science and Ideology in the Policy Sciences**

James D. Wright, Peter H. Rossi, and Kathleen Daly, **Under the Gun: Weapons, Crime, and Violence in America**

Walter L. Wallace, **Principles of Scientific Sociology**

Robert C. Liebman and Robert Wuthnow (eds.), **The New Christian Right: Mobilization and Legitimation**

Paula S. England and George Farkas, **Households, Employment, and Gender: A Social, Economic, and Demographic View**

Richard F. Hamilton and James D. Wright, **The State of the Masses**

James R. Kluegel and Eliot R. Smith, **Beliefs About Inequality: Americans' Views of What Is and What Ought to Be**

James D. Wright and Peter H. Rossi, **Armed and Considered Dangerous: A Survey of Felons and Their Firearms**

Roberta G. Simmons and Dale A. Blyth, **Moving into Adolescence: The Impact of Pubertal Change and School Context**

Carolyn C. Perrucci, Robert Perrucci, Dena B. Targ, and Harry R. Targ, **Plant Closings: International Context and Social Costs**

Robert Perrucci and Harry R. Potter (eds.), **Networks of Power: Organizational Actors at the National, Corporate, and Community Levels**

David Popenoe, **Disturbing the Nest: Family Change and Decline in Modern Societies**

John Mirowsky and Catherine E. Ross, **Social Causes of Psychological Distress**

James D. Wright, **Address Unknown: The Homeless in America.**

George Farkas, Robert Grobe, and Daniel Sheehan, **Human Capital or Cultural Capital? Gender, Ethnicity, Poverty, and Success in School**

Paula England, **Comparable Worth**

Alice S. Rossi and Peter H. Rossi, **Of Human Bonding: Parent–Child Relations Across the Life Course**

G. William Domhoff, **The Power Elite and the State**

Social Causes of
Psychological Distress

John Mirowsky

Catherine E. Ross

Aldine de Gruyter
New York

About the Authors

John Mirowsky is Associate Professor of Sociology, University of Illinois at Urbana-Champaign. A major contributor to professional journals, Dr. Mirowsky was the recipient of the 1985 Reuben Hill Award of the National Council on Family Relations. He is currently studying the effects of optimism vs. realism and personal control and interpersonal support on distress.

Catherine E. Ross is Associate Professor of Sociology, University of Illinois at Urbana-Champaign. Dr. Ross has published extensively in numerous journals and is currently studying the interplay of job conditions, parental responsibilities, and marital arrangements for women and their effect on mental health.

Copyright © 1989 by Aldine de Gruyter

ALDINE DE GRUYTER
A Division of Walter de Gruyter, Inc.
200 Saw Mill River Road
Hawthorne, New York 10532

Library of Congress Cataloging-in-Publication Data
Mirowsky, John, 1949-
    Social causes of psychological distress / John Mirowsky and
Catherine E. Ross.
        p. cm. — (Social institutions and social change)
    Includes bibliographies and index.
    ISBN 0-202-30354-3. — ISBN 0-202-30355-1 (pbk.)
    1. Affective disorders—Social aspects. 2. Stress (Psychology)
3. Social psychology. I. Ross, Catherine E., 1953- . II. Title.
III. Series.
    [DNLM: 1. Social Environment. 2. Socioeconomic Factors.
3. Stress, Psychological—etiology. WM 172 M676s]
RC537.M56 1989
155.9'2—dc20
DNLM/DLC
for Library of Congress   89-6703
                                                                CIP

Printed in the United States of America
10 9 8 7 6 5 4 3 2 1

Contents

V. Conclusion

Chapter Nine: Why Some People Are More Distressed Than Others

Appendix: Description of Data Sets and Measures

Acknowledgments

We thank the people who gave us access to their data over the years, especially Joan Huber, Richard Hough and Dianne Timbers, and William Cockerham and Guenther Lueschen. All these people, their data sets, and funding agencies are described in the Appendix to this book. We thank the Research Board of the University of Illinois at Urbana-Champaign for supporting our data collection. We thank all the people who read and commented on various drafts of this book, especially James Kluegel, Alan Ross, and Collin Vanuchelen.

Our book is dedicated to the people who started us thinking.

I

Introduction

CHAPTER ONE

Introduction

Understanding the Connections between Social and Personal Problems

Why are some people more distressed than others?

Imagine a man who left his inner city high school at the first opportunity, without a degree and without basic skills; who spent years unemployed or underemployed; who finally got a factory job that he managed to hold onto long enough to make a down payment on a house and to start a family; who was among the first laid off when the product his factory produced could not compete with similar items made where labor costs are lower; and whose unemployment compensation has run out.

Imagine a woman who married young because she was pregnant; who had two more unplanned children in quick succession; who took a boring and unpleasant job at minimum wage because her husband could not support the family; whose husband says she trapped him into marriage, is embarrassed that she has a job, and gives her little help with the children and housework; who cannot always find someone to look after the children, cannot afford day care, and cannot afford to miss work; whose boss gave her a bad report for being absent or late too often; and who has just learned that she is pregnant again.

The despair these people feel is deeply personal. Their problems are deeply social (Mills, 1959). More than that, it is the despair that identifies the social facts as social problems.

One of the core areas addressed by sociology is the study of social stratification—of inequalities in income, power, and prestige. We would not be as interested in these inequalities if the poor, powerless, and despised were as happy and fulfilled as the wealthy, powerful, and admired. Sociology springs from humanistic empathy and concern as much as from scholarly and scientific curiosity. The observation that blacks are disproportionately poor leads to an investigation of the racial differences in education, employment, and occupation that account for this circumstance. A table comparing the additional income blacks and whites can expect for each additional year of education is as intrinsically interesting as any dinosaur bone or photograph of Saturn. But something more than scientific curiosity underscores our interest in the table. We understand that racial differences in status and income are a problem in the human as well as in the academic sense. It is the inequality in misery that makes the other inequality meaningful.

The traditional division of academic turfs can mask the connection between personal and social problems (Pearlin and Lieberman, 1979). Researchers who study personal problems often speculate on how these problems arise from the social milieu. Those who study the structure of society and its institutions often guess about their effects on the subjective quality of life. Speculation and guessing have their hazards. The researcher who considers a particular social condition distressing may be projecting values, preferences, and emotional responses not shared by people in the situation. An error of this sort is unacceptable in social science.

The cautious sociologist often concentrates on a social condition and leaves its emotional consequences unmentioned, which creates a reassuring appearance of objectivity. Speak of status mobility, but do not mention the bitterness of failure or the pride of success. Speak of marital status, but do not mention the comforts of marriage or the loneliness and hardship of divorce. Speak of employment status, but do not mention the reassurance of a regular paycheck or the worries and doubts caused by unemployment. This avoids the appearance of attributing one's own feelings to others.

Critics of "value-free" social science say that researchers cannot help projecting their own values, beliefs, and feelings. The demographer who studies divorce rates knows that becoming divorced is usually a disturbing transition and that being divorced is often a lonely and impoverished state. Though the researcher may compile figures that represent the currents of marital dissolution without prejudice or bias, the very choice of divorce as an object of study is value laden. Some critics go so far as to argue that we should drop all pretense of value-free social science and be unabashed advocates of openly declared causes.

The trouble with advocacy is that it begins with the choice of a conclusion for which suitable arguments and facts are then selected or created. Advocates believe that debate and struggle result in a natural selection of the truest and most correct arguments and facts, which is akin to the medieval lord's belief that victory in battle proves the legitimacy of one's cause. The arguments and facts that evolve from the debate and struggle of advocates may simply appeal to the prejudices and self-interests of the greatest number, or they may simply represent the prejudices and self-interests of the wealthy or powerful—those who can control advocates. Whatever the role of advocacy in politics, its value in scholarship is limited—a temporary stance for the development of hypotheses. Advocacy provides possibilities, not answers.

There are two ways that social scientists avoid advocacy. The first is to resist projecting personal beliefs, values, and responses as much as possible, while recognizing that the attempt is never fully successful. Social science can be relatively, if not absolutely, value free. The value-free social scientist looks at society in ways that do not demand moral agreement. Two demographers can calculate the same divorce rate, although one sees it as a measure of human tragedy and the other as a measure of human freedom.

The second way social scientists avoid advocacy is by making the values of the subjects the values expressed in the research. Typically, this takes the form of opinion or attitude surveys. Respondents are asked to rate the seriousness of crimes, the appropriateness of a specific punishment for a given crime, the prestige of occupations, the fair rate of pay for a particular job, or the largest amount of money a family can earn and not be poor. The aggregate judgments, and variations in judgments, represent the values of the subjects and not those of the researcher. They are objective facts with causes and consequences of interest in their own right. In addition, they provide "objective" definitions of value-laden terms such as "serious," "fair," and "poor." They are objective in the sense that they are not mere reflections of the researcher's own feelings.

The two approaches are useful, but have their limitations. The demographers can calculate divorce rates without deciding whether the rates indicate suffering or release from suffering. Ultimately, though, if the divorce rate is increasing, people may want to know which of the two it is. The survey researcher can ask the public's opinion, but does the public really know? Respondents might simply project cultural stereotypes. And what if judgments differ among the happily married, unhappily married, never married, currently divorced, and divorced but remarried? Whose opinion carries the greatest weight?

There is a way to evaluate the subjective quality of social conditions without imposing the judgments of either the researcher or public—explicitly and objectively measure feelings such as fear, anxiety, frustration, anger, guilt, despair, depression, demoralization, joy, fulfillment, and hope, then map the relationship of these feelings to social conditions and positions. For instance, we might find that women with jobs outside the home are happier than housewives. If so, it is *not* our opinion. It is *not* public opinion. It is a social fact. This is the alternative we have chosen.

The inequality of misery is the most fundamental inequality. The founders of the United States recognized this in the first sentence of the Declaration of Independence, which says that the pursuit of happiness is an unalienable and self-evident right. When sociologists and economists study the unequal acquisition and accumulation of valuables, they study the pursuit of happiness. The subjective quality of life is the ultimate valuable. Goods, services, wealth, and prestige are the means or markers of acquired value, but not the value itself. As means, they may or may not be effective. As markers, they may or may not coincide with happiness. The correspondence is a matter for study. Our study of unequal distress has three primary aspects.

Distress as a Sign of Social Problems

The misery, demoralization, or distress a person feels are not the problem. They are consequences of the problem. Misery is not only real, it is realistic. Suffering contains a message about the causes of the suffering; a message that can be read, understood, and acted upon. We are not looking for a drug to suppress the misery. While such drugs have humane uses, they are palliative. A drug that suppresses anguish does not remove its cause. We are not attempting to find a way to talk people into believing things are better than they seem. An illusion cannot dispel a distressing reality; it just makes the reality more perplexing. We are looking for information on how people feel under various circumstances. The information can be used to make informed decisions about personal and communal lives. If you would rather not be distressed, and would rather that others are not distressed, then you may find the information useful.

Gradations in Distress

Distress has many forms, suffered more or less. Situations are not good or bad, they are better or worse. We do not see our task as dividing people into two categories: happy and fulfilled, or miserable and distressed. We certainly do not see our task as dividing people into the categories sane and insane, or well and ill. Insanity and mental illness are largely categorical names for the clipped, extreme tail of a distribution, like the words tall, fat, or smart. We see no great divide, no natural boundary, between common and uncommon misery, but look at all the shades and tones of distress.

"Ordinary" People in the Community

There are many kinds of "ordinary" people. Social scientists often speak of them as a composite—the mythical "average person," who is 55% female, 70% married, has 1.7 children, 12.5 years of education, and so on. The composite flattens a range and variety of experiences and situations into a single profile. When the various types of ordinary people are compared, the dimensions and textures of social reality become visible. The lives of ordinary people in the community constitute a huge natural experiment beyond anything that could or would be produced in a laboratory. The contingencies and exigencies of life differentially frustrate, strain, challenge, and empower. The inequality of misery is a fact of everyday life, produced by unequal resources, opportunities, limitations, and demands. In this study, we compare the rich, middle class, and poor; those with good jobs, bad jobs, and no jobs; men and women; the young, middle-aged, and old; the single, married, divorced, and widowed; blacks and whites; Hispanics and Anglos; Catholics, Protestants, Jews, and the nonreligious; school dropouts, graduates, and postgraduates. Practically and ethically, no laboratory can affect the personality, mind, and emotions with the force and power of everyday life. To the extent that society is a creation of human action, it is an experiment in the causes of misery and happiness. We observe and report the outcomes of that experiment—the lives and fortunes of ordinary people.

A Preview

Social Causes of Psychological Distress is, first and foremost, a statement of our view and our understanding. Much of what we see and understand comes from the work of other scholars, including sociologists, demographers, psychologists, epidemiologists, psychiatrists, and social workers. Throughout the book we strive to give credit where it is due and to describe accurately the ideas and findings attributed to the work of others. However, this volume is not a summary of the field. We look to the findings of others to answer our questions, and to the ideas of others to stimulate and discipline our own. Our colleagues gave us a lot of good material to work with. We cut and assembled that material into our own construction—our representation of the social causes of distress.

Our book summarizes, synthesizes, and elaborates our observations and thoughts from a decade of research. It also presents many new results.

This volume is divided into five major parts. Part I is this introduction in which we sketch our view and outline subsequent chapters.

In Part II, "Researching the Causes of Distress: Sociology Compared to Psychiatry and Psychology" (Chapters 2 and 3), we describe how sociologists study psychological distress. The sociologist's approach to studying the causes of psychological distress differs from that of the psychiatrist or psychologist. Part II highlights two distinctive elements of the sociological approach: looking for gradations in distress rather than diagnosing mental illness, and interviewing people in the community rather than experimenting in laboratories.

In Chapter 2, "Measuring Psychological Distress", we describe psychological distress and the ways of assessing its gradations. By psychological distress we mean the unpleasant subjective states of depression and anxiety, which have both emotional and physiological manifestations. We call the emotional component mood, and the physiological component malaise. We contrast the diagnostic approach of psychiatry with our own approach. The diagnostic approach assumes that psychological problems are the manifestations of discrete disease entities that invade and disturb the human organism. We believe the entities are mythical—a linguistic throwback to the eighteenth and nineteenth century science of infectious diseases.

In the last part of Chapter 2, we evaluate three distinct hypotheses concerning relationships among types of psychological symptoms. The galaxy hypothesis says that symptoms of the same type (e.g., depression) generally appear together and symptoms of different types (e.g., depression versus schizophrenia) generally do not. The nebula hypothesis says that all psychological symptoms tend to appear together, in an amorphous sea. The spectrum hypothesis says that symptoms of a similar type go together more than symptoms of different types, but one shades into another (e.g. anxiety to depression to paranoia to schizophrenia). A map of the correlations among

91 symptoms in a community sample shows a spectrum of symptoms with an overall pattern like a color wheel. It shows no evidence for discrete diagnostic entities, or for an undifferentiated mass of symptoms.

Chapter 3 is called "Real-World Causes of Real-World Misery." It contrasts our population-based survey method with the experimental method of psychology, and begins with a discussion of the ways in which cause is established in the human sciences. There are three formal criteria for establishing cause: (1) association—two things go together more than expected by chance; (2) nonspuriousness—the reason they go together is not just because they happen to result from the same prior condition; and (3) causal order—one of the things cannot be the cause of the other, so it must be the consequence.

Survey researchers talk to large numbers of people in the community who are representative of the larger population. We discuss the way survey research meets the three criteria of cause, using as an example the idea that low income causes depression. Because the most difficult criterion to establish is the direction of the cause, we discuss causal order in detail. Practically, population researchers such as sociologists look to six kinds of information to judge causal order: (1) the things that do not change, (2) common sequences, (3) the things that rarely change, (4) common knowledge, (5) follow-up, or longitudinal, data, and (6) patterns and their explanations. Because explaining patterns is the heart of causal analysis, we discuss the sixth type of information in the greatest detail, contrasting the "social selection" versus "social causation" views on the association between low income and depression.

Next we talk about experimental studies of distress. The essence of an experiment is that a researcher manipulates an hypothesized cause and randomly assigns subjects to different levels of exposure to this cause. We discuss the practical, inherent, and philosophical limitations of experiments. Practical limitations include stable traits that cannot be manipulated, weak manipulation, trivial manipulation, analog manipulation, and unrepresentative subjects. Although the practical limitations of experiments can be reduced, the inherent limitations cannot. The core inherent limitation is that the laboratory is not the world. As a consequence, experiments cannot show patterns of distress in the real world; they cannot show causal direction in the real world; and they cannot explain why observed patterns of distress exist. The philosophical limitation of experiments is that they treat subjects as objects.

Despite practical, inherent, and philosophical limitations, the prestige of randomized, controlled trials is so great in the scientific community that many social psychologists are loath to give them up. In the next section of Chapter 3, we describe four ploys that preserve the *appearance* of a randomized, controlled trial while skirting the substance. A genuine experiment on the causes of distress manipulates personalities, world views, or social characteristics in a way calculated to make some subjects more distressed than others. But a researcher cannot produce a personality, world view, or social characteristic in a 1- or 2-hour laboratory session that is more salient than those the subject came in with. Instead, psychologists studying distress conduct various ersatz experiments. We call these substitute experiments, pseudo-experiments, para-experiments, and experiments in imagination. On close examination, most experiments on the causes of depression are simply cross-sectional surveys of small and grossly unrepresentative samples.

In Part III, (chapters 4 and 5) we describe the "Social Patterns of Distress." Even the most elementary information about social patterns is remarkably recent. The earliest community surveys were published in the early 1960's (Gurin, Veroff, and Feld, 1960; Srole *et al.*, 1962; Leighton *et al.*, 1963). These and subsequent studies published by the early 1970's (Dohrenwend and Dohrenwend, 1969; Myers, Lindenthal, and Pepper, 1971; Warheit, Holzer, and Schwab, 1973) discovered and confirmed four basic social patterns. Chapter 4 outlines and discusses these "established patterns": (1) women are more distressed than men; (2) married people are less distressed than the unmarried; (3) undesirable life events are associated with distress; and (4) higher income, education, and occupational prestige are associated with less distress. Most of the research, well into the late 1970's, attempted to confirm patterns, specify them precisely, rule out spuriousness, and discover whether the associations represented social cause or social selection. The four established patterns revealed likely social causes of distress. They also explained other patterns. In particular, blacks are more distressed than whites largely because of lower income and education, worse jobs, poorer neighborhoods, greater unemployment, and the like.

The established patterns are common knowledge to sociologists now, but were far from known in 1960. Cultural myths and human variety often cloud the facts. Many people in the general public and in the social and behavioral sciences believed that men who face competition, uncertainty, responsibility, and noxious environments on the job are more distressed than housewives in the relatively protected environment of the home. Many believed that single people with few responsibilities or restrictions are less distressed than married people constrained by family ties and responsibilities. Many believed that the executive or employer scrambling to make deadlines, meet payrolls, and negotiate conflicting demands is more distressed than the employee who simply has to punch a clock and do as he is told. All these beliefs proved untrue. Research establishing the basic social patterns dispelled these myths and pointed to the possibility of other myths and false beliefs.

Chapter 5, "New Patterns: Questioning Cultural Myths," discusses our new research that goes beyond the established patterns, testing the validity of four widely held beliefs:

Most parents love their children, and see them as one of the great joys and blessings of life. Because of this, many people believe that children increase parents' sense of well-being. On the contrary, surveys show that people with children are more distressed than those without. This is because parents sometimes find it difficult to support and care for their children. Love may make the burden seem worth carrying; it does not make the burden lighter.

Many people believe that religion provides succor and peace of mind. In fact, religious belief may soothe some, but no more than the absence of belief soothes others. Distress is as low among nonbelievers as among those with strong religious beliefs. It is the people in between—the weakly religious rather than the nonreligious—who are most distressed. Perhaps religion generates guilt in order to encourage conformity. Such guilt could be assuaged by conformity or avoided by nonbelief, leaving the weakly religious most distressed.

In our time and place, we celebrate the trim body as a cultural ideal. Words such as fat, plump, and chubby carry pejorative connotations. If people judge themselves as they believe others judge them, then we would expect overweight people to view themselves critically. One would think distress would increase with the amount a person is overweight, particularly a woman, since women are expected to be attractive (i.e., thin). Our survey results do not confirm this expectation. There is no detectable association between overweight and distress. It makes no difference whether the people are women rather than men, young rather than middle-aged, or single rather than married. Maybe the social onus is overstated. Maybe people do not judge themselves as they believe others judge them. Dieting is distressing, being overweight is not.

Ours is a youth-oriented culture. We think youth is the best time of life, and the years of young adulthood may be recalled as a time of hope and joy. In any generation, young adulthood is seen as a time of boundless prospect and vigor. It's all downhill from there . . . or so we thought. Our survey results show that depression and anxiety are high among young adults. Anxiety decreases progressively in subsequent age groups. Depression decreases up to the 45-year-old group, stays low until age 55, then increases progressively in groups aged 60 and beyond. This pattern has been stable for at least a decade, suggesting that it reflects the life cycle in our society, and not the different historical events experienced by people currently of different ages.

With the basic social patterns established and new ones emerging as various cultural beliefs are tested, the purpose of research shifts to "Explaining the Patterns," which is the subject of Part IV (chapters 6, 7, and 8). If the observed patterns are not imaginary, then why do they exist? Establishing the facts is a great step forward, but it is only the first step. We need to advance understanding beyond the raw observation and confirmation of patterns. We want to know why gender, marital status, events, and socioeconomic status influence distress, and especially if there is a common thread connecting these and other social causes of distress. If possible we want to interpret the set of observed patterns with a smaller set of underlying explanations.

There are two steps needed in arriving at explanations for the social patterns of distress. The first is generative: thinking of the possibilities and testing whether there is support for them. The second is selective: pitting one explanation against another and seeing which explains more. Current research is somewhere in the middle of this process. As it stands, the established and new patterns have sparked at least eight distinct explanations. Ideally, we would like to reduce that to one. "Explaining the Patterns" describes each, and the reason it might be the explanation for the social patterns of distress.

Not long after the results of the first community surveys were published, one explanation became rapidly and widely accepted. That is that life change, positive or negative, causes distress (Holmes and Rahle, 1967). The popularity of this explanation was phenomenal, despite weak supporting evidence. Only after a decade or more of accumulating counterevidence was this explanation put to rest in scientific circles. No doubt there are many in the general public who still believe this scientific myth.

Chapter 6 is about "Life Change." Life events initiate major changes in a person's daily life. They include transitions such as the death of a spouse, birth of a child, move to a new home, loss of a job, marriage, graduation, and so on. These events do not occur often in any one person's life, but are likely to occur within a lifetime and are common in the community as a whole.

Two physicians, Holmes and Rahe, had subjects rate the amount of readjustment demanded by each of 43 events (Holmes and Rahe, 1967). They found that subsequent physical illness increased with the sum readjustment weight of a person's events in the previous year (Holmes and Masuda, 1974). Not long after these results were published, popular magazines began featuring do-it-yourself checklists for assessing one's own Social Readjustment Units (SRUs). If you experienced a lot of changes last year, magazines warned, you might need help to deal with the resultant stress.

Despite impressive rationales based on endocrinology and biological equilibrium, there was never much evidence that life change per se is distressing. The early studies failed to distinguish between desirable and undesirable changes. Later research by us and others found that only the undesirable changes are associated with distress (Ross and Mirowsky, 1979; Vinokur and Selzer, 1975). Weighting events by their SRU is superfluous. Counting the number of undesirable events is sufficient. No matter how you add them up, though, life change events do not explain the basic social patterns of distress. For instance, only a small part of the effect of socioeconomic status is a result of differences in the rates of undesirable events in the lives of those of different status. Also, there is little difference between men and women or the married and unmarried in their rates of undesirable life events.

It is not change itself, or even undesirable change, that is most important. There are two critical factors that largely determine the psychological impact of life events: (1) the conditions that produce the events or follow from them (Gersten *et al.*, 1974); and (2) an active and instrumental response to the events, rather than a passive and fatalistic one (Wheaton, 1980, 1983; Pearlin *et al.*, 1981). These, more than the events themselves, account for the social patterns of distress.

Chapter 7, "Alienation," discusses five factors that in our view represent important explanations for social patterns of distress, displacing life change as the explanation. In social psychology, alienation is a rift in social identity. It is a tear in the normally seamless connection between the individual and society. There are five basic types of alienation: powerlessness, self-estrangement, isolation, meaninglessness, and normlessness (Seeman, 1959, 1983). Speculation about the emotional impact of alienation leads social scientists to predict five corresponding social-psychological requirements for well-being: control, commitment, support, meaning, and normality. Each type of subjective alienation arises from a corresponding objective condition.

Powerlessness, self-estrangement, and the other subjective forms of alienation are not "just in your mind." They are realistic perceptions of objective social conditions. They are the link between social conditions and emotional well-being or distress.

Objective powerlessness is a condition in which the individual is unable to achieve desired goals. It leads to subjective powerlessness, the sense that important outcomes are beyond one's control—the consequences of chance, fate, or powerful others. It is important for people to feel that they are in control of their own lives, to a large extent, because a sense of control bolsters the will to think about problems and do something about them. A person who feels powerless sees little reason to think about the causes of problems and their possible solutions and little reason to try to solve the problems. The tragedy of a sense of powerlessness is that it is destructive even when it is largely justified. If most of the bad things that happen to a person are unavoidable and genuinely beyond the individual's control, that person may develop a general sense of powerlessness. Consequently he will not see that many other problems can be avoided or solved and thus will not take effective action against these problems. A firm sense of personal control makes a person attentive, active, and (ultimately) more effective. Beyond that, it promotes a self-assurance that directly counteracts demoralization and distress.

Alienated labor is a condition in which a worker does not decide what to produce, does not design the production process, and does not own the product. Self-estrangement is a corresponding sense of being separate from that part of one's thoughts, actions, and experiences being controlled by others. Work is drudgery. It has no intrinsic value. There is no pride in it. Rewards lie outside the activity itself. At best one is compensated. At worst, one is forced by circumstances to submit. Work is unalienated if the person participates in decisions, controls the work process, and feels the work is a part of him or herself. Unalienated labor is typified by participation in churches, political parties, civic or charitable organizations, clubs, and hobbies. Because these activities are voluntary and unpaid, they are necessarily expressive of the self rather than estranged from it. Commitment to one's activities implies an identification that gives purpose and meaning to one's life. One's actions express rather than subjugate one's self. Freedom of action is a principal value, inherent in the human organism (Rotter, 1966). The frustration of this freedom is distressing.

Isolation is a condition of detachment from networks of communication, obligation, and liking. Social integration is the opposite condition, indicated by the density of a person's social network, the number of relationships, and the frequency of contact. Social support is the corresponding sense of being someone important in the eyes of others, being cared for and loved, being esteemed and valued as a person, and of having someone who will listen, understand, and help when needed. Social integration is necessary, but not sufficient, for a sense of social support, which reduces distress by increasing a sense of security. This is clearly an important component of well-being. However, there are many indications that integration and mutual obligation can be excessive and overly restrictive, limiting personal freedom and thus counteracting the desirable aspects of social support.

Disorganization is a condition in which there are no guidelines for action and evaluation or in which there are a welter of inconsistent guidelines. Meaninglessness is the corresponding sense that the world is unintelligible, and that life is without purpose. A sense of meaningful existence seems important to well-being for two reasons. A world that cannot be understood cannot be controlled. In a chaotic world, all outcomes are determined by chance. Beyond the issue of control, people usually require a sense of purpose, significance, and value in their lives. A meaningful life, like a grammatical sentence, a delightful song, a stirring speech, or a beautiful sight, conforms satisfyingly to standards even if they are unarticulated. If the standards are in disarray, or if the world seldom conforms, a person might feel a vague and general dissatisfaction, with consequent distress.

Structural inconsistency, role stress, and a disordered life cycle make it difficult or impossible to meet normal expectations. Structural inconsistency is a condition in which standard goals are reinforced but access to effective, legitimate means is restricted. Role stress is a disjunction or inconsistency in the system of roles, so that normal obligations cannot be met. A disordered life cycle is one in which the usual sequence of major transitions is disrupted or contravened.

Structural inconsistency produces normlessness, defined as the belief that socially unapproved behaviors are required to achieve one's goals (Seeman, 1959). Lack of faith in community standards often leads normless individuals to displace the pursuit of prestige and respect with the pursuit of elementary pleasures. The normless individual falls back on intrinsic gratification and pragmatic efficiency as guides that do not require faith in others. Other people exist to be manipulated, cheated, robbed, or used. They provide gratification, but not comfort. Because of the need to disguise actions and purposes, and protect against preemption and retaliation, normlessness results in mistrust, paranoia, and anxiety.

Role stress produces role strain, which is the frustrating sense of not being able to understand or meet the normal expectations of one's roles. There are three types of role stress: (1) Role conflict exists when two legitimate roles produce incompatible or mutually exclusive demands. (2) Role ambiguity exists when it is not clear what is expected. (3) Role overload exists when role demands overwhelm the resources and capabilities of the individual. Most people, most often, want to meet their obligations as spouses, parents, children, friends, citizens, employees, co-workers, and members of a given group. The inability to do so produces frustration and guilt, with consequent distress. The plight of employed women with children is an outstanding example of role stress in contemporary American society. Although the current reality is that most adult women hold jobs outside the home, relatively few couples have fully adjusted their marital and family lives to this circumstance. Women still have primary responsibility for work around the house and for child care. While employment is emotionally beneficial for women on average, the average conceals a large minority of employed women who have children, who get little or no help with child care from their partners, and who find it very difficult to arrange day care. These women are extremely distressed.

A disordered life cycle is a condition similar to role stress in its nature and effects. Each society tends to have a normal sequence of roles, statuses, and transitions over the lifetime. Transitions that happen out of their usual sequence create moral and practical dilemmas. Getting married is normal after graduation, but a problem if done while the couple is in high school. Getting pregnant is normal after marriage, but a problem before. Losing one's parents is normal by age sixty, but a problem at age six. The more common a given sequence of events and transitions, the greater the cultural, social, and personal preparation for it, and the less distress it engenders.

Although life change and alienation are the most commonly offered explanations of the social patterns of distress, there are two other contenders. Both have long histories as ideas and issues in the humanities and social sciences. They are "Authoritarianism and Inequity," discussed in Chapter 8.

Authoritarianism has two components most relevant to distress: inflexibility and mistrust. Authoritarianism is a complex world view that grows from situations that limit horizons and opportunities and that demand conformity and obedience. Insular personal networks and a lack of exposure to the views of other cultures, historical periods, and sectors of society create a sense that the familiar, traditional order has a universal and unique validity that transcends time, place, and situation. Tradition and authority are seen as compelling guides to behavior. Compliance with the dictates of tradition and authority are considered ethical and effective.

Inflexibility in dealing with practical and personal problems is one consequence of the authoritarian world view. Each problem is seen as having a single solution, which is known intuitively by the individual or by authorities. Inflexibility produces distress in two ways. It limits the person's ability to solve practical problems because it places severe limitations on the range of possible solutions and the means of evaluating solutions. To the authoritarian, if things are done the proper way, ineffectiveness and undesirable consequences are irrelevant, or a sign of evil forces contradicting and undermining proper order. Inflexibility also limits the person's ability to solve interpersonal problems. If there is really only one right way, available through intuition, then any contradictory desire, belief, or action of another is necessarily invalid and malicious. Any difference evokes moral outrage and righteous indignation. Such responses make negotiation nearly impossible. In an authoritarian world, there is no incentive to understand and express individual desires and beliefs, much less to adapt oneself to the individual desires and beliefs of others.

Mistrust is another distressing consequence of the authoritarian world view. It can result from the authoritarian premise that for one person to have more, another person must have less. To some extent, this view is a holdover from land-based peasant economies. Land is more-or-less fixed in quantity. If land is the basic measure of wealth, then one person's wealth increases only at the expense of another's. The "zero-sum" view has intrinsic appeal if technology and productivity stagnate. If community wealth is not visibly increasing, then one person's wealth will seemingly necessitate another's poverty. If there is an inherent scarcity of wealth, power, and prestige, then people must be constantly alert to the threat of exploitation and victimization. Under the circumstances, many consider it rational to exploit and victimize others, believing it is a matter of "eat or be eaten." The consequent fear and guilt are distressing in themselves. By blocking coalition, cooperation, and negotiation, the atmosphere of mistrust also increases distress by reducing effectiveness.

Ideas about inequity go back to Aristotle. Human beings have a sense of right and wrong. Injustice and unfairness arouse frustration and anger in the victim and sympathizers and apprehension and guilt in the exploiter. While other theories predict that the victims of an unfair relationship are distressed by it, equity theory is distinct in predicting that the exploiters are also distressed. People have a conscience—a built-in mechanism for self-punishment. People can choose to be unscrupulous, but at an emotional price. Furthermore, even an exploiter devoid of guilt must fear retaliation and retribution from the victim and sympathizers. It is also possible that exploitative relationships are less productive than cooperative ones. Victims often resist and frustrate the will of exploiters. The exploiter may have more control than the victim, but still less than could be had through cooperation. Equity theorists generally argue that exploiters are less distressed than victims but more distressed than people who are neither victim nor exploiter.

Part V (chapter 9) is the "Conclusion." Chapter 9 is called, "Why Some People Are More Distressed than Others." Of all the things that might explain the social pattern of distress, a sense of control over one's own life stands out as a critical link. The patterns of distress reflect the patterns of autonomy, opportunity, and achievement in America. The realities of socio-economic status—amount of education, type of employment or lack of it, family income—have a profound influence on a person's sense of control. Minority status is associated with a reduced sense of control partly because of lower levels of education, income, and employment, and partly because for members of minority groups, any given level of achievement requires greater effort and provides fewer opportunities. Undesirable events also decrease a sense of control because they imply powerlessness to avoid them. Old age is associated with low control. As resources, networks, and social power decrease, so does the sense of control and well-being.

The barriers of class and status, the misfortunes of life, and the losses of old age are impersonal oppressors. The personal worlds of family and faith hold out the hope of an alternative source of power. That hope can be realized, but it can also be undermined. Marriage increases the sense of control for both men and women by increasing the average household income and by creating a partnership of mutual effort. However, marriage increases control more for men. For some women, marriage increases subordination and dependency, which can counteract its positive effects on their sense of control. Like marriage, religion's effect on control depends on specifics. Religion can increase control by providing purpose, direction, and the strength to solve problems. But religion can pressure the individual to conform, to submit his or her will to the communal will, and to substitute prayer for active problem solving.

As stated earlier, knowing the facts helps one to understand the social causes of distress, and explaining the facts helps more. Explaining the facts succinctly helps the most. In the business of explanation, less is more. Powerlessness, self-estrangement, isolation, meaninglessness, normlessness, inflexibility, mistrust, and inequity each explain at least a part of what we know about distress. Each concept has a body of theory and research. Each is a plausible factor in the social patterns of distress. Each captures some of the truth, but we see one explanation that contains the others. We see a single thread that connects all the explanations—control.

The sense of control is implied by all the other explanations. The occurrence of undesirable events implies powerlessness to deter them. Self-estrangement is the enslavement felt when labor is alienated. Isolation leaves a person without allies and supporters. Meaninglessness implies a chaotic world beyond control. Normlessness and role stress arise when standard approaches and understandings are taxed beyond their limits. Inflexibility reduces the ability to solve problems and negotiate solutions. Mistrust undermines the ability to cooperate and achieve mutual goals. The victims of inequity suffer a situation not of their preference and choosing. The exploiters mistake power over others for the power to achieve ends. Every other explanation refers, directly or indirectly, to the individual's sense of control. Self-estrangement, isolation, meaninglessness, normlessness and role stress, inflexibility, mistrust, victimization, and perhaps even exploitation, undermine the sense of being master of one's own fate—the main force that shapes one's own life.

Control improves well-being, but there are limits to its psychological benefit. Autonomy—the ability to control one's own life—is crucial to psychological well-being; but authority—the ability to control the lives of others—is not. Control over another in marriage implies inequity. Control over others at work often implies conflict and frustration. Supportive relationships are based on the ability to negotiate and compromise, not to get one's way in opposition to others. Inequity, conflict, and lack of support are distressing. Emotionally beneficial power is the ability to achieve goals, not the ability to win conflicts. We discuss the limits of control as an important focus of future research.

The second part of Chapter 9 asks, "Social Causes of Psychological Distress: How Important Are They?" First, how much of all distress is attributable to social factors? Second, how serious is the distress that is socially patterned? To address the first question we look at the collective impact of seven social factors on depression. These are: family income, education, minority status, gender, age, the sense of personal control, and the sense of social support. We divide symptoms of depression into two parts: base and excess. The base represents the symptoms we would find if all segments of society had the same level of symptoms as the best ten percent, defined in terms of the seven social traits. Of all the symptoms reported, 48.6% are base, and 51.4% are excess. At least half of all the symptoms of depression are attributable to social factors. In the bottom ten percent of society, 72% of all symptoms are excess above the base—symptoms the people would not have if they were in the most advantaged ten percent of society.

Social factors account for a great deal of distress, but do they account for severe psychological distress? To address this second question, we defined extreme distress as a level of symptoms greater than that evidenced by 95% of the population. Approximately 61% of these people would qualify for a psychiatric diagnosis (Boyd et al., 1982). If we split society into two halves soioeconomically, better and worse, the worse half of society has 83.8% of all severe distress. The advantaged half has only 16.2%. Stated another way, the odds of being severely distressed are 5.9 times greater in the worse half than in the better half.

Next we look at genetics and biochemistry as alternative explanations of distress. The current popularity of genetic and biochemical explanations of distress comes from recent advances in genetic theory and psychopharmacology. Despite the impressive bodies of research in these areas, neither genetic nor biochemical factors have been shown to account for any substantial part of the differences in levels of distress found in our society. In particular, there is no evidence that the social patterns of distress reflect genetic or biochemical abnormalities.

Finally we ask, "What Can Be Done to Prevent Distress?" We summarize our views on preventing psychological distress under three main headings: (1) Education: the headwaters of well-being; (2) a good job: providing an adequate income, a measure of autonomy, and a minimum of strain between the demands of work and family; and (3) a supportive relationship: fair and caring.

We are social. We think. We feel. These things come from the organism. The basic link between powerlessness and distress may come from the organism. But the man out of work, the employed woman wondering if her children are all right, the black facing discrimination, the divorcee alone and uncertain, the old person losing everything, the young family struggling to make ends meet—their distress comes from the world we have created for each other and for ourselves. It comes from society. These are the social causes of distress.

II

Researching the Causes of Distress:
Sociology Compared to Psychiatry
and Psychology

CHAPTER TWO

Measuring Psychological Distress

What is Psychological Distress?

Depression and Anxiety

Distress is an unpleasant subjective state. It takes two major forms. The first is depression: feeling sad, demoralized, lonely, hopeless, worthless, wishing you were dead, having trouble sleeping, crying, feeling everything is an effort, and being unable to get going. The second is anxiety: being tense, restless, worried, irritable, and afraid. Depression and anxiety each have two components: mood and malaise. The mood refers to negative feelings such as the sadness of depression or the worry of anxiety. The malaise refers to bodily states, such as the listlessness and distraction of depression or the autonomic ailments (headaches, stomachaches, dizziness) and restlessness of anxiety. Depression and anxiety are related in two ways: The maps of their social high and low zones are very similar, and a person who has one also tends to have the other (although not necessarily at the same time). Figure 2.1 shows some examples of symptoms of depression and anxiety, separating mood and malaise.

One widely used measure of distress is Langner's (1962) index. It is typical of distress indexes in general and was the standard in community research for many years. Langner's index is a checklist of 22 questions that were chosen from a much longer list because they best distinguish between people with psychiatric problems and those without. The items selected on this basis turned out to be questions about depression and anxiety, although Langner was not trying to measure any specific form of mental problem. There are questions about depressed mood ("Do you sometimes wonder if anything is worthwhile anymore" "In general, would you say that you are in very good spirits, good spirits, low spirits, or very low spirits?") and malaise ("Have you had times when you couldn't take care of things because you couldn't get going?") There are questions about anxious mood ("Are you the worrying type?") and malaise ("Do you feel weak all over much of the time?" "Are you bothered by acid or sour stomach several times a week?" "How often are you troubled with headaches or pains in the head?"). Langner's index was intended to be used as a quick and easy way of screening individuals for further evaluation and possible treatment. Its greatest success, though, was in assessing and comparing the level of psychological distress in various segments of the population.

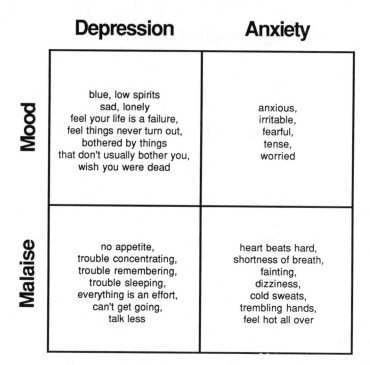

Figure 2.1. Examples of items measuring depression and anxiety, separated into mood and malaise components. Respondents are asked how often they feel this way (i.e., in low spirits). The depression items are from the Center for Epidemiologic Studies' Depression Scale (CES-D) and the Diagnostic Interview Schedule (DIS); anxiety items are from the Langner index and the DIS. In the case of depression, mood may also be thought of as having two components: depressed affect and lack of positive affect. The latter includes the absence of feeling happy, enjoying life, and feeling hopeful about the future.

The content of indexes measuring distress has changed over the years. Early community studies, in the early 1960's, usually asked about malaise, such as cold sweats, heart palpitations, and other physical symptoms (Gurin, Veroff, and Feld, 1960; Srole *et al.*, 1962). Current studies ask more questions about mood, such as feeling afraid, lonely, or sad. This transition is typified by the contrast between the Gurin index and the Center for Epidemiologic Studies' Depression Scale (CES-D). In *Americans View Their Mental Health*, Gurin, Veroff and Feld (1960) measured distress with an index composed entirely of items referring to malaise such as dizziness, trembling hands, and difficulty getting up in the morning. This index was also used in Myers' New Haven follow-up study that began in 1967 (e.g., Myers, Lindenthal and Pepper, 1975). In contrast, the CES-D is composed primarily of items such as feeling depressed, fearful, lonely, and sad or not feeling as good as other people, hopeful about the future, or happy, and not enjoying life (Radloff, 1977). The CES-D is used in the National Center for Health Statistics' Health and Nutrition Examination Survey (HANES) (e.g., Eaton and Kessler, 1981), in a large-scale public health survey in Los Angeles (Frerichs, Aneshensel, and Clark, 1981), in a national survey of married couples (Ross, Mirowsky, and Huber, 1983), and others (e.g., Lennon, 1982; Tausig, 1982), and has largely replaced the Langner index as the standard.

There are a number of reasons for the shift from physiological to psychological indicators of distress. First, researchers have discovered that people are far more willing to report their emotional feelings in community surveys than anyone expected, so that questions about headaches, sweaty palms, and heart palpitations, which were used to mask the intent of measuring a respondent's emotional state, are unnecessary. Some early studies hired psychiatrists to ask direct questions about emotions, but today, the same results are achieved regularly and reliably by telephone surveys using lay interviewers with the same training as interviewers for an opinion poll. Second, malaise may indicate physical health problems as well as emotional ones, particularly in aging populations (Johnson and Meile, 1981) or other groups that have unusually high rates of health problems [such as Mexican immigrants to the United States (Wheaton, 1982)]. The use of physiological symptoms of distress could bias results in favor of an association between distress and disease, hospitalization, injury, and disability (Thoits, 1981). Many researchers feel that it is safer to use purely psychological indicators. On the whole, though, studies of "physiogenic bias" find that while it exists, it is not great and does not account for the major social patterns of distress. Measures of dread, anxiety, sadness, hopelessness, worthlessness, guilt, enervation, distraction, and psychophysiological distress are interrelated. For most purposes they are interchangeable indications of demoralization and distress (Dohrenwend et al., 1980). Sometimes different types of distress (such as depression and anxiety) have different patterns that provide insight into the nature of a particular social condition(e.g., Mirowsky and Ross, 1984; Wheaton, 1983), but more often the patterns match and tell the same story about who is distressed and why.

Not "Mental Illness"

Distress is conceptually distinct from a number of other mental problems that are sometimes collectively called "mental illness." The term distress does not refer to personality disorder such as being antisocial or paranoid, thought problems resulting from old age or drug abuse, extreme mood swings, alcoholism, or hallucinations and delusions, although distress may be associated with all of these. Also, there is a wide range of distress, but only the more extreme levels would be considered mental illness. Most people in the community do not have severe emotional problems, although a substantial minority do. Much distress is the psychiatric equivalent of the common cold.

If distress is not mental illness, why bother to study it? There are several reasons. The most important is that misery is still miserable, even if it is a normal response to a stressful situation rather than a symptom of disease. Distress also has social costs, some of which are obvious, such as the person whose distress keeps him awake at night so that he feels run down during the day and has trouble working or getting along with others.

Some costs of distress are less obvious. For instance, psychological distress often creates problems in our medical care system. People with backaches, stomachaches, headaches, and other forms of malaise often seek medical care. At least 20% of all visits to primary care physicians are for symptoms of physiological malaise with no detectable physical cause (Locke and Gardner, 1969; Hiday, 1980). Because the same symptoms can result from serious medical illness, the physician takes a history, does a physical, follows up with diagnostic tests, and, because false positives are inevitable, sometimes treats people for illnesses they do not have. This is an expensive, dangerous, and ineffective way to care for people who are depressed or anxious. For sociologists there is a final reason to study distress. The maps of emotional high and low zones reveal a great deal about the nature of life in different social circumstances.

Depression and anxiety are highly correlated. People who suffer from one usually also suffer from the other. Because of this, researchers often count up both types of symptoms without bothering to distinguish between them. The same is true of mood and malaise. Unless a researcher is interested in how physical illness, injury, or hospitalization affect psychological distress, the mood and malaise components do not need to be distinguished. If a researcher is interested in the effect of physical illness on psychological distress, he or she distinguishes mood from malaise to avoid confounding cause and effect.

Distress and Well-Being as Opposite Poles

Well-being and distress are opposite poles on a single continuum: more well-being means less distress and more distress means less well-being. Well-being is a general sense of enjoying life and feeling happy, hopeful about the future, and as good as other people. Lack of these positive feelings is related to depression and anxiety. It is useful to think of a continuum from happy and fulfilled at the well-being end to depressed and anxious at the distress end.

The fact that well-being and distress are opposite poles of the same emotional dimension is so obvious that many readers may think it does not need to be said. Yet, some researchers say that positive and negative affect are distinct dimensions of mood, and not just opposite poles (e.g., Bradburn, 1969). The reason given is that the negative correlation between measures of well-being and of distress is not perfect (not −1.0). Depending on how well-being and distress are measured, the estimated correlation ranges from −.50 (Ross and Mirowsky, 1984) to near zero (Bradburn, 1969). These correlations seem to suggest that well-being and distress are at least partially independent moods.

There are two reasons why the negative correlation between well-being and distress is less than perfect, even though they are opposite poles of a single dimension of mood. The first is random measurement error. There is always a certain amount of randomness in the processes of communicating and recording. Like the background noise in a radio broadcast, this randomness can be minimized but never totally eliminated. Random error in measures of well-being and distress reduces the size of the apparent correlation, because the random part of one measure is necessarily uncorrelated with the random part of the other. However, it is possible to estimate the percentage of the recorded communication that is random, and then estimate the correlation that would be found if communication and recording were perfect. By our estimate, the corrected correlation is approximately −.70 (Ross and Mirowsky, 1984).

The second reason the correlation is less than perfect is that some people express their feelings less than others. Differences in expressiveness crosscut differences in mood: the worse a person's mood the less well-being and more distress he or she reports, but the less expressive a person is the less of *both* he or she reports. By our estimate, differences in expressiveness account for 30% of the nonrandom differences in reported distress. Differences in mood account for the other 70%.

Differences in expressiveness are easy to take into account, and investigations show they have little effect on the results of studies (Ross and Mirowsky, 1984b; Gove *et al.*, 1976; Gove and Geerken, 1977a). Women are more expressive than men, but this does not account for the higher levels of anxiety and depression reported by them, since they also report fewer days of enjoying life and feeling happy, hopeful about the future, and as good as other people (Ross and Mirowsky, 1984). Other sociodemographic differences in expressiveness are not as great as that between the sexes, and do not account for the social patterns of distress. Well-being increases and distress decreases with greater education and income, with fewer personal losses and economic hardships, and with marriage. Well-being and distress have opposite sociodemographic patterns because they are opposite ends of the same continuum.

In contrast to other researchers, notably Campbell, Converse, and Rodgers (1976), we do not consider satisfaction a part of well-being. Well-being and distress are the poles of one dimension; satisfaction and discontent are the poles of another. Satisfaction implies a convergence of aspiration and achievement that reflects resignation as much as it does accomplishment. Whereas distress often results from deprivation, discontent results from deprivation *relative to one's expectations*. Although the two may often go together, the instances in which they do not are important to sociological theory. For example, education increases average income and thus increases both well-being and satisfaction with one's income; but among people in the *same* income bracket, higher education increases well-being but *decreases* satisfaction with that level of income (Mirowsky, 1987). By the same token, a worker is more satisfied with low pay, but also more distressed, if he has a high school rather than a college education. Rising expectations tend to reduce satisfaction with a given level of achievement, while simultaneously enhancing the sense of well-being.

Distress and Other Psychological Problems

Depression and anxiety are especially useful indicators of the subjective quality of life. They are the most common types of psychological problems, experienced by everyone to some degree at some time. However, there are other types of psychological problems. These include other affective symptoms like anger and guilt, and cognitive symptoms like mistrust and paranoia, delusions, and other disordered thought processes.

Other affective symptoms are often associated with depression. In particular, persons who feel depressed often feel angry and guilty. Weissman and Paykel (1974) describe women who are depressed, partly because of being powerless and dependent vis-à-vis their husbands. The women get angry at their husbands, take it out on their children, and then feel guilty, which makes them even more depressed.

Cognitive problems such as schizophrenia are conceptually distinct from affective problems such as depression. Anxiety, guilt, anger, and lack of positive feelings are basically emotional. Problems such as schizophrenia are basically disorders of the thought processes rather than emotions. Although affective problems have cognitive components, and vice versa, their defining characteristics are different. Cognitive symptoms including seeing things other people do not see, hearing things other people do not hear, believing other people can hear your thoughts, feeling possessed or controlled by forces or beings, thinking you have enemies who want to harm you, being sure everyone is against you, believing you are being plotted against, feeling it is safer to trust no one, having nightmares, and having unusual thoughts. Many of these symptoms indicate the delusional thinking of paranoid schizophrenia. Although affective and cognitive problems are conceptually distinct, the same types of people who have a lot of cognitive problems also have a lot of depression and anxiety.

Alienation also is not distress. While alienation is a state of mind, distress is a state of feeling. An alienated person has a sense of not controlling outcomes in his or her own life, or of being an agent of someone else's intentions, or of life having no meaning or purpose, or of not being someone of importance and value to others, or of the social rules being in disarray, inapplicable, or hostile to his or her own interests. These perceptions may be profoundly distressing, but they are not distress itself. Distinguishing between alienation and distress allows researchers to ask several empirical questions that are of theoretical interest: to what extent are alienation and distress correlated; under what conditions is the correlation stronger or weaker; to what extent, and under what conditions, do those who suffer as a consequence of alienation recognize the cause of their distress?

Diagnosis

Psychological Problems—Real, but not Entities

Psychological problems are not discrete. They are not something that is entirely present or entirely absent, without shades in between. Psychological problems are not alien entities that invade a person and wreak mental havoc, though psychiatrists speak of depression and other psychological problems as if this were the case. The psychiatrist detects the presence of an entity, determines its species, and selects an appropriate weapon against it. The imagery of detection follows from the language of discrete entities. This categorical language is the legacy of nineteenth century epidemiology and microbiology, according to which a person is diseased or not. The disease is malaria or not, cholera or not, schistosomiasis or not, and so on. A language of categories fits some realities better than others; it fits the reality of psychological problems poorly.

The Linguistic Legacy of Infectious Disease Epidemiology

In the eighteenth and nineteenth centuries, the fledgling science of epidemiology made its first major advances. Epidemiology studies the causes of disease by comparing the amount of disease in different groups of people. In the early days, epidemiologists gathered the birth, death, and census data collected by churches and local government. Much of this information was kept for the purpose of tithing and taxation, or to warn wealthy urbanites of impending plagues (Susser, 1973). The early epidemiologist counted the number of deaths in an area, divided by the number of persons living in the area, and compared the ratio with similar figures for other areas or for the same area at other times. Differences in death rates were correlated with environmental differences between areas or changes over time. Counts of persons and counts of deaths lent themselves naturally to a language of categories. When London parishes began recording counts of death resulting from cholera, John Snow discovered the connection between outbreaks of the disease and the contamination of drinking water with sewage. Snow demonstrated the power of the new science by closing a contaminated well and thus stopping an epidemic (Susser, 1973). Based on his observations, Snow thought cholera might be caused by an invisible, self-reproducing organism living in contaminated water. His speculation was confirmed 30 years later, when Koch and Pasteur showed that the cholera *Vibrio* is the responsible agent.

As the science of epidemiology developed, it spawned a host of concepts based on the underlying method of sorting and counting people and comparing ratios of various counts. These are concepts familiar to anyone who studies epidemiology today: point prevalence, period prevalence, incidence, attack rate, risk, relative risk, attributable risk, standardized morbidity, proportionate mortality, and so on. Every one of these concepts presupposes the ability to sort people into two groups: those who have a particular disease and those who do not. This distinction is not always easy to make. Another set of concepts describes the ability to detect the true underlying presence or absence of the disease: sensitivity, specificity, true positive rate, false positive rate, true negative rate, false negative rate, likelihood ratio, and so on. In essence, these concepts measure how much one is more or less certain a person does or does not have the disease. Alternatively, we could say that they measure how well a particular piece of information, or the information on a particular patient, fits our concept of the disease. These terms stretch the dichotomy at the heart of epidemiology to cover a dimensional and shaded reality. So do other terms such as infectivity, pathogenicity, virulence, and resistance. In a time when health problems such as hypertension, alcoholism, diabetes, hypercholesterolemia, and obesity are forcing the language of epidemiology and medicine to describe gradations, and not just distinctions, psychiatry has developed a passion for diagnostic schemes.

Reification of Categorical Assessment in Psychiatry

Why does psychiatry use and promote a categorical language if psychological problems are not discrete entities? Today, psychiatry wants to look and sound like other medical specialties. The older Freudian psychiatry was not always well received in the "bugs and drugs" world of medicine. Physicians familiar with talk about lesions, toxins, and organisms felt queasy when the talk turned to repression, transference, and the desire to sleep with your mother and kill your father. To the extent that Freudian analysis was considered the treatment for all psychological problems (or at least all neuroses), exact and uniform diagnostic categories and procedures were not essential; the insight of a specific analysis was most important. In other medical specialties, professional authority was (and is) based on the claim of having the proper treatment for each disease and the proper diagnosis for each patient. Diagnosis links the problem presented by a particular patient to the cataloged information and accumulated lore of medicine.

Psychiatry has come to equate categorical assessment with true science. The method of research and the form of ideas in nineteenth century epidemiology and microbiology are built into the official language of medicine, and if psychiatry is medicine, then it must use the official language. Instead of shaping the methods and language of psychiatry to suit its dimensional and graded subject, psychiatrists and psychiatric epidemiologists insist that there must be discrete entities hidden in the shades of psychological problems. The following quote is from a debate in the *Archives of General Psychiatry*: " . . . Without some diagnostic criteria for who is "in" or "out" of a diagnostic class, such as depression, it is not possible to decide whether a given person or group of persons are clinically depressed as distinct from unhappy and discontented because of social deprivation or the frustration of their personal wishes. Nor is it possible to assess risk in a way that would generate more specific clues to possible etiologies. The concept of 'risk' implies 'risk for what?' The 'what,' we maintain, are discrete disorders." (Weissman and Klerman, 1980, p.1424).

According to this statement, clinical depression is and must be a discrete entity, otherwise the concept of risk and the standard machinery of clinical and epidemiologic research would not apply. There is a word that is not used in everyday conversation but is used by philosophers, linguists, cultural anthropolgists, and others who study the relationship between ideas and the things they represent. The word is "reify." Reifying is treating an abstraction as if it has material existence. This is known as "the fallacy of misplaced concreteness" (Srole and Fischer, 1980, p.1425). The person who feels bad is real, the person's feelings are real, the psychiatrist's act of classifying the patient's problem is real, the consequences of the psychiatrist's act of classification are real. However, the entity "diagnostic depression" is *not* real. It is a linguistic pigeonhole into which some cases are placed. Speaking of the diagnosis "depression" as if it *is* depression is reifying. The shape of the pigeonhole is mistaken for the shape of reality.

The Alternative to Diagnosis: Assessing the Type and Severity of Symptoms

We do not have to place people in diagnostic categories in order to know which subpopulations suffer more than others. Counting the number of persons in a diagnostic category is easily replaced by counting the number of symptoms of a particular type that various people have. The latter strategy avoids the proliferation of diseases, each with its own name and mythical status as unique, discrete entities. We need to remember, though, that a category of symptoms is a mental pigeonhole too. People are the real entities. The symptoms are merely things that some people feel or think or do more than others, for reasons we would like to know. Some of those things appear together more frequently than others, and those are the ones we treat as a single type of symptom.

It is useful to think in terms of the *type* and *severity* of psychological problems. Depression is one type of psychological problem. Anxiety is another. Each type of problem ranges from not at all severe to very severe, on a continuum. People score at all points on the continuum—from very few symptoms to many symptoms. People can get a severity score for each type of psychological problem.

Contrast this with the diagnostic approach. Imagine two people on either side of some arbitrary cutoff that defines depression. Although the type and severity of their problems are very similar, one has just enough symptoms to be diagnosed as depressed, the other is just short of enough. This diagnostic imposition ignores their similarity. Imagine another two people, one happy, fulfilled, and productive and the other demoralized, hopeless, and miserable, but just short of meeting the criteria for a diagnosis of depression. The imposition of a diagnosis ignores their differences. Diagnosis throws away information about the similarity of some cases and the dissimilarity of others.

Reliability versus Certainty: The Fallacy of the Two-Category Scale

Throwing away information does not help us understand problems—it hinders us. Many people, including many scientists, erroneously believe that the accuracy of an assessment is improved by making crude distinctions. For example, a typical bathroom scale is able to measure weight accurately within a range of plus or minus 2 pounds. This means that if a person's true weight is 140 pounds, there's a 99% probability that the bathroom scale will say the person's weight is in the range from 138 to 142 pounds. It is unlikely the scale will give the person's exact, true weight, and it would be sheer chance if it did. Nevertheless, the bathroom scale is almost certain to register within 2 pounds of the person's true weight, and will usually show correctly which 5- or 10-pound range the person's weight is in. The broader the ranges, the more likely a bathroom scale is to correctly show which range the person's weight is in. The broadest range would divide everybody into two categories: heavies and not heavies, and almost everyone would be correctly classified. The current bathroom scale, which almost never shows a person's true weight, could be modified so that it only shows whether a person is heavy or not. Suppose you are trying to loose weight. Which bathroom scale would you choose? The old one that is almost never correct, or the new and improved one that is almost always correct?

The fallacy of the two-category scale lies in confusing certainty and reliability. In psychometrics (the science of measuring psychological states and traits), reliability is the amount of exactness of reproduction that can be achieved with a given measure. Reliability in psychometrics is analogous to fidelity in electronics. Fidelity is the degree to which a system, such as a radio or television, accurately reproduces the essential characteristics of its input. The symphony one hears on the radio is never exactly like the symphony one hears in the concert hall, but no one would ever suggest improving the broadcast by reducing all sounds to the presence or absence of a single tone. Imagine listening to a broadcast altered in that way and trying to figure out what music is being played. Reliability increases with the precision of assessment. A measure of length is more reliable if the ruler is marked in inches than if the ruler is marked only in feet. Reliability is lowest if measurement is dichotomous—a simple yes or no, in or out, heavy or not, diagnosed or not.

As an assessment becomes broader, it becomes less sensitive to meaningful changes or differences, *and the ratio of information to random noise declines*. The bathroom scale that has a random error of plus or minus two pounds has exactly the same amount of random error when we paint out all the little marks and replace them with a red zone for heavy and a white zone for not heavy. The crude split has eliminated almost all of the information without eliminating any of the random error. Broader categories increase the *certainty* of an assessment but decrease its *reliability*, and it is *reliability*, not *certainty*, that we need. If we reduced everything to a single category, our certainty is perfect but it would be meaningless.

When a full range of symptoms is split into only two categories, such as: enough symptoms for a diagnosis of depression; and not enough symptoms for a diagnosis of depression, most of the information is lost, but all the random error remains. The diagnosis "depression" is a profoundly insensitive measure. As a consequence, it can be difficult to find meaningful changes or differences in diagnosed depression. For example, a recent community study finds that education and family income do not predict whether a person will get a diagnosis of depression or not (Weissman, 1987). One of the researchers concludes that "depression equally affects the educated and uneducated, the rich and poor, white and black Americans, blue- and white-collar workers" (Weissman, 1987, p.448). Nothing could be further from the truth. No theory, whether social, psychological, genetic, or environmental, predicts that the poor, the uneducated, blacks, and blue-collar workers have the same exposure to the causes of depression as the rich, the educated, whites, and white-collar workers. With a sufficiently insensitive measure, we cannot hear the suffering of millions, and cannot see the causes of the suffering.

A Person Does Not Have to Be Diagnosed to Be Helped

Although the argument is often made that categorizing people as ill versus well is necessary so that those considered ill can be treated, a diagnosis is not necessary for treatment. Anyone who feels bad and seeks or is referred for treatment can be treated. We do not need to label people as depressives, schizophrenics, or alcoholics in order to recognize that they feel bad, that their thoughts are disorganized and bizarre, or that they have problems with alcohol. Certainly the type and extent of a person's problems needs to be assessed, but the assessment does not need to be categorical. A person does not have to be diagnosed to be helped.

Diagnosis might actually be detrimental to treatment. Once a person is diagnosed, the diagnosis may be treated as the person's preeminent trait. Mark Vonnegut is a good example. He writes of his experiences with serious psychological problems in *The Eden Express* (1975). He had severe levels of schizophrenia (thought disorder). His functioning was impaired, and his problem lasted for months or more. He was diagnosed as schizophrenic, and within the diagnostic paradigm this was correct. However, Vonnegut had other psychological problems as well. His anxiety was so severe he would often panic. His depression led to long crying spells, black moods, and suicide attempts. But because Vonnegut was "schizophrenic," his depression and anxiety were ignored or treated as merely secondary. His label made those who were trying to help him, and Vonnegut himself after he accepted the diagnosis, less likely to address and solve his other problems. He was a person with high levels of schizophrenia, depression, and anxiety who was not treated for the depression and anxiety because he was labeled schizophrenic.

Many people with problems of one type also have problems of another type. Even if types of symptoms are distinct, we cannot neatly assign individuals to a set of mutually exclusive diagnostic categories, saying some are depressed, others are anxious, and others are schizophrenic. Attempts to produce a set of exhaustive and mutually exclusive diagnostic categories lead to a proliferation of diagnoses that describe people who happen to have symptoms from more than one cluster. Thus, we get diagnostic categories like "schizoaffective," which is given when the clinician can't decide whether to diagnose schizophrenia (disorganized and bizarre thoughts and perceptions) or affective disorder (severe depression and anxiety). Worse than the introduction of unnecessary complexity, such a practice may obscure the fact that the causes of some symptoms on which a diagnosis is based are different from the causes of other symptoms on which it is based. Even with a profusion of categories for people who are between categories or just outside a category (e.g., schizophreniform disorder), a large minority of patients cannot be classified (Srole and Fischer, 1980).

How a Diagnosis Is Made

Symptoms, Function, and Duration: Assessing, Splitting, Totting-up, and Excluding

Although diagnostic schemes vary somewhat, all are based on descriptions in the *Diagnostic and Statistical Manual of Mental Disorders* (DSM-III and III-R) of the American Psychiatric Association. (Psychiatrists are now working on DSM-IV.) The general criteria for diagnosis are the presence of symptoms, impaired functioning, and prolonged duration of the symptoms. Each criterion has a cutoff point below which the person does not qualify for a diagnosis of a particular disorder. In addition, diagnostic categories are considered mutually exclusive, so alternate diagnoses must be ruled out. For example, to obtain a diagnosis of depression, schizophrenia must be ruled out. Depression with a medical cause, such as infection, anemia, or life-threatening disease, is also excluded from the diagnostic category of depression, as is depression caused by a death in the family.

There are four steps in making a diagnosis. The first is *assessing* the level of symptoms, extent of impaired functioning, and duration of problems. Note that level, extent, and duration all refer to assessments of degree or amount. The second is *splitting* each assessed amount at some cutoff point, so that differences in degree are collapsed into two categories: amounts that meet the criterion and amounts that do not. The third is *totting up* so that all possible combinations of met/unmet on the three criteria are represented in a single overarching split. The fourth is *excluding* cases that also meet other criteria considered preeminent (such as recent bereavement).

Diagnosis combines assessment with judgment. Questioning, observing, and recording symptoms, functioning, and duration is assessment. Using the answers, observations, and records to assign a case to a category is judgment. The two kinds of tasks can be divided in time or between actors (e.g., nurse and physician). In research they are often divided into a questionnaire or protocol for assessment, and an "algorithm" or set of rules for making a judgment. In early community mental health studies, the judgments were made by psychiatrists who examined the records of assessed symptoms, functioning, and duration. Today, the judgments are often made by computers following preset rules.

Diagnosing Major Depression: An Example

To illustrate psychiatric diagnosis, we will see how two diagnostic instruments are used to diagnose major depression. The first is the Schedule for Affective Disorders and Schizophrenia (SADS), which is used to make a diagnosis based on the Research Diagnostic Criteria (RDC) (Endicott and Spitzer,

1979; Spitzer and Endicott, 1978). The SADS is a questionnaire and protocol for assessing symptoms, functioning, and duration. The RDC is a set of criteria for deciding on a diagnosis given the information in the SADS. Together these are often called the SADS/RDC. The second is the Diagnostic Interview Schedule (DIS) (Robins et al., 1979; Robins, 1986). Both instruments were developed for research. Both have been used in community surveys using trained interviewers who are not psychiatrists (Weissman and Myers, 1987), the most recent of which are large community surveys done in various sites throughout the United States, called Epidemiologic Catchment Area (ECA) surveys (Eaton et al., 1986).

We discuss the SADS/RDC first because they are more standardized than the equivalent clinical protocols and rules in the Diagnostic and Statistical Manual-III, although the gist is the same; and they are more explicit and detailed in describing how a diagnosis is made than the latest research diagnostic instrument, the Diagnostic Interview Schedule. The SADS/RDC, the DSM-III, and the DIS have common roots. Spitzer and Endicott based the RDC on the Feighner criteria (Feighner et al., 1972). As head of the task force to develop the DSM-III, Spitzer based the DSM-III on the RDC to the extent that committee decision-making would allow (Robins, 1986). The DIS, developed for the ECA studies, also has its roots in the Feighner criteria and the diagnostic instrument used to make diagnosis based on these criteria, called the Renard Diagnostic Interview.

The SADS interviewer first assesses dysphoric (or depressed) mood by asking the respondent, "How have you been feeling? Describe your mood. Have you felt depressed (sad, blue, moody, down, empty, hopeless, as if you didn't care)? How often? Does it come and go? How long does it last? How bad is the feeling?" Based on the person's response, the interviewer records the frequency and severity of depressed mood from not at all depressed to constant unrelenting extremely painful feelings of depression. Similar scales record the frequency and intensity of feelings of inadequacy, self-reproach, and worthlessness, suicidal tendencies, appetite problems, inability to concentrate, loss of interest or pleasure, loss of energy, and other elements of depression (Spitzer and Endicott, 1977).

After the questions about specific symptoms, the interviewer makes a global assessment of the subject's level of functioning. The assessment ranges from "good functioning in all areas, many interests, socially effective," to "major impairment in several areas such as work or family relations," to "needs constant supervision for several days to prevent hurting self or others," or "makes no attempt to maintain minimal personal hygiene."

Once the assessments are made and recorded, the Research Diagnostic Criteria are applied. The *symptom criterion* has two conditions, which must both be met: (1) dysphoric mood characterized by feeling depressed, blue, sad, hopeless, irritable, worried; and (2) at least five of the following symptoms: poor appetite or increased appetite, sleep problems, loss of energy, psychomotor retardation or agitation, loss of interest or pleasure in usual activities, self-reproach, diminished ability to concentrate, and thoughts of suicide. Although the SADS assessment records the frequency and intensity of each symptom, the criteria only refer to the presence or absence of symptoms. The *duration criterion* is that dysphoric mood has lasted at least one week. The *functioning criterion* is that the person sought or was referred for help, took medication for the problem, or had impaired functioning at home with family, at school, at work, or in social situations. Again, although the SADS assessment records the frequency and intensity of dysfunction, the criterion only refers to its presence. If all three criteria are met, if the person is not bereaved, if the person is not suffering from a medical illness that could cause the symptoms, and if there are no signs of schizophrenia, the person is diagnosed as having major depression.

The example illustrates the fact that diagnosing current major depression is a process of collecting information and then ignoring most of it. Information is thrown out in the splitting, totting up, and excluding processes. Splitting dispenses with much of it. Differences in the frequency and intensity of each symptom are ignored by counting only the presence or absence of each. Information on the number of symptoms is thrown out by ignoring less than five, and treating any number greater than or equal to five as alike. Information on the duration of symptoms is thrown out by ignoring episodes of less than a week, and treating all episodes of more than a week as alike. Differences in the type of dysfunction are ignored by lumping them together, and differences in the extent of dysfunction are ignored by counting only the presence or absence of some sign of dysfunction.

The totting up and excluding processes throw out information by ignoring the distinction between an emotional state and its causes and consequences. When symptoms, functioning, and duration are totted up into one global judgment, the distinctions *among* the three dimensions are ignored, as well as the distinctions within each. This may be a problem, since the things that cause a greater number, frequency, and intensity of symptoms may not be the same things that cause greater dysfunction. The extent of dysfunction depends on the level of performance normally demanded by a person's situation. It is often the case that the same factor that decreases the probable level of distress also increases the dysfunction produced by any given level of distress. Employed engineers are less distressed than unemployed construction workers, but an employed engineer having difficulty concentrating is more impaired than an unemployed construction worker with the same symptom.

Psychiatrists often treat the act of seeking help as an indication of dysfunction because problems in functioning are often the primary motive a person has in seeking help, or that friends, family or co-workers have when referring a person for help. Once again, however, the same factors that decrease the probable level of distress often increase the likelihood of the person or his/her associates seeking help. In particular, people with higher levels of education, income, and occupational status have lower average levels of distress, but at any given level of distress they are more likely to seek and get treatment. This phenomenon is so pronounced that mental health professionals once believed that depression and anxiety increased with education, income, and occupational status (Hollingshead and Redlich, 1958). The overwhelming evidence to the contrary is one of the most important contributions made by surveys based on randomly selected community residents, rather than on patients in treatment.

By failing to distinguish between symptoms and the dysfunction that they cause, the diagnosis of depression necessarily has a lower correlation with education, income, and occupation than the actual mood does. The social patterns of dysfunction and help seeking tend to cancel the social patterns of distress. The hotel maid may feel miserable, but she still does her job as well as anyone expects. The same degree of distress may be so common in her social world that it seems normal to her and her friends and family. Even if she wanted help she probably could not afford it.

The practice of excluding depression caused by medical illness or loss of a loved one from the diagnosis of depression also obscures social patterns. Exclusion rules ignore the distinction between the emotional state and its cause or concomitant. The rules typically presuppose that each distinct cause necessarily produces a distinct disorder, even if the disorders are not otherwise distinguishable. Psychiatrists cannot tell the difference between grief and major depression without knowing if a patient has lost a close friend or relative. As a practical matter, it is worth noting whether a depressed person has recently lost a loved one, just as it is worth noting other possible causes of the depression. There is no reason to assume that each cause produces a unique emotional state. One consequence of excluding depression caused by medical illness or loss of a loved one is that social patterns are obscured. The elderly and poor have more illness and higher death rates among their loved ones than do the young and well-to-do. The emotional distress caused by this illness and loss is discounted in studies of diagnosed major depression.

As an example, Boyd *et al.* (1982) describe the case of an 85-year-old woman who lives alone, without friends or family nearby. She is afraid of being robbed and will not leave her apartment. She scores very high on any measure of depressive symptoms. She has not sought help. Because her social roles are limited to begin with, she has no impairment of social functioning. She is incapacitated by arthritis. She does not get a diagnosis of depression.

The latest diagnostic instrument, used in the Epidemiologic Catchment Area (ECA) surveys, is the Diagnostic Interview Schedule (DIS). The symptoms of depression are the same in the DIS as in the SADS [feelings of depression, loss of interest or pleasure (in things usually enjoyed, including sex), appetite problems, feelings of worthlessness, sleep problems, trouble thinking or concentrating, loss of energy or restlessness, and suicidal tendencies]. However, the format for assessing these problems is different. The DIS questions used to diagnose major depression are shown in Appendix A to this chapter.

The first major difference is that the DIS combines the assessment of problems with the cutoff rules, whereas the SADS/RDC keeps them separate. The SADS first counts symptoms and then splits them into enough for a diagnosis versus not enough for a diagnosis. The DIS goes right to the split. For example, people are first asked, "In your lifetime, have you ever had two weeks or more during which you felt sad, blue, depressed or when you lost all interest and pleasure in things that you usually care about or enjoyed?" The intensity and duration of the feelings are compressed into a simple YES or NO. All other symptoms of depression are also recorded in a YES/NO format. (See Appendix A to this chapter.)

The second major difference is the focus on lifetime problems, with current problems simply part of the lifetime assessment. (The SADS assesses current and lifetime problems with two distinct schedules.) As mentioned above, the DIS begins to asking, "In your lifetime, have you ever . . . ." It is well established in survey research that people can most accurately report current or recent states. People have much more difficulty remembering things that happened years ago, and memory is heavily influenced by current feelings. Yet it is not until close to the end of the section of major depression that the person is finally asked, "Are you in one of these spells of feeling low or disinterested and having some of these other problem now?"

There are other differences between the DIS and the SADS. Unlike the SADS, the DIS does not emphasize impaired functioning as a criterion for receiving a diagnosis. In the SADS, an important indicator of impaired functioning is the act of seeking or being referred for treatment. The National Institute of Mental Health recognized the problem of using this as a criterion for diagnosis: If, by definition, a person is not depressed if he or she does not seek treatment, then there is no need for more psychiatric services.

There are other slight differences between the SADS and the DIS. For instance, the duration criteria for symptoms in the DIS is two weeks instead of one. Both cutoffs are arbitrary.

In sum, diagnostic instruments ignore information on the level of a person's problem, instead splitting the information into a crude YES or NO distinction. They also confound information on symptoms, their causes, and their consequences. The latest "advance" in diagnostic instruments used in research (the DIS) makes these problems worse.

Diagnosing Schizophrenia

Many people might agree that depression is not a categorical problem; that this is a reified notion of disease that does not reflect reality. But the same people might disagree about schizophrenia, arguing that the diagnostic approach *is* appropriate here. We do not think so. Symptoms of schizophrenia can also be measured on a continuous scale. Wheaton (1985b, pp. 162–163) uses a scale of schizophrenic (cognitive) symptoms, scoring each according to how often the respondent reported it (never, rarely, sometimes, often, very often), and then adding the scores together. The respondents were asked, "How often in the past year, have you felt that your mind was dominated by forces beyond your control; felt sure everyone was against you; heard voices without knowing where they came from; had trouble thinking; believed you were being plotted against; thought people were saying things about you behind your back; seen things that other people did not see; heard your thoughts being spoken aloud; heard your thoughts being broadcast or transmitted; felt you did not exist at all; felt possessed by the devil; felt you had special powers; had trouble thinking; had visions. The interviewer also recorded if the respondent made up words or gave answers that had little to do with the questions.

We are most aware of people who have severe symptoms of schizophrenia, who cannot function, and who have had the problem for a long time—those who would qualify for a diagnosis of schizophrenia. In fact, cognitive symptoms, like affective ones, can be scaled, and people placed along the continuum. People can score from no cognitive symptoms, to mild, moderate, and severe levels. There are actually many people in the community who have mild or moderate cognitive problems. They sometimes see things that others do not see, or feel that their minds are controlled by outside forces, but their problems are not severe and do not interfere with functioning.

Thus, even in the case of schizophrenia, the diagnostic approach does not reflect reality. As with depression, information on possible social, psychological, and genetic causes should be collected and correlated with schizophrenia. So should information on the duration and consequences of schizophrenia. Nothing is gained, and much is lost, by reducing that information to a diagnosis. It is likely that susceptibility, onset, severity, duration, and dysfunction have different causes that obscure each other when all are thrown into a single diagnostic pot.

A Sea of Troubles

Two things are classified in diagnosis: people and symptoms. People are hard to classify. They often have more than one type of psychological problem, and each form is graded and variable, not just present or absent. Perhaps symptoms are more readily classified. Each person could have a profile of scores representing their levels of anxiety, depression, schizophrenia, and so on, with each score counting the person's symptoms of the respective type. But how do we know which symptoms belong in which index? How unambiguously distinct are the types of psychological problems?

Types of Psychological Symptoms: Galaxies, Nebula, or Spectra?

Do the diagnostic categories used by psychiatrists reflect real discontinuities in types of problems, or are they simply conceptual overlays? Do the diagnostic concepts reflect natural boundaries between types of symptoms? There are two predominant opposing views about the distinctiveness of the types of psychological symptoms. Both are compatible with the fact that individual persons can have mixed and graded problems. One we will call the galaxy hypothesis and the other the nebula hypothesis. According to the galaxy hypothesis, symptoms are clustered by type. Symptoms of a similar type cluster together, and symptoms of different types are separated by large, empty regions. Clusters may be close to each other or far apart. For instance, depression and anxiety clusters may be closer than depression and schizophrenia clusters. However, each is a distinctive cluster, separated from the others by empty space. The types of problems are clearly separate. In contrast, the nebula hypothesis states that symptoms are randomly distributed and do not cluster according to type—they are an undifferentiated pool. The only meaningful quality of the nebula is its overall severity—types are not distinct. (See Fig. 2.2.)

Are the types of psychological problems distinct galaxies, or merely a random, undifferentiated nebula of symptoms? Debates over this issue are often acrimonious (e.g., Srole and Fischer, 1980, versus Weissman and Klerman, 1980). The weight of scientific opinion shifts one way or the other from time to time, but the issue is not settled, largely because the debate is over conceptual schemes with little reference to the data on real people and real symptoms.

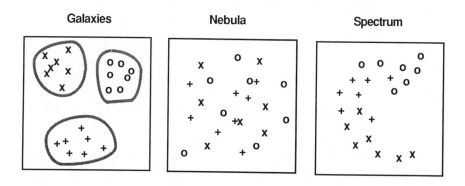

Figure 2.2. The galaxies, nebula, and spectrum hypotheses. o's, +'s, and x's each represent a type of symptom such as paranoia, depression, and anxiety.

There are two alternatives to the opposing galaxy and nebula views. Dohrenwend and his colleagues present one compromise view. They argue that there is a large pool of symptoms indicating "nonspecific psychological distress" (Dohrenwend *et al.*, 1980). Like fever or pain, the nonspecific symptoms tell us whether or not a person has a problem but not which problem. Then there are specific symptoms that distinguish one type of problem from another, such as false beliefs and perceptions, mania, guilt, or problem drinking. In our analogy, this would be a large random nebula with definite galaxies interspersed.

Another alternative is the spectrum hypothesis. According to this view symptoms of each type cluster together—symptoms of depression cluster together, symptoms of anxiety cluster together, and so on—but the clusters are *not* clearly separate and are not separated by empty space. One type shades into the next. Symptoms of depression cluster together, as do symptoms of anxiety, but there are no clear boundaries, and there are areas where symptoms of different types are mixed.

Mapping the 4095 Correlations among 91 Symptoms

Using modern psychometric techniques, we can map the location and clusters of symptoms in correlational space. This shows what symptoms are associated with each other, and, most importantly, does it without our having to guess in advance what the pattern looks like. Using a technique called multidimensional scaling, and making no assumptions about the nature of psychological problems, we map what people report (Kruskal and Wish, 1978; Schiffman, Reynolds, and Young, 1981). Then we can superimpose categories of symptoms on the map of actual correlations. This will show us how our ideas about categories of symptoms fit actual patterns of correlation.

Before showing the actual map thus derived, we need to summarize how the method works, what the results mean, the nature of the data used, and the reason that data was chosen. The mapmaking begins by selecting a set of symptoms, a sample of people, and a way of noting each individual's symptoms. All pairs of symptoms are correlated across individuals. The correlation is a number that theoretically ranges from -1 to $+1$. The correlation is positive if the two symptoms tend to be present together and absent together. In other words, if a person in the sample has one of the symptoms, he or she is more likely than average to have the other one too. If a person in the sample does not have one of the symptoms, he or she is less likely than average to have the other. The more this is true, the larger the positive correlation. If two symptoms always appear together, and never appear without each other, the correlation would be $+1$. (In practice, correlations are usually much smaller.)

The technique of multidimensional scaling results in a map of the correlations among the symptoms. Each symptom has a location on the map, just as each city or town has a location on a road map. The proximity of two symptoms on the map represents the size of their correlation with each other and the similarity of their profiles of correlations with all the other symptoms. The map summarizes the correlations among all the symptoms. Without the map it is very difficult to see and think about all the relationships at once. In our analysis, we look at the correlations among 91 symptoms—a total of 4095 correlations. That's more numbers than anyone can think about at once. Ninety-one points on a map are relatively easy to comprehend. The closer two symptoms are on the map, the higher the correlation between them, and the more similar their patterns of correlation with the other symptoms.

To make the map, the computer program designed for this task begins by giving each symptom a random location. Then it measures the distance between all the pairs of locations and compares the distances to the respective correlations. If two symptoms are farther apart than their correlation says they should be, the program moves them closer together. If the symptoms are too close, they are moved farther apart. The program keeps shuffling the points around until the fit of the distances to the correlations stops improving.

The correlations we use come from a community survey of 463 people living in El Paso, Texas, and Juarez, Mexico, called the Life Stress and Illness Project. Although it is not a nationwide survey, we used this survey because it has, to our knowledge, one of the most complete list of symptoms of all types of psychological problems of any community study. The symptoms were chosen from standard research indexes and diagnostic questionnaires. They represent the symptoms found in survey research measures such as the Langner, Gurin, and CES-D indexes, and in diagnostic instruments such as the Schedules for Affective Disorder and Schizophrenia (SADS) and the Diagnostic Interview Schedule (DIS). (A complete list of the 91 symptoms is given in appendix B to this chapter.) *These are the symptoms on which psychiatric diagnosis is based.* They represent the problems of the overwhelming majority of all patients seen and diagnosed by psychiatrists.

The persons interviewed in the study were selected by careful random sampling to represent the typical range of people living in El Paso and Juarez. Most people in these communities have some symptoms, which range in severity from mild to moderate. Very few are psychiatric patients or have ever been psychiatric patients, although some may be. All were interviewed in their homes, in English or Spanish, depending on the person's preference. One of the original purposes of the study was to find out if the pattern of correlations among symptoms depends on the subjects' language and culture. In these data, it does not. The patterns are essentially the same for the Mexicans as for the Anglos (Mirowsky and Ross, 1983b). The two groups are therefore combined.

For most of the symptoms, the people were asked how often they had it or

Special

Exciting Schemes

Thoughts Broadcast
Thoughts aloud

Afraid to Go Out   Felt Dead
Nothing Turns Out Enemies   Plotted Against

Thoughts Race Suicidal   Talk Behind My Back
No Interest   Suspicious Nothing Worthwhile
Felt Evil Deserve Punishment
Fear Closed Places Afraid Might Do Wrong
Fear Something I Should Die Repeat Act
Useless Thoughts   Don't Talk
Mind Not Work   SelfBlame Wish I'd Die
LoseThoughts Worthless Strange Thoughts
Guilty Can't Concentrate
Anxious Worry a Lot   Fears All Against Me
Felt Like Crying   Blue Hopeless
Restless   No Get Go
Nothing Turns Out Useless Confused Lonely
Lose Temper Do Over 'n Over Too Excited
Irritated Low Spirits
Brood Sick from Anger
Irritable   Don't Care
Can't Remember   Moody
Can't Stay Asleep
Fear Attack   Muscles Twitch
Helpless Wake Early
Can't Fall Asleep
Oversleep

Tired

Nightmares

Poor Appetite
Worry   Cold Sweats
Weak

Dizzy

depression-mood **depression-malaise** *anxiety-mood* ***anxiety-malaise***

Figure 2.3. Multidimensional scaling of psychological symptoms. See Appendix B to Chapter 2 for the categorization and wording of each symptom. Data are from the Life Stress and Illness Project.

how often it happened in the previous 12 months. The response categories were never, almost never, sometimes, fairly often, and very often (coded 0 through 4, respectively). Seven of the items are based on the interviewer's observation of the person's behavior during the interview, with specific behaviors noted as observed or not. Most people do not have, or rarely have, most of the symptoms, but everyone has some symptoms, and every symptom is reported by some people.

Powers

Possessed
Visions

See Things

Trust No One

Hear Voices   *Dominated by Forces*
Sick from Drink

Drink & Argue

Drink & Miss Work

Tearful

Makes up Words

Blurred Speech

Moves Around
Drumming
Not Listening
Weight Loss
Nervous

Hot All Over

Fidgeting

Breathless

Hands Tremble

Palpitations

paranoia   *schizophrenia*   **alcoholism**

In order to show the relationship between the pattern of correlations and diagnostic concepts, we've classified symptoms into five main categories: depression, anxiety, schizophrenia, paranoia, and alcoholism. These distinctions help us read the map, *but they do not determine the findings.* Our assignment of symptoms to categories follows standard research and diagnostic practice (American Psychiatric Association, 1980; Wheaton, 1985b). We've subdivided the symptoms of depression and anxiety into two subgroups: mood and malaise. The feelings and body states typically go together, but survey researchers sometimes separate the two to avoid "physiogenic bias"—the possibility that an illness could create malaise that has nothing to do with underlying depression or anxiety (Johnson and Meile, 1981).

A Circular Spectrum

Our final map is shown in Fig. 2.3. The pattern is like a spectrum with the ends connected. It is not separate galaxies, nor is it an amorphous nebula. It is not separate galaxies against a backdrop of an amorphous nebula. It is a circle of association—a circumplex. It is like a color wheel, shading from blue to green to yellow to orange to red to purple to violet to blue. In order to fit all the words on the map, we stretched the horizontal axis (in a ratio of 3:2 compared to the vertical axis). Although the figure looks like an oval, the actual pattern is close to a perfect circle. There are regions of similarity on the circumference that correspond roughly with research and clinical distinctions. Beginning at 12 o'clock and moving counterclockwise, there is schizophrenia, paranoia, extreme depression and anxiety, a large amorphous area of depression and anxiety, sleep problems, physical symptoms of anxiety, signs of restlessness and tension during the interview, signs of alcoholism during the interview, drinking problems, and then schizophrenia again.

The symptoms of schizophrenia cluster together at the top of the map. Seeing things other people do not see, having visions, hearing things other people don't hear, thinking your thoughts are broadcast or spoken aloud, feeling dead, and feeling possessed and dominated by forces beyond your control cluster together. Notice, however, that heavy drinking is also associated with hearing voices, seeing things, and feeling dominated by forces beyond your control.

At the top left of the map, symptoms of paranoia cluster together between schizophrenia and depression/anxiety and shade into both. Paranoia is a cognitive problem. In the lexicon of psychiatry, it is a delusion, at the heart of which is the belief that others are out to harm you. Paranoid schizophrenia is the most common type of schizophrenia, and some think all schizophrenia has a paranoid component (Meissner, 1978). According to psychiatric diagnostic schemes, cognitive problems are clearly distinct from emotional (or affective) ones like depression and anxiety. Yet the results of the multidimensional scaling show that paranoid beliefs are strongly associated with depression. Believing that you have enemies who wish to harm you, that others are talking about you behind your back, that you are being plotted against, and that everyone is against you is strongly associated with depression, especially with the feelings that nothing is worthwhile and nothing ever turns out right, with suicidal feelings, and with the feeling that you deserve punishment. In the community, suspicion and paranoia are associated with other cognitive symptoms of schizophrenia *and* with feelings of depression.

Following the circle of symptoms counterclockwise, we see a large group of symptoms of depression and anxiety, including both mood and malaise. Even though depression and anxiety are conceptually distinct, in reality people who have one tend to have the other. Although the map does not indicate it directly, depression and anxiety are the most common types of psychological problems. That is why there are so many variations on these forms. The large cluster at the top includes serious symptoms of depression, like wishing you were dead and feeling that others would be better off if you were dead, following by blaming yourself and feeling worthless and guilty as we continue around the circle, and by feeling blue, lonely, hopeless, and that nothing ever turns out right. Interspersed among symptoms of depression are symptoms of anxiety, which include feeling irritable, anxious, restless, and worried. Toward the bottom of this large cluster are the sleep problems characteristic of depression (and anxiety), including trouble falling asleep, waking early and not being able to get back to sleep, feeling tired, sleeping too much, and having nightmares.

At the bottom of the map are symptoms of malaise that indicate anxiety, including cold sweats, feeling weak, dizzy, breathless, hot all over, and feeling that your heart is beating hard. These symptoms shade into behavioral symptoms of anxiety as recorded by the interviewer's observations: that the person is restless, fidgeting, not listening, and nervous.

On the right of the map are symptoms of alcoholism, including the interviewer's observations of behavior such as blurred speech, and the person's reports of troubles due to drinking. Notice that the tearfulness of the person during the interview, while conceptually a symptom of depression, is actually associated with drinking. Drinking problems shade into seeing things, hearing things, and feeling dominated by forces beyond one's control. We are back to schizophrenia.

This map of people's reports of their symptoms makes it clear that, while there are distinct types of symptoms, there is also a lot of overlap. Depression and anxiety, including mood and malaise, are found together. Paranoia, a cognitive symptom, is closely associated with the affective symptoms of depression and anxiety. People who think that enemies are out to get them, that others are plotting against them and talking behind their backs, are likely to feel depressed. Schizophrenia is a distinct cluster, but in some cases, these symptoms appear to be the result of heavy drinking.

The conceptual overlay reflects the pattern of association, but the correspondence is far from perfect. The correlations among symptoms indicate that psychological problems are not clearly distinct, nor are they completely nebulous. There are loci of association, but the regions overlap and blend from one to the next. The symptoms form a spectrum of association in which the ends are linked—a circumplex. The large, amorphous area of depression and anxiety on the left at first seems consistent with Dohrenwend's idea about "nonspecific psychological distress." However, it is not nonspecific. It is clearly depression and anxiety. It shades into paranoia toward the schizophrenia end. Furthermore, it is not simply a backdrop for more specific forms. It is as much a distinct place on the circular spectrum as is schizophrenia or alcoholism.

Several things not apparent from the figure should be mentioned. First, the symptoms in one place in the circle are positively correlated with the symptoms in any other place: people who have one type of problem tend to have others. To some extent, this reflects the fact that all the types of psychological problems are more common among persons with lower education, less desirable jobs, lower family income, and less comfortable living conditions. To some extent it may represent a cascade of problems, with one type resulting in another. Thus, the diagnostic insistence on mutually exclusive categories—that a person *cannot* be depressed if he or she is schizophrenic, for example—does not reflect reality. It also belies the notion that one type of symptom substitutes for another. For instance, some claim that the poor and the well-to-do, or women and men, face the same amount of stressful demands, but that under stressful conditions they simply express their problems in different ways. The well-to-do become depressed, the poor drink; women become depressed, men drink. This implies that one problem substitutes for the other and is *negatively* associated with the other. This is not the case. Persons who drink heavily are more depressed, not less.

Second, as mentioned earlier, depression is the most common type of psychological problem, experienced by everyone to some degree at some time. Anxiety is the second most common type. Thus, in looking at social patterns of distress, we focus on depression and anxiety. In most cases, the patterns would be the same if we examined other forms of psychological problems, but not in all. When we speak of psychological distress, we are referring to symptoms of depression and anxiety. However, in Part IV, we will look briefly at other psychological forms on the map: particularly paranoia and schizophrenia.

Conclusion: The Story of a Woman Diagnosed

Superimposing a diagnosis on a person's symptoms and situation does not add information, it takes information away. Worse than that, it entices us to believe a hidden entity has been revealed. The mythical entity insinuates itself into the role of a named actor, and the symptoms and situation dissolve into mere signs of its presence. Current psychiatric theory favors the view that the detected entities are physiological dysfunctions arising from anatomical abnormalities that developed because of a pathological genetic inheritance. This explanation is often firmly believed, despite the fact that diagnoses are made without reference to direct measure of genetic inheritance, anatomy and histology, or physiology. Diagnoses are almost always made entirely by reference to symptoms and history. Nevertheless, the *presumed* presence of the entity justifies biochemical treatment and obviates a continuing search for social and environmental causes. To illustrate, we end this chapter with the story of a woman diagnosed.

The story appeared as an "in-depth report" on an evening news program aired nationally on the Public Broadcasting System (PBS). The program is well known for its balanced and revealing exploration of opposing political views. Unfortunately, the same techniques often are not applied to coverage of health issues. The "medical miracles" format often supercedes the "opposing views" format. The story in question had a clear and simple message: Depression is an illness that can be diagnosed by doctors and treated with drugs; if you have the telltale signs, see your doctor.

The woman is in her late 20s or early 30s. She appears intelligent and educated. She is married, a mother of preschool-aged children, and a full-time housewife. Her husband has a good job and provides for the family. They live in a pleasant home with a yard the children can play in. She has not suffered any major failure, loss, threat, or undesirable event: no death of a loved one, no life-threatening disease, no marital breakup. As far as she can tell, she has no reason to feel bad. Nevertheless, she found herself drifting into a deepening state of apathy, lethargy, and sadness. As her energy dwindled, she found herself becoming unresponsive to the children and letting things go around the house. She went to her family doctor, who found no evidence of the medical problems that might produce a profound lethargic state (e.g., anemia, fever, infection, vitamin deficiencies). Her physician diagnosed major depression, prescribed standard antidepressive medication, and referred her to a psychiatrist. Unfortunately, her symptoms did not respond to drug treatment, so her psychiatrist enrolled her in a clinical trial of a new drug. During the interview, she said she felt a little better than before, but far from well. She expressed her belief that the origin of her problem is organic, and (somewhat less certainly) that her psychiatrist would find the right drug to solve her problem.

Within the context of psychiatry, the woman's diagnosis of major depression is correct. She has the symptoms that characterize depression: feeling sad, blue, hopeless, lethargic, and distracted; the symptoms have been around more than a few weeks; she sought help. Her family physician ruled out medical disease. She does not have symptoms of schizophrenia or other psychiatric disorder. She, her physician, and her psychiatrist can see nothing in her recent history or present circumstances that would normally result in depression. By default, they presume she is suffering the consequences of an insidious and unseen organic dysfunction that may the due to an unfortunate genetic inheritance.

Apparently, the woman, her physician, and her psychiatrist are unaware that the role of housewife and mother of young children is not the idyllic state our culture says it is. As detailed in parts of chapters 4, 5, and 7, women who are solely housewives are, on average, more depressed and anxious than women who also have jobs outside the home; women with young children (whether employed or not) are more depressed and anxious than women with older children or no children in the home. The combination of being a housewife with young children at home is particularly distressing. The difference in distress cannot be attributed to differences in other traits of the women, such as age, education, or family income. This is not to say that all housewives and mothers of young children are miserable. But many women find the economic dependency, restrictions, isolation, and menial labor distressing.

The combination of cultural values and preconceptions, along with genuine love for the children and husband, make it difficult for many women to recognize or admit that they find the role of housewife and mother ungratifying. These women may find the psychiatric interpretation of their symptoms appealing, to the extent that it helps them avoid an interpretation they are inclined to avoid. In such a case, drug treatment does not solve the basic problem, but it may make the situation more tolerable to the woman, and improve her performance in it. (Also see Chapter 3, Fig. 3.2.) If she is treated long enough, her children will get older, her emotional state may improve, and she can be taken off the drug and declared cured. The woman's diagnosis of major depression is functional, in that it provides an interpretation and response that does not challenge or threaten her preconceptions, values, and family relationships. The diagnosis is dysfunctional, in that it helps her hide from a problem she must recognize and understand in order to solve.

Appendix 2.A. The Diagnostic Interview Schedule— Major Depression

1. In your lifetime, have you ever had two weeks or more during which you felt sad, blue, depressed or when you lost all interest and pleasure in things that you usually cared about or enjoyed?

      Yes_____
      No_____

2. Has there ever been a period of two weeks or longer when you *lost your appetite?*

      Yes_____
      No_____

3. Have you ever *lost weight* without trying to—as much as two pounds a week for several weeks (or as much as ten pounds altogether?)

      Yes_____
      No_____

4. Have you ever had a period when your eating increased so much that you *gained* as much as two pounds a week for several weeks (or ten pounds altogether)?

      Yes_____
      No_____

APPETITE SUMMARY: CHECK YES_____If YES in 2, 3, or 4.

5. Have you ever had a period of two weeks or more when you had *trouble falling asleep*, staying asleep or with waking up too early?

      Yes_____
      No_____

6. Have you ever had a period of two weeks or longer when you were *sleeping too much?*

      Yes_____
      No_____

SLEEP SUMMARY: Check YES_____If YES in 5 or 6

7. Has there ever been a period lasting two weeks or more when you felt *tired out* all the time?

      Yes_____
      No_____

TIRED OUT SUMMARY: Check YES_____If YES in 7

8. Has there ever been a period of two weeks or more when you talked or moved *more slowly* than is normal for you?

Yes_____
No_____

9. Has there ever been a period of two weeks or more when you had to be *moving all the time*—that is, you couldn't sit still and paced up and down?

Yes_____
No_____

SLOW, RESTLESS SUMMARY: Check YES_____If YES in 8 or 9

10. Has there ever been a period of several weeks when your *interest in sex* was a lot less than usual?

Yes_____
No_____

SEX SUMMARY: Check YES_____If YES in 10

11. Has there ever been a period of two weeks or more when you felt worthless, sinful or guilty?

Yes_____
No_____

WORTHLESS SUMMARY: Check YES_____If YES in 11

12. Has there ever been a period of two weeks or more when you had a lot more *trouble concentrating* than is normal for you?

Yes_____
No_____

13. Have you ever had a period of two weeks or more when your *thoughts* came much *slower* than usual or seemed mixed up?

Yes_____
No_____

TROUBLE THINKING SUMMARY: Check YES_____If YES in 12 or 13

14. Has there ever been a period of two weeks or more when you *thought* a lot *about death*—either your own, someone else's or death in general?

Yes_____
No_____

15. Has there ever been a period of two weeks or more when you felt like you *wanted to die*?

Yes_____
No_____

16. Have you ever felt so low you *thought of* committing *suicide*?

Yes_____
No_____

17. Have you ever attempted *suicide*?

Yes_____
No_____

DEATH SUMMARY: Check YES_____If YES in 14, 15, 16, OR 17.

CHECK ITEM. REFER TO SUMMARY BOXES.

_____Fewer than 4 summary boxes checked YES. [*No diagnosis of major depression.*]

_____4 or more summary boxes checked YES, and NO in question 1. Go to question 20.

_____4 or more summary boxes checked YES, and YES in question 1. Go to question 18.

18. You've said you've had a period of feeling depressed (blue, sad, etc.) and also said you've had some other problems (mention all checked YES in 2–17). Has there ever been a time when the feelings of depression and some of these other problems occurred together, that is within the same month?

Yes_____
No_____

19. (If "NO" to question 18): So there's never been a period when you felt depressed at the same time you were having some of these other problems?

Yes, has been a period_____
No, never been a period_____   [*No diagnosis*]

20. You said you have had periods when (mention all checked YES in 2–17). Was there ever a time when several of these problems occurred together— that is, within the same month?

Yes_____
No_____   [*No diagnosis*]

21. (If "YES" to question 20): When you were having some of these problems at about the same time, were you feeling okay, or were you feeling low, gloomy, blue or uninterested in everything?

Low or equivalent_____
Okay_____   [*No diagnosis*]

22. (If "low or equivalent" to question 21): What's the longest spell you've ever had when you felt depressed (blue, sad, etc.) and had several of these other problems at the same time?

More than 2 weeks_____

Less than 2 weeks_____   [*No diagnosis*]

23. Have you had more than one spell when you felt depressed (blue, sad, etc.) and had several of these other problems at the same time?

Yes_____

No_____

24. Did this spell (or any of those spells) occur just after someone close to you died?

Yes_____

No_____

25. Have you had any spell of depression along with these other problems (mention some problems checked YES in 2–17) at times when it wasn't due to a death?

Yes_____

No_____   [*No diagnosis*]

26. Are you in one of these spells of feeling low or disinterested and having some of these other problems now?

Yes_____

No_____

27. When did your last spell like that end?

Within last 2 weeks_____
Within last month_____
Within last 6 months_____
Within last year_____
More than 1 year ago_____

28. Now I'd like to know about the time when you were feeling depressed (sad, blue, etc.) for at least two weeks and had the largest number of these problems at the same time. How old were you at that time?

_____years old

During that spell of depression (blues, sadness, etc.), which of these other problems did you have? For instance, during that spell:

29. Did you lose your appetite?

Yes_____
No_____

30. Did you lose weight without trying to—as much as two pounds a week for several weeks (or as much as ten pounds altogether)?

Yes_____
No_____

(Questions 29–44 are the same questions as 2–17, phrased in the format shown in 29–30. Respondents are only asked about these symptoms during the worst spell if they answered "YES" to them in questions 2–17; that is, if they answered earlier that they had ever had them for a period of more than two weeks).

(Questions 24 and 25 show the exclusion of depression due to death of a loved one from the diagnosis of depression. Other exclusion criteria are not shown, but are assessed by probes in which the interviewer questions whether symptoms are due to physical illness, drugs, or other psychiatric problems.

Appendix 2.B. 91 Symptoms

(Each question was phrased, "How often in the past 12 months have you_____." Responses were recorded as never, almost never, sometimes, fairly often, or often.)

Schizophrenia

DOMINATED BY FORCES: felt that your mind was dominated by forces beyond your control
HEAR VOICES: heard voices without knowing where they came from
SEE THINGS: seen things or animals or people around you that others did not see
VISIONS: had visions or seen things other people say they cannot see
POSSESSED: felt that you were possessed by a spirit or devil
SPECIAL POWERS: felt you had special powers
• FELT DEAD: felt that you did not exist at all, that you were dead, dissolved
THOUGHTS ALOUD: seemed to hear your thoughts spoken aloud—almost as if someone standing nearby could hear them
THOUGHTS BROADCAST: felt that your unspoken thoughts were being broadcast or transmitted, so that everyone knew what you were thinking
AFRAID MIGHT DO WRONG: felt afraid that you might do something seriously wrong against your own will
STRANGE THOUGHTS: had unusual thoughts that kept bothering you

USELESS THOUGHTS: had useless thoughts that kept running through your mind

Paranoia

TRUST NO ONE: felt it was safer to trust no one
PLOTTED AGAINST: Believed you were being plotted against
TALK BEHIND BACK: felt that people were saying all kinds of things about you behind your back
ENEMIES: felt you had enemies who really wished to do you harm
SUSPICIOUS: been very suspicious, didn't trust anybody
ALL AGAINST ME: been sure that everyone was against you

Depression—Mood

NOTHING WORTHWHILE: wondered if anything was worthwhile anymore
SUICIDAL: thought about taking your own life
NOTHING TURNS OUT: felt that nothing turned out for you the way you wanted it to
DESERVE PUNISHMENT: felt you deserved to be punished
SHOULD DIE: felt that others would be better off if you were dead
FELT EVIL: felt that you have done something evil or wrong
WISH I'D DIE: wished you were dead
WORTHLESS: felt very bad or worthless
SELF-BLAME: blamed yourself for something that went wrong
HOPELESS: felt completely hopeless about everything
LONELY: felt lonely
FELT LIKE CRYING: felt like crying
GUILTY: felt guilty about things you did or did not do
USELESS: felt useless
LOSE TEMPER: lost your temper
LOW SPIRITS: been in low spirits
BROOD: brooded over unpleasant thoughts or feelings
DON'T CARE: just didn't care what happened to you
MOODY: been moody and unhappy
HELPLESS: felt completely helpless
TEARFUL: the respondent cried or was tearful

Manic

EXCITING SCHEMES: had times when exciting new ideas and schemes occurred to you one after another
THOUGHTS RACE: became so excited that your thoughts raced ahead faster than you could speak them

Depression–Malaise

DON'T TALK: became very quiet and didn't talk to anyone

NO INTEREST: showed no interest in anything or anybody

CAN'T CONCENTRATE: had trouble concentrating or keeping your mind on what you were doing

LOSE THOUGHTS: kept loosing your train of thought

MIND NOT WORK: felt that your mind did not work as well as it used to

BLUE: had periods of feeling blue or depressed that interfered with your daily activity

NO GET GO: had periods of days or weeks when you couldn't take care of things because you couldn't "get going"

CONFUSED: felt confused; had trouble thinking

SICK FROM ANGER: got angry and afterward felt uncomfortable, like getting headaches, stomach pains, cold sweats and things like that

CAN'T REMEMBER: began having trouble remembering things

STAY ASLEEP: had trouble staying asleep

WAKE EARLY: had trouble with waking up too early and not being able to fall asleep again

OVERSLEEP: had trouble with oversleeping: that is, sleeping past the time you wanted to get up

TIRED: troubled by feeling tired all the time

NIGHTMARES: been bothered by nightmares

POOR APPETITE: had poor appetite

WEAK: felt weak all over

WEIGHT LOSS: experienced any weight loss of 10 lb. (5 kg) or more over the past year, without going on special diets

Manic

TOO EXCITED: felt so great (excited, talkative or active) that it was difficult to concentrate

Anxiety-Mood

WORRY A LOT: worried a lot about little things

ANXIOUS: felt anxious about something or someone

IRRITATED: were easily irritated

IRRITABLE: been bothered by being irritable, fidgety, or tense

WORRY: I am a person who is the worrying type

Panic

AFRAID TO GO OUT: felt afraid to leave the house because you were afraid something might happen to it

FEAR CLOSED PLACES: been afraid to be in closed places
FEAR SOMETHING: feared something terrible would happen to you
FEARS: had special fears that kept bothering you
FEAR ATTACK: feared being robbed, attacked, or physically injured

Anxiety-Malaise

Autonomic

MUSCLES TWITCH: had trouble with your muscles twitching or jumping
CAN'T FALL ASLEEP: had trouble falling asleep
COLD SWEATS: had cold sweats
DIZZY: had dizziness
BREATHLESS: had shortness of breath when you were not exercising or working hard
HANDS TREMBLE: had your hands tremble
PALPITATIONS: had you heart beating hard when you were not exercising or working hard
HOT ALL OVER: suddenly feel hot all over

Behavioral

RESTLESS: had periods of such great restlessness that you could not sit in a chair for very long
FIDGETING: the respondent kept fidgeting and squirming
NERVOUS: the respondent appeared nervous and fidgety
NOT LISTENING: the content of the respondent's answers often have little or nothing to do with the questions asked
DRUMMING: the respondent drums on surfaces with fingers or taps on floor
MOVES AROUND: the respondent kept getting up and moving around restlessly

Obsessive

REPEAT ACT: had to repeat an act over and over again though it was hard to explain to others why you did it
DO OVER AND OVER: found yourself doing the same things over and over again to be sure they were right

Alcoholism

BLURRED SPEECH: the respondent's speech was blurred
MAKES UP WORDS: the respondent makes up new words
DRINK & MISS WORK: missed work or been late to work because of drinking
DRINK & ARGUE: had arguments with your family because of your drinking
SICK FROM DRINK: had trouble with your health because of drinking

CHAPTER THREE

Real-World Causes of Real-World Misery

Establishing Cause in the Human Sciences

Why are some people more distressed than others? That is the question—the issue, the thing to be explained. The answer is found in the reality of people's lives: the hard facts and tough realities, the problems that must be faced, and the problems that cannot be faced. It is not found in fantasies or the subconscious, or in laboratories and clinics.

To learn why some people are more distressed than others, we must first find out *who* is more distressed: who feels happy, energetic, fulfilled, and hopeful; who feels miserable, run down, empty, and worried. The "who" is a list of attributes pointing to a reality shared by some that is different from the reality shared by others. It includes being wealthy, middle class, working class, or poor; having a college degree, a high school degree, or no degree; having a job or not; being white or black, male or female, single, married, divorced, or widowed; being young, middle-aged, or old; being the boss or the bossed.

Once we know the social patterns of distress, we look for explanations. The patterns suggest and reveal the social causes of psychological well-being and distress. In this chapter we show how researchers in the human sciences —the sciences that study people—determine whether one state causes another. We discuss the criteria used in all the human sciences to establish cause, and compare the two major study designs: experiments and surveys. We argue, in contrast to what many other scientists believe, that surveys and not experiments are the best way to find out why some people are more distressed than others.

Finding Causes: The Three Criteria

How do we know one thing causes another? Commonly, a cause is that which produces an effect, result, or consequence; the person, event, or condition responsible for an action or result. Logically, a cause must exist for an effect to occur. In modern human sciences, the effect is viewed as an alteration of probabilities, rather than a determination of outcomes. Probabilities can be altered by individual or communal choice and effort, aggregate behavior, historical trends, environmental constraints, biological events, and so on.

The probability of an American earning more than the average income is increased by finishing college compared to only finishing high school, and by having been born white rather than black. Thus, education and race both cause variation in earnings, even though one is an achieved status and the other ascribed, even though some high school-educated blacks earn more than some college-educated whites, and even though the causal connections might not exist in another society or in the future.

Philosophers interested in cause have argued for centuries about necessity, sufficiency, responsibility, and inevitability. The debates become especially thick where humans are the objects of study, because of human free will. Many scientists are tired of the debate. Some try to avoid using the idea of cause. More commonly, scientists use terms that express the underlying idea without using the actual word: terms such as increased risk, increased probability, effect, determinant, or risk factor. Whatever the terms, the idea is much the same.

Human sciences say that one thing causes another if three criteria are met: association, nonspuriousness, and causal order (e.g., Hirschi and Selvin, 1967; Cole, 1972; Mausner and Bahn, 1974). Things are associated if they appear together more than would be expected by chance. The association is not spurious if it exists for reasons other than historical coincidence and other than the two simply resulting from a common cause. The association is ordered if one thing leads and the other follows, rather than vice versa. Association, nonspuriousness, and causal order are individually necessary and collectively sufficient to show that one thing causes another.

The relationship between cigarette smoking and lung cancer is a good example of an established cause (Mausner and Bahn, 1974). Smoking is associated with lung cancer: People who smoke are more likely to get lung cancer than people who do not. After four decades of research, there is no sign that the association is spurious: Smoking is connected with lung cancer by more than historical accident or a common antecedent. For example, men smoke more than women, and also have higher rates of lung cancer. It is possible that men have more lung cancer than women for some reason other than smoking. Thus, it is possible that cigarette smoking and lung cancer are associated because men smoke more than women, and coincidentally happen to have more lung cancer than women. If this were the entire reason for the association, then men who smoke would have the same rates of lung cancer as men who do not. In reality, just the opposite is true: men who smoke have higher rates of lung cancer than men who do not, and women who smoke have rates of lung cancer similar to those of men who smoke. If one compares smokers and nonsmokers matched in age, education, type of job, race, ethnic origins, weight, drinking habits, and anything else that can be measured, smokers have higher rates of lung cancer than the nonsmokers. The real difference is between smokers and nonsmokers.

Researchers have not tried every imaginable comparison and never will, but they have tried a great many, and the connection between smoking and lung cancer remains. However, it is *possible* that a gene makes some people susceptible to both tobacco addiction and lung cancer, with no other connection between the two. If so, then the association between smoking and lung cancer is spurious, and both are simply due to a genetic factor that researchers did not take into account. In reality there is no evidence that such a gene exists. No one has shown that smokers and nonsmokers matched on genotype have the same rates of lung cancer. The "what if" argument is nothing more than speculation.

What is the order of the connection between smoking and lung cancer? Can we rule out the possibility that lung cancer causes smoking? It seems we can. Smokers usually pick up the habit in their teenage or young adult years. Lung cancer appears 30 or 40 years later, in late adulthood. Among people who used to smoke but quit, the rate of lung cancer decreases as the number of years since they smoked increases. Thus lung cancer does not cause smoking. Smoking causes lung cancer.

As the example shows, evaluating an association requires judgment. The evidence is never totally unequivocal. There is no way to check off "YES" or "NO" for each criterion without thought, no matter what the study design. The data provide evidence, but the researcher makes the judgment. It is possible, given everything we know, that smoking does not cause lung cancer. The evidence is never absolute proof. In this case, it is also hard to believe, given what we know, that smoking does not cause lung cancer. The evidence of association, nonspuriousness, and causal order is substantial.

Population Studies of Distress

Sociologists ask people about their lives in the community, at work, and at home—in other words, the world that they live in. Mostly this is done by phoning or visiting large numbers of people who are selected randomly to represent the entire population. Everyone has an equal chance of being interviewed: those who sought help and those who did not, the middle class and the poor, men and women, those for whom visiting a psychiatrist is shameful and those for whom it is acceptable, those with access to care and those without it. Unlike clinical studies, this avoids the biases of basing conclusions on people who have sought help: those with the time, money, or inclination to visit a psychologist or psychiatrist.

Statements about social causes are statements of probability. Suppose we say that poverty causes depression. This means that the poor have higher average levels of depression than the well-to-do. It does not mean that *all* poor people are depressed; in fact, many are not. It does not mean that all depressed people are poor. Some poor persons are less depressed than some rich ones. Poverty increases a person's risk of depression. It puts one at a *relative* disadvantage. In addition, social causes are not sole causes. When we say that poverty causes depression *we do not mean it is the only cause.* Poverty is one of many causes.

Survey research establishes cause the same way all research on humans does: by meeting the three criteria. For example, consider the idea that lower income causes higher levels of depression.

Association

First, is lower income associated with higher levels of depression? To see if this is the case, we must compare persons at various income levels. A sample of poor people alone would be insufficient. Suppose poor people average 20 symptoms a week. If people who are not poor also average 20 symptoms a week, there is no association. While this point may seem too obvious to mention, a lot of studies miss it. It is amazing how often researchers interested in the effects of poverty talk only to poor people, how often those interested in the effects of being female talk only to women, how frequently those interested in the effects of being part of a minority group talk only to blacks or to Hispanics, or how often those interested in the causes of depression talk only to the depressed. Comparison is essential for establishing an association. By randomly sampling from the large and varied population of a city, state, or nation, the survey researcher is assured of a representative range of comparisons and contrasts. Random sampling gives everyone in the population the same chance of being interviewed. As a consequence, a random sample contains people at all levels of income in much the same proportion as in the population. The very rich sometimes refuse to talk to interviewers. The extremely poor often cannot be contacted, especially those living on the street or staying wherever they can find shelter. Nonetheless, random community samples usually have the variation needed for comparison.

Nonspuriousness

Second, are low income and high levels of depression really connected, or is the association spurious? We know that blacks, Hispanics, women, and the elderly are on average both poorer and more depressed than non-Hispanic whites, men, and young or middle-aged adults. Perhaps there are hidden genetic, organic, or cultural factors that make these groups both poorer and more depressed. If there are, then there may be no causal connection between low income and high levels of depression; the two may only have common antecedents. However, when we look at people of comparable race, ethnicity, gender, and age, we find that the relationship between income and depression still exists. This would not be the case if the association merely reflected differences in race, ethnicity, gender, and age. There is no evidence that the association is spurious.

Causal Order

Third, does low income cause depression, or is it the other way around? This is the really tough question. We know that depression is associated with lethargy, listlessness, and malaise—qualities that do not contribute to success. On the other hand, we know that housewives are more depressed the less their husbands' incomes. A housewife's depression is less likely to cause her husband's lack of success than her own. Similarly, young people just entering the labor force are more depressed the less their parents earn. The son's or daughter's depression seems unlikely to be the cause of the parents' lack of success. We also know that retired people are more depressed than others. Much of the association between retirement and depression (but not all) is due to low income. Retirement is mandated by social norms, organizational rules, and public laws. It is more likely that the drop in income due to retirement causes depression, than that depression causes retirement and a drop in income. Thus, we conclude that low income causes depression.

Judging Causal Order

Of the three criteria, the easiest one to judge is association. All we need to do is think of the appropriate questions, ask them of a representative sample of people, and correlate the responses. Ruling out a spurious association is a bit more difficult. We need to think of what might make the things we are interested in correlated without one causing the other. Then we need to measure those things as well, and take them into account. Usually this requires adjustment of the association, using statistical methods such as multiple regression (Tufte, 1974; Pedhazur, 1982). Technically, we never completely rule out spuriousness because we never adjust for every imaginable possibility. Practically, though, the more possibilities we rule out the more convinced we become that the association is not spurious.

Of the three criteria, the most difficult one to judge is causal order. Which is the cause and which the consequence? (There's a reason the old conundrum about the chicken and the egg has been around so long.) The paragraphs that follow describe six ways that sociologists judge causal order.

Some Things Do Not Change

Sometimes the causal order is obvious. This is usually the case if one of the variables is an ascribed status. For example, on average, women are more depressed than men. The association between gender and depression is not spurious. It is implausible that depression causes people to become women, because gender is fixed at birth. The social status is attached to the individual's morphology before the first cry. So we say that something about being female is a cause of depression, rather than the other way around. Ascribed statuses, such as gender, race, year of birth, and national origin, are largely fixed by accidents of birth. For the most part, they are not optional, not a matter of choice, and not changeable. They are not produced by the individual's attitudes, feelings, beliefs, or experiences, so causal order is not a question.

Common Sequences

Causal order is established by common and well-known sequences. For instance, people usually finish high school, then get a job that pays a certain wage. We might ask people the kind of job they have, the amount of money they earn, and the highest grade or year of school they have completed. If we find an association between level of education and job prestige, we can assume with good reason that education preceded job status. We can also assume that certain jobs pay certain wages, not that one's wages determine what kind of job one gets. Other well-established sequences might include: the prestige of one's first job precedes the prestige of one's second job, service in World War II precedes attitudes in 1980, grades in high school precede grades in college, marriage precedes divorce, and so on.

Some Things Change More Readily Than Others

Causal order can be established by the "relative stickiness" of the variables (Davis, 1985). We know that some things do not change readily: where people live, their religion, the kinds of jobs they have. Other things change more easily: preferences and attitudes, especially for certain political candidates, brands of products, and so on. Therefore, if a person's religion is associated with his preference for a political candidate, we can assume that the person's religion affected preferences, not that preference for a certain candidate led the individual to become Protestant or Catholic or Jewish. This is not to say it could never happen the other way around. It is just that religious change is unlikely to account for much of any association. Research shows that 90% of adult Americans practice the same religion they were brought up in. About 5% have switched to having no religion. Most of the rest have switched from one Protestant denomination to another, higher-status one. Information such as this often allows us to judge the causal order of an association.

Common Knowledge

Causal order is judged based on understandings about the world. For example, we find that women who have jobs *and* children *and* husbands who do not share the child-care responsibilities are very depressed compared to employed women without children, or employed women with children whose husbands share child care. One could argue that a woman first becomes depressed (for organic reasons, say), and the depression leads her to get a job, have children, and do all the child care herself. This is possible, but implausible. We know that depression decreases motivation. It seems unlikely that depression drives women to take on a number of roles. It is more likely that role strain, overload, and conflict increase depression.

Longitudinal Data

Causal order is established with longitudinal data—information collected from the same people at two or more points in time. We can ask people about their income and symptoms in 1988, then ask the same people again in 1993. Then we can see if poverty in 1988 is associated with an *increase* in depression over the subsequent period. Low income at the beginning of the period cannot result from subsequent increases in depression, so we assume that low income caused the increase. A number of longitudinal studies find that low socioeconomic status increases psychological distress (Pearlin *et al.*, 1981; Wheaton, 1978). It is also true that distress retards socioeconomic progress (Kohn and Schooler, 1982), but this rebound effect is a relatively small part of the total association. Interestingly, to our knowledge the longitudinal studies in community mental health have never shown the causal order assumptions of previous cross-sectional analyses to be wrong. So far, the causal order judgments based on other considerations proved correct when tested.

Patterns and Their Explanations

Causal order is established by explaining the association. If an association is causal, what are the mechanisms? If being female, or black, or poor causes depression, how does it do so? What are the consequences of being female, black, or poor that might be depressing? If we measure those consequences and show that they account for the association with depression, then we have explained the association. *Patterns plus their explanations* are the essence of cause. Because explaining patterns is the heart of causal analysis, we give an extensive example of the process.

We know that low income is associated with depression. In general, we think that the reality of day-to-day lives affects well-being. Perceptions and feelings do not just spring out of people's heads; they come from experience. What consequence of low income might result in depression? One real possibility is economic hardship—difficulty providing for the family's needs. A family is an economic unit bound by emotional ties. It is in the home that the larger social and economic order impinges on individuals, exposing them to varying degrees of hardship, frustration, and struggle. The chronic strain of struggling to pay the bills and feed and clothe the family on an inadequate income takes its toll in feelings of depression—in feeling run down, feeling that everything is an effort, that the future is hopeless, in an inability to shake the blues. Nagging worries produce restless sleep. There is not much to enjoy in life. When life is a constant struggle to get by, when it is never taken for granted that there will be enough money for food, clothes, and medical care, people feel worn down and hopeless. There is no relief from the struggle—it pulls at the person day after day in the form of another bill, an unexpected injury or sickness that needs treatment, or facing the week before payday with less than a week's worth of food money.

Does economic hardship explain the association between low income and depression? Economic hardship is assessed by asking, "During the past twelve months, how often did it happen that you did not have enough money to afford food for your family? Clothes for your family? Medical care for your family? How often did you have trouble paying the bills?" (Pearlin et al., 1981). A random sample of 680 married couples throughout the United States was interviewed by telephone and asked these questions, as well as questions about family income and symptoms suffered in the past week (Ross and Huber, 1985). The answers are summarized in indexes of income, economic hardship, and depression (see the description of the *Women and Work* study in the Appendix to the book).

Let us look at the pattern of association. The degree to which a pair of variables goes together is measured with a correlation coefficient, which is positive if more of one goes with more of the other and negative if more of one goes with less of the other. The correlation between income and economic hardship is about $-.35$; the correlation between economic hardship and depression is about $+.30$; the correlation between income and depression is about $-.10$ (Ross and Huber, 1985). To see what this pattern tells us, let's look at two competing causal models.

The social cause model says that higher income reduces economic hardship, and economic hardship increases depression. As illustrated in Fig. 3.1, the social status of having low income results in the psychological state of depression through economic hardship. The numbers over the arrows are the correlation coefficients reported above. In a causal chain, correlations are the simplest case of path coefficients, which can be multiplied to get total effects. According to the model, the total causal effect of income on depression is $(-.35) \times (+.30) = -.105$. This value, predicted by the social cause model, is very close to the actual correlation of $-.10$ between income and depression reported above.

The social selection model says that depression causes low income, and higher income reduces economic hardship. As illustrated in Fig. 3.2, the psychological state of depression increases the family's economic hardship through low income. According to the model, the total causal effect of depression on economic hardship is $(-.10) \times (-.35) = +.035$, which is *not* close to the observed correlation of $+.30$ reported above.

Social Cause Model

-.105 = (-.35)(.30)

-.105 = predicted correlation between family income & depression

-.100 = observed correlation between family income & depression

.005 = observed - predicted

Social Selection Model

+.035 = (-.10)(-.35)

+.035 = predicted correlation between depression & hardship

+.300 = observed correlation between depression & hardship

.265 = observed - predicted

Figure 3.1. Social cause and social selection models of the association between income and depression. Data are from the Women and Work Study (see the Appendix to this book for measurement of the variables and description of the sample).

The observed pattern of correlations fits the social cause model much better than the social selection model. This information as a whole strongly suggests that low income causes depression. Other pieces of information strengthen this judgment. For example, education should help people get more out of their money. The results show that higher education reduces the association between low income and economic hardship, which in turn reduces the association between low income and depression (Ross and Huber,

1985). Other research shows that economic hardship results in a sense of powerlessness—of not being master of one's own life (Pearlin *et al.*, 1981). The sense of powerlessness connects economic hardship to depression, as well as low income to depression. The way the pieces fit together says a great deal about cause and effect. The patterns and their explanations tell us who is more distressed, and why.

Experimental Studies of Distress

The essential difference between experiments and surveys is manipulation. In an experiment, the researcher does something to the subjects and observes the consequences. The modern experiment holds out the hope of meeting the three criteria of cause without requiring judgment—without depending on common knowledge or outside information. Wherever there is room for judgment, there is room for misjudgment. Social scientists are acutely aware that common knowledge, assumptions, and presuppositions can represent false stereotypes, prejudices, and mistaken beliefs. The process of judgment is one of stating the assumptions, questioning them, looking for their implications, and checking them against objective information. The modern experiment *seems* to offer a logical sword that will cut through this Gordian knot. While the modern experiment works very well for many purposes, it does not work for others. In particular, experiments cannot tell us why some people are more distressed than others. This can be explained by examining the theory behind experiments and their practical, inherent, and philosophical limitations.

The Theory Behind Randomized Experiments

A randomized experiment works in the following way. The researcher enlists a number of subjects who are divided into two or more groups based on the outcome of a random process, such as flipping a coin. The researcher puts the individual members of the groups through experiences that are alike in every way, the sole exception being the experimental treatment, which is the same for all members of the same group, and different for each group. The researcher assesses the outcome in all subjects, using the same means of assessment for all. Measures of the outcome are averaged for all members of the same group, and the averages are compared across groups.

The experimenter attempts to create an association by exposing the groups to different treatments. If the difference between groups in average outcome is greater than might typically be found by chance, then the results demonstrate an association between treatment and outcome.

The experimenter attempts to eliminate spuriousness by randomly assigning subjects to treatments. It is totally a matter of chance as to which persons wind up in which group. As a result, the groups are roughly comparable in terms of the proportion of females, average age, average IQ, proportion espousing any particular political affiliation, average family income, average distress, and any other factor, known or unknown, imagined or unimagined, that might affect the outcome. The larger the number of subjects, the more this is true. If the groups are reasonably large, then any association between treatment and outcome is probably not due to pretreatment differences in the composition of the groups. In other words, the association is not spurious.

The experimenter attempts to estabish causal order by actually manipulating the independent variable—the supposed cause. The groups are alike to begin with. The only consistent difference in their experiences is the treatment, introduced by the experimenter. If there is an association between the manipulated experience and the assessed outcome, it cannot be that the outcome caused the experience. It must be that the experience caused the outcome.

The essence of an experiment is that an experimenter *does* something to the subject. (Survey researchers, like all observational researchers do nothing to the subjects. They just observe the natural variation in the real world, usually by asking people questions about their lives and recording the answers.) Like any other form of research, the experiment is designed to meet the three criteria of cause. In an experiment, the researcher *produces* variation in the presumed cause and sees whether it affects the presumed consequence. In an observational study like a survey, the researcher *examines* whether the natural variation in the presumed cause produces the presumed consequence.

Experiments are the best way to evaluate the effectiveness of treatments. This is because treatments, such as drugs, surgery, or counseling, are interventions, actions taken by a therapist or researcher to produce a desired effect. Because intervention is the essence of an experiment, the randomized controlled trial is the preferred method of evaluating treatments. The power of experiments to evaluate treatments often leads researchers to prefer it as a method, even if the research question is not about treatments.

Practical Limitations of Experiments

There are practical limitations of experiments on human subjects. To some extent they flow from the ethical limitations on doing things to human beings to see what happens, but to some extent control is simply beyond the experimenter's powers. There is a limit to how effectively one human being's life can be designed by another. No one can completely constrain another person. Some things require cooperation. At some level, freedom is not just a right, it is a fact.

The major practical limitations of experiments are stable traits, weak manipulation, trivial manipulation, analog manipulation, and unrepresentative volunteers.

Stable traits pose a special problem. Ascribed characteristics such as sex, race, or age, are beyond manipulation. Others could be manipulated in theory, but would involve many practical problems. Personality traits fall into this category. Personality is, by definition, a set of stable traits shaped over the years. It is the sum of experiences and developmental changes, shaped by a substantial and enduring reality. Experiments tend to be brief experiences limited in scope. It is very difficult to change, in a short time, the presuppositions, habits, preferences, and inclinations accumulated over years.

Weak or limited manipulation plagues many experiments. It is unethical to push some things too far, such as strain, threat, and helplessness—anything that, in theory, causes depression, anxiety, or malaise. Other things are ethical but impractical to manipulate greatly. Experiments often manipulate money rewards ranging from $5 to $10. This is tiny compared to the corporate rewards ranging over thousands and tens of thousands of dollars. The experimental manipulation is two or three orders of magnitude weaker than the forces it supposedly represents.

Problems with stable traits and weak manipulation lead some experimenters to substitute trivial manipulations. For example, we know there is a correlation between overweight and high blood pressure. Does excessive weight elevate blood pressure? To answer the question experimentally, we would have to randomly assign subjects to gain weight, stay the same weight, or lose weight. We would have to follow them long enough for substantial gains or losses to occur, and look at the differences in blood pressure across groups. The practical difficulties are obvious. In a typical trivial manipulation, the experimenter, instead, divides the subjects into two groups: overweight and not overweight. Within each weight class the subjects are randomly assigned to experience or not experience a loud and unexpected bang. Blood pressure is then measured. The difference in blood pressure between bang and no-bang conditions is greater for the overweight subjects than for those who are not overweight. So what? The experiment still does not tell us if being overweight causes high blood pressure because weight was not manipulated to increase or decrease blood pressure.

Many experiments on human subjects are simply analogies to reality that may or may not be apt. For example, much depression might result from overwhelmingly difficult or impossible circumstances. To see if frustration and failure cause depression, the experimenter gives one group an anagram that can be solved and gives another group something that looks like an anagram but is not, and that cannot be solved. The experimenter finds that the subjects doomed to failure report being more frustrated and annoyed with the task than do the subjects with a solvable problem. In what way is the unsolvable anagram like a life of poverty, being laid off, or having cancer? Can it really represent them? How much is the experimentally induced frustration and annoyance like the demoralization, powerlessness, depression, anxiety, and malaise felt by the poor, the unemployed, and the sick?

The final practical problem with experiments is that the samples are usually biased. The subjects are an odd group bearing an uncertain similarity to the population as a whole. Typically, experiments use convenient samples of college students or people in institutions such as the army or prison. Since the subjects rarely represent the general population, the results can only be generalized to others similar to the subjects in the experiment. Experimental researchers often assume that people are people, and that the knowledge gained in experiments on college freshmen taking psychology courses applies to everyone. The assumption is false. Going to college is a social advantage. About 22% of Americans have had some college and about 23% have a college degree or more. About half the people in the United States have never been to college—the half with less opportunity. Students are also younger and less experienced than the general population. In addition, the students in experiments are paid to participate, required to participate, or voluntarily donate their time. There is no reason to think the experimental subjects represent students in general, even at their own schools.

Inherent Limitations of Experiments on Causes

The practical limitations of experiments on humans can be reduced by effort, ingenuity, and resources. The inherent limitations cannot. In the last analysis, the laboratory is not the world. The relevance of effects induced in the laboratory to phenomena observed in the world is inherently uncertain. Experiments cannot show patterns of distress in the real world; they cannot show causal direction in the real world; and they cannot explain why observed patterns of distress exist.

Experiments cannot show patterns: they cannot show who is more distressed than others. Their core inherent limitation is that they do not account for observed differences in distress because they do not observe those differences. The cause manipulated in an experiment may not be the important one. One example comes from epidemiology: it is possible to produce high blood pressure in rats by inducing lesions in the blood vessels of the kidney (renovascular lesions). When the same lesions are found in human hypertensives, the hypertension can usually be cured with vascular surgery. However, it is clear from cross-sectional surveys such as the National Health and Nutrition Examination Survey that very little of the hypertension observed in the community is due to renovascular disease. The vast majority of high blood pressure is caused by obesity and a sedentary life-style—which are difficult to manipulate in experiments. Nevertheless, diet and exercise are things that individuals can and often do control, so the information is useful to people interested in reducing their blood pressure. This is just one example of an established experimental cause which is largely irrelevant as a cause (in the case of high blood pressure) in the population.

The uncertain relevance of the cause found in an experiment to real-world variation means that experiments do not resolve the question of causal order in the real world. Doing something to the subjects and seeing what follows establishes the causal order within the experiment. Finding an effect of the manipulation does not rule out the possibility or primacy of the opposite effect. Suppose an experimenter randomly assigns subjects to two groups. One group is given a drug that makes them feel depressed, the other is given a placebo. On average, the subjects given the drug feel and act more helpless than those given the placebo. Thus, depression causes helplessness *in the experiment*. This does not rule out the possibility that helplessness also causes depression. It does not tell us which effect accounts for the association between helplessness and depression in the community. In theory, doing both experiments might provide an answer, if an effect is demonstrated in one direction but not the other. Practically, though, the failure to find an effect in one direction might be due to weak manipulation. At best, the experiment demonstrates a possibility.

Establishing causal order is supposedly one of the strengths of experiments. It is the reason that many researchers use experimental methods when they are inappropriate, impractical, or unable to answer the real question. Yet experiments cannot say which is the cause and which the effect in the real world, they can only form conclusions within the experiment. Perhaps it is better to trade the simplicity of unreality for the complexity of reality.

Experiments can show whether or not the manipulation has an effect, but they cannot explain *why* the effect does or does not exist. Experiments can measure different outcomes, but they cannot show the links among outcomes. They cannot tell us which outcome is the explanation and which is the ultimate consequence. To answer that question we must return to the logic of observational research and causal analysis.

For example, unemployment and poverty are common among mothers who are single, divorced, and separated, and may be a cause of the high levels of depression in these groups. Suppose we are considering a policy of providing unmarried mothers with jobs that pay a decent wage, and we want to evaluate the policy with an experiment. We randomly assign some unmarried mothers to an intervention in which employment is provided, while the control group receives no treatment. We might find that the experimental group—those mothers who got jobs—had lower levels of depression than the control group after six months. Jobs decrease depression among unmarried mothers. The policy is a success, and even though we do not know why the jobs decreased depression, we know that they do. It may be that jobs decrease depression by decreasing poverty, or by increasing self-esteem, or by increasing the control these women feel over their lives, or by increasing interaction with and support from co-workers. We could even measure various outcomes—say, earnings, self-esteem, and depression. But the experiment does not show whether higher earnings decrease depression, or whether higher self-esteem decreases depression, or whether lower depression increases self-esteem or earnings.

Suppose the experiment had found no differences in depression between the control and experimental groups. In this situation, we have no idea what is happening. Possibly, jobs do not affect mental health. However, sometimes an experimental intervention has unintended side effects that counteract the desired effect. If this is the case, the independent variable appears to have no effect on the outcome, because two intervening processes counteract each other. Possibly, employment among unmarried mothers has some positive and some negative effects, which, in essence, cancel each other out. The experiment cannot tell us why we found no effect, just that we did. Maybe this is what is happening. Jobs have the positive effects of decreasing poverty and increasing self-esteem, personal control, and social support, as described above. But jobs also greatly increase time pressures on unmarried mothers, compared to staying home. When a mother gets a job, she has to arrange child care, get her child to day care in the morning and pick him or her up after work, cope somehow when the child is sick, and so on. This mother now has a double work load of paid work and child care. Possibly, jobs increase depression, on the one hand, by way of increasing time demands and work overload, but decrease depression, on the other hand, by way of decreasing poverty and increasing control, esteem, and support. The experiment cannot show why the independent variable had an effect or no effect on the outcome.

An experiment can tell us the consequences of the intervention but not the relationships among the consequences. The experiment itself could show that jobs increase time pressures on mothers, and that jobs increase depression among mothers. It cannot show the association between time pressure and depression within the experiment. This part is purely observational. We can correlate the two and conclude that jobs increase depression by increasing time pressure, but this is nonexperimental evidence. It could be that jobs increase felt time pressures by increasing depression. We must assume a causal order between the two. Because the experiment itself does not tell us the sequence of its consequences, it cannot explain its own consequences.

Patterns plus their explanations are the essence of cause. Experiments cannot show the patterns of distress in the real world, cannot show the causal direction in the real world, and cannot explain the patterns.

Inherent Limitations of Experiments on Treatments

As noted earlier, experiments are the best way to evaluate the effectiveness of treatments such as drugs or counseling, which are interventions. However, many misinterpret the meaning of treatment experiments, deeming that the effectiveness of a treatment says something about the cause of the problem. This is incorrect, for two reasons.

First, we cannot know what makes people depressed unless we compare them to people who are not depressed. An experiment evaluating the effectiveness of drugs versus counseling in reducing depression only uses subjects who are depressed.

Second, we cannot discover the cause of depression by seeing what treatments are effective in reducing it. For example, novocaine may relieve the pain of a toothache. Drilling and filling the tooth may eliminate the pain. But the cause of the toothache was not the absence of novocaine or filling; the cause was probably decay induced by too much sugar in the diet, or the lack of fluoride. Likewise, psychiatric or psychological treatment studies do not tell us what causes depression. Just because a drug works to alleviate the condition does not mean the original cause was chemical. Treatments may relieve depression without removing its cause: they may be palliatives, not cures (see Fig. 3.2.). Effectiveness of treatments does not tell us what causes depression. An effective treatment may not be as effective as removing the cause. An effective treatment may in fact be a liability if it deters the search for the problem causing the depression and a solution to the problem. This brings us to what we, as sociologists, see as the philosophical limits of experiments.

Philosophical Limitations of Experiments

Possibly the most important limitation of experiments is their view of the relationship between researcher and subject. The whole point of an experiment is to develop ways in which objects and outcomes can be manipulated. The philosophical problem arises when the objects are humans, and the outcomes are human thoughts, feelings, and actions. The intent of an experiment is to give control to the manipulator, not to the manipulated. The validity of treating actors as objects is uncertain at best. There is a world of difference between manipulating and informing. Recall the blood pressure example. Informed individuals can and often do control their own blood pressure by exercising and practicing good eating habits. The big money, though, is in selling and prescribing antihypertensive medication. By their very nature, experiments look for a lever to put in the hands of a professional. The value of manipulating rather than informing is uncertain enough in a case such as hypertension. When we talk about psychological distress, the wisdom of giving control to the professional rather than the subject becomes extremely questionable. By all indications, distress is caused by helplessness, powerlessness, and the sense that others and chance control one's life. The search for experimental and professional means of manipulating these states is ironic, and probably futile.

Treatment as Cure

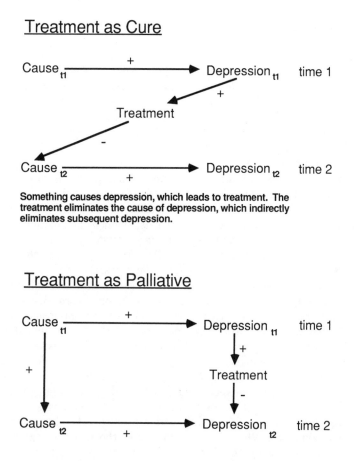

Something causes depression, which leads to treatment. The treatment eliminates the cause of depression, which indirectly eliminates subsequent depression.

Treatment as Palliative

Something causes depression, which leads to treatment. The treatment alleviates some depression, but not all because the cause is still there.

Figure 3.2. Treatment as cure versus treatment as palliative.

Ersatz Experiments on Personality and Depression

Ersatz refers to a substitute that is an inferior imitation. Ersatz experiments try to look like true experiments, but lack an essential ingredient: manipulation of the suspected cause. The prestige of experiments is so great in some sciences that researchers are loath to abandon the method. When absolutely forced to by the nature of the phenomenon, researchers in those sciences cling to the appearance of experiments while relinquishing the logical form. Better to substitute an inferior imitation than to design a study that is frankly no experiment at all. Keeping the appearance while abandoning the logical form serves two essential functions. First, it reassures reviewers, editors, funding agencies, and colleagues that the research is real science done by real scientists. Second, it deflects serious and difficult questions that are normally asked about the adequacy of a nonexperimental study, particularly questions about spuriousness, causal order, and representativeness of the sample. The popularity and prevalence of ersatz experiments attests to their survival value.

Ersatz experiments rely on substitution and paraphernalia to produce an illusion of relevance and validity. The problem is that a genuine experiment is difficult, impossible, or unethical, so a feasible experiment or a survey in experimental guise is substituted. The rituals, symbols, and paraphernalia of laboratory science sustain the illusion. Four aspects of genuine experiments appear frequently in ersatz experiments: (1) *laboratory setting*—the subjects come to the researcher; (2) *intervention*—the researcher does something to the subjects and observes their response; (3) *equipment*—special machines, tools, and setups are used to elicit, observe, or record responses; (4) *randomization*—subjects are exposed to different interventions on a random basis. As we will show, the mere presence of these elements does not guarantee a genuine experimental design. The essence of an experiment is in its logic, not in its trappings.

There are four types of ersatz experiments: substitute experiments, pseudo-experiments, para-experiments, and experiments in imagination. In reality, most ersatz experiments mix two or more of the forms to create a more substantial illusion of validity and relevance. The four types have different weaknesses. When types are combined, the mind is distracted from the weakness of one by the fact that the other does not have the same weakness. However, two ersatz experiments do not add up to a genuine experiment, whether they are published separately or together.

To illustrate the four types of ersatz experiments, we selected examples from a flow of studies trying to answer one question: what is the effect of personality on the development of depression? Personality is, by its nature, difficult to manipulate. There are many definitions of personality, but all say it is a stable and general trait of the individual that is manifest in a variety of behaviors and circumstances. Some think personality is organic or genetic in origin, others think it is the result of one's personal history, and still others think it is the combination of these things. Regardless of one's view, personality is not easy to manipulate in a laboratory. In addition to the practical difficulties, the individual personality is sacred in our society; it would be unethical to manipulate it just to see what happens.

One hypothesis about personality is that certain habitual ways of interpreting events and outcomes are depressing. Specifically, depression results from habitually seeing bad events as caused by something about oneself that does not change much over time and that affects all aspects of one's life (Peterson and Seligman, 1984). [These habitual ways of interpreting the causes of events are called attributional styles in the *revised* learned helplessness paradigm (Peterson and Seligman, 1984).] To test this hypothesis experimentally, a researcher would have to manipulate subjects' habitual interpretation of bad events, and observe subsequent changes in depression. To minimize the possibility of a spurious association, the experimenter would randomly assign some subjects to habitually see bad events as caused by something about themselves that does not change much and that affects all aspects of their lives, and assign others to habitually see bad events as caused by something not about themselves or not affecting their whole lives. It is clear why a decade of research and literally hundreds of studies have not produced a single genuine experimental test of the hypothesis. Personality (specifically, habitual ways of interpreting events) is the hypothesized cause of depression, but it cannot be produced in a laboratory. Yet most studies addressing the question look like experiments.

Psychology is a discipline that idolizes experiments. To many psychologists the experiment is not just a method, not even just the ideal method, it is the only method capable of establishing causal relationships. This prestige is based on the fact that experiments produced impressive and useful bodies of information about perception, cognition, and behavioral conditioning. The glow from these achievements enhances the status of all experiments and all studies that look like experiments.

This is not to suggest that psychology has nothing to say about the subjects of interest to us. Many psychologists do surveys, even though they must struggle against the prejudices of their colleagues (Block, 1977). Many of the indexes used by sociologists to assess beliefs and feelings were developed by psychologists. Most importantly, though, the sociologist's interest in alienation, anomie, demoralization, fatalism, and powerlessness is paralleled by the psychologist's interest in external locus of control, learned helplessness, and self-blame. The ideas and findings of one enhance and enrich those of the other.

Substitute Experiments

A substitute experiment is a study in which a variable that can be manipulated is substituted for a variable of interest, or a subject that can be manipulated is substituted for one that can not. In essence, an experiment that can be done is substituted for the one that can not. The substitute experiment is an analogy. The researcher hopes that the substitute is governed by the same laws that govern the phenomenon of interest. If so, the results of the substitute experiment are similar to the results that would be found if the genuine experiment could be done. The plausibility of this hope is determined by factors outside the experiment.

The classic substitute experiment replaces humans with animals. Clearly, a hypothesis about the effect of habits of interpretation on depression cannot be studied in animals. We have no way of asking them their thoughts. Nevertheless, a substitute experiment is possible. The researcher can manipulate something other than the human subjects' habitual interpretations, and can look at outcomes other than depression. In a section labeled "Laboratory Experiments" of a review article called, "Causal Explanations as a Risk Factor for Depression: Theory and Evidence," Peterson and Seligman (1984) summarize six studies. Only one looks at depression at all. The others substitute the following for depression: difficulty manipulating a shuttle box, difficulty solving anagrams, lower self-esteem, lower expectations for success in convincing other students to donate blood, and lower actual success convincing other students to donate blood. None of the studies manipulates habitual interpretations. They substituted the following: the presence and escapability of unpleasant noise, success or failure at an experimental task, and interpretation of the cause of success or failure on the experimental task. How good are these surrogates? How do we know the little world of the experiment is not too little? The studies themselves cannot tell us.

Pseudo-experiments

A pseudo-experiment is a study in which there is a measurement intervention but no manipulation of the variables of interest. At least one of the variables of interest is measured and treated as a preexisting trait. A laboratory manipulation is used to elicit a response, which is measured and correlated with the preexisting trait. The measurement intervention makes the study seem like an experiment, but the intervention did not establish causal order and did not rule out spurious association.

An excellent example of a pseudo-experiment was published by Martin, Abramson, and Alloy (1984), titled "Illusion of Control for Self and Others in Depressed and Nondepressed College Students." (This example and the ones that follow are from the *Journal of Personality and Social Psychology*.) If people who feel responsible for bad things are more depressed, then perhaps people who feel responsible for good things are less depressed. The researchers thought that susceptibility to an illusion of control might protect people from depression. Those who cannot sustain the illusion wind up depressed. The researchers recruited 108 undergraduates who were paid for their participation in the experiment. The subjects were asked to report their symptoms and were divided into depressed and nondepressed categories based on the number and severity of these symptoms. They were brought into a laboratory, complete with one-way mirrors, and told to watch a yellow light and decide within 3 seconds whether to press a red button that supposedly controlled a green light in some nonobvious way the subject was to figure out. Each time a subject supposedly turned on the green light, the subject won a quarter. In actuality, the subject had no control over the green light and the number of quarters won. After the trial, the subject rated his or her amount of control over the green light, on a scale of 0 to 100.

The researchers' description of their setup and procedure provides some classic examples of ersatz-experimental folderol. Here is a choice excerpt: "The stimulus display panel . . . consisted of a black wooden standup platform, 23 cm × 23 cm, facing the subjects, on which a yellow light and a green light were positioned 5 cm from the top of the platform equidistant from the vertical center of the platform. The lights were spaced 11.5 cm center to center across the platform. The response apparatus was a grey metal box, 5.5 cm × 7 cm × 4 cm, with a spring-loaded red button in the center of the top . . ." (Martin, Abramson, and Alloy, 1984, p. 128). This litany provides absolutely no information on the adequacy of the study or the inferences that may be drawn from its results. It does sound very scientific, though.

Here's the result, laid bare: the depressed subjects were less likely to think they controlled the green light and the number of quarters won. What does this mean? It means there is a negative correlation between depression and susceptibility to an illusion of control in an ambiguous (not to mention unreal) situation. Do the manipulation and intervention reveal the causal order? No. Susceptibility to the illusion could cause depression. Depression could cause susceptibility to the illusion. Do the manipulation and intervention rule out spuriousness? No. It could be that students from higher socioeconomic backgrounds are more confident and less depressed. The negative correlation might represent nothing more than two advantages of socioeconomic status, with no causal effect of either on the other. The result is nothing more than an unadjusted, cross-sectional correlation between a measure of depression and a measure of susceptibility to an illusion of control in an unrepresentative sample of 108 college students.

The fact that one measure is a response evoked in a laboratory does not elevate a study to the status of a genuine experiment. Nevertheless, it typically deflects three important questions that are always asked about correlations found in survey research: Which is the cause and which the consequence? Does either cause the other, or do they merely have a common precursor? Does the sample in which the correlation was found adequately represent the larger population, or is the correlation confined to the small group in which it was observed? Despite a section on "important cautions" in their discussion, Martin, Abramson, and Alloy never raise these questions, let alone answer them.

In the study above, the researchers correlated an evoked response with preexisting levels of depression. It is also possible to correlate an evoked response with preexisting tendencies to consider oneself the cause of bad outcomes. Alloy, Peterson, Abramson, and Seligman (1984) use this variant of the pseudo-experiment in a paper titled "Attribution Style and the Generality of Learned Helplessness." There are plenty of props, including lights, buttons, noises, and a hand shuttle box [". . .a 24 × 5 × 6 in. (61 × 13 × 15 cm.) box with a 3-in. (7 cm.) knob protruding from the top and sliding on a 19 in. (48 cm.) straight channel."] The researchers found that students who tend to consider themselves the cause of bad events are more readily discouraged when performing laboratory tasks. Once again, we do not know whether the habit of interpretation causes the tendency to get discouraged, or vice versa. Once again, we do not know if there is any causal connection at all, because the correlation might simply reflect the different socioeconomic origins and experiences of the students. Once again, we do not know if the sample in which the correlation was observed in any way represents a larger population. (Interestingly, the subjects in this study appear to be the same 108 students at the University of Pennsylvania that participated in the study above.) Once again, the researchers do not raise these critical questions about their results, and the peer reviewers and editor do not demand that the questions be raised (let alone answered). Once again, the pseudo-experimental design deflects questions asked of nonexperimental research.

Para-experiments

A para-experiment is a study in which a pseudo-experiment is grafted onto a substitute experiment. The para-experiment is the crowning achievement of ersatz-experimental design. It befuddles the critical mind because the pseudo element brings in at least one of the variables that is really at issue, and the substitute element brings in something that can be experimented on. The para-experiment may be the most successful form of ersatz-experiment. It is a mainstay of psychological research on personality and depression. In fact, some of the studies described so far are para-experiments. We focused on one element or the other in order to make it clear how each works. Now we examine how both elements work together.

Recall, for example, that Martin, Abramson, and Alloy (1984) studied subjects' sense of control over a task with an ambiguous and surreptitiously random connection between performance and outcome. They found a negative correlation between the sense of control and preexisting depression. To make this look more like a genuine experiment, the researchers needed to bring in a variable that they could randomly assign. They chose to have some of the subjects observe experimental confederates performing the task and rate the confederate's control over the outcome. The subjects got the same rewards as the confederates they watched. A fixed portion of the depressed and the same portion of the nondepressed were randomly assigned to perform the task themselves and rate their own control. Depressed students saw more control over the task if somebody else was performing it. Nondepressed students saw less control over the task if somebody else was performing it.

What does this add? In regard to depression, there is still no experiment. They still do not alter the sense of control and observe changes in depression. All they have done is introduce a second measure of interpretive tendencies.

Picture a similar study without the paraphernalia. We randomly assign a portion of the depressed students, and an equal portion of the nondepressed students, to answer this question: "In general, do you control the good things that happen in your life?" The rest of the depressed and nondepressed students answer this question: "In general, do other people control the good things that happen in your life?" We find that the depressed are more likely to say "NO" to the first question, and are more likely to say "YES" to the second, than are the nondepressed. Without all the flashing lights, it's pretty clear that these are just two ways of getting at the same thing. The random assignment of questions merely obscures the fact. We could just as well have asked all the subjects both questions. It would be clear that the difference in answers measures a single trait: the sense that people other than yourself control good outcomes.

If we add the paraphernalia back in, the picture is clearer. Martin, Abramson, and Alloy could have exposed all subjects to both conditions. The difference between the sense of personal control and the sense of the confederate's control in an ambiguous situation measures a single trait: the degree to which you believe that people other than yourself control good outcomes. The correlation of that trait with depression is nothing more than a correlation. The assignment of some subjects to one condition and the rest to another condition is deceptive. It hides the fact that the result is merely a correlation of one preexisting trait (depression) with another preexisting trait (the tendency to sense that others besides yourself control good outcomes). Neither trait is actually manipulated nor is either trait shown to cause the other. A spurious correlation between the two traits due to social background or personal history is not ruled out. Nothing in the study assures us that the correlation exists outside the students in the study.

Experiments in Imagination

An experiment in imagination is a study in which subjects are asked to imagine an intervention and their response to it. The researcher looks for different imaginary responses under different imaginary conditions. The experiment in imagination may be a new ersatz-experimental form. It seems to be emerging from "The Attributional Style Questionnaire" (the ASQ) (Peterson, Schwartz, and Seligman, 1981). This questionnaire asks subjects to imagine experiencing certain good and bad events and to imagine the primary cause of each. Then the subjects rate how much the cause is something about themselves rather than others or circumstances, whether the cause is persistent, and whether the cause affects all areas of their life. The subjects also rate how helpless and how guilty they would feel if each event happened to them. The correlation of imagined helplessness and guilt with the qualities of the imagined events and their imagined causes is an experiment in imagination.

The originators of the ASQ admit that it is a survey questionnaire and not an experiment (Peterson and Seligman, 1984). Nevertheless, the procedures surrounding its use are those of experimental psychology and not those of survey research. Results are presented in the style of an experiment. Few studies using the ASQ address the issue of causal order or possible spuriousness. None that we know of uses a representative sample of *any* defined population. Published results typically blend imagined, semi-imagined, and real correlations with little or no attempt to highlight the different statuses of each (e.g., Peterson, Schwartz, and Seligman, 1981).

Other researchers are adapting the ASQ so that it can better serve the essential functions of an ersatz-experimental design. A notable adaptation appears in Russell and McAuley's article (1986), "Causal Attributions, Causal Dimensions, and Affective Reactions to Success and Failure." They randomly assign some students to imagine themselves experiencing good events. The remaining students are assigned to imagine themselves experiencing bad events. The randomization ploy greatly enhances the scientific appearance of an experiment in imagination.

Explaining Real Patterns

Laboratory experiments are never going to tell us why some people are more distressed than others. By their very nature, laboratory experiments shut out the world that people live in. When the experimenter hangs up his lab coat, shuts the light, and locks the door, he steps into the forces that make some people more distressed than others. He says good night to the student lab assistant, who did poorly on a statistics test the day before. He says good night to the secretary, who is on the phone trying to find out if her child got home from an early school closing all right. He passes the janitor, who is unlocking the broom closet and thinking that the university's budget cut means a new round of layoffs. He gets on the bus behind an old woman, who pauses at each step to rest and has difficulty counting the right change to give the driver. On the way home, the bus takes the experimenter past the hospital where an ambulance has just arrived; around the edge of the slums where there are kids playing in the street and teenagers hanging out and adults sitting on stoops or at windows staring; past the graveyard where he sees a fresh mound of dirt next to a precise rectangle cut in the earth; into the pleasant suburb where he signals the driver to stop at his block. Unless the experimenter thinks about what he has seen on the ride home, unless he finds some way to talk to the people he passed, he will never learn why some people are more distressed than others.

III

Social Patterns of Distress

CHAPTER FOUR

Established Patterns

Community Mental Health Surveys

Before the 1960's little was known about social patterns of emotional well-being and distress. Mental health studies looked at people in psychiatric treatment or in institutions such as the Army or mental hospitals. Ideas about social stress were based on clinical interviews with small numbers of patients or on records of groups in unusual circumstances. The first representative community surveys uncovered several unexpected findings.

All the findings we discuss are based on community surveys of mental health. Large, representative samples of people in the community are interviewed either in person or by telephone. This avoids the biases of basing conclusions on people who have sought help; people with the time, money, or inclination to do so. Everyone has an equal chance of being interviewed: those who sought help and those who did not, the middle class and the poor, men and women, those for whom visiting a psychiatrist is shameful and those for whom it is acceptable, those with access to care and those without it.

The research we discuss uses multiple regression or some form of multivariate analysis to statistically control for confounding factors (Tufte, 1974). This allows researchers to draw conclusions about the effect of one factor (e.g., marital status) independent of others (e.g., age or education).

Four basic social patterns of distress were revealed in early community surveys done in the 1960's and in many surveys conducted since: (1) women are more distressed than men; (2) married persons are less distressed than unmarried persons; (3) the greater the number of *undesirable* changes in a person's life the greater his or her level of distress; (4) the higher a person's socioeconomic status (defined by education, job, and income) the lower that person's level of distress. These findings are now well established and thus may seem obvious, but they were not common knowledge thirty years ago.

Before community surveys, many theorists believed that responsibility, commitment to work, and upward mobility were stressful, whereas dependency, protection, and freedom from responsibility were not. Three decades ago women had little economic responsibility. Men had to go out and beat the world or be beaten by it, daily braving the rigors of commuter traffic and workplace tension. Women could stay home contentedly (so it was assumed) ministering to the needs of the family, kept safe by protecting males. Many were surprised to learn that women have higher levels of depression, anxiety, and malaise than men. Some people thought that married people,

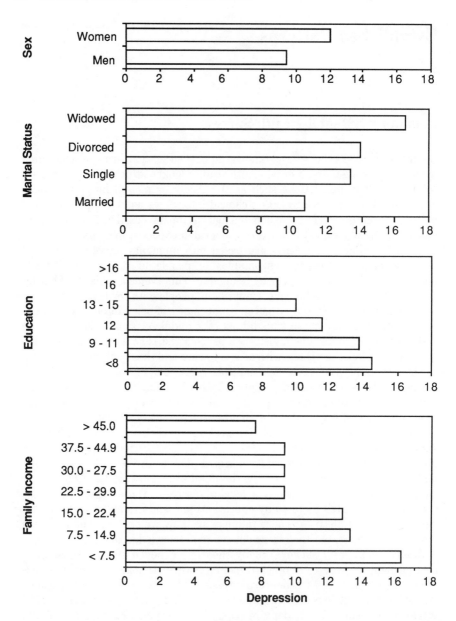

Figure 4.1. Mean depression levels in different categories of sex, marital status, education, and family income, based on 2000 adults in the United States from the Women and Work Study, described in the Appendix. Depression levels are measured by a ten-item depression scale also described in the Appendix to this book.

especially married men, faced burdensome responsibilities whereas singles led a free and happy life. In fact, married people have lower levels of distress than singles, especially married men. Similarly, many assumed that executives and others at the top of the status hierarchy were made tense and anxious by heavy responsibilities (a view reinforced by the heart disease literature on "type A personality"), while those at the bottom were relatively carefree and content. Harried executives, rushing to the next meeting, might envy laborers with few responsibilities; but in fact, power, responsibility, and control have been found to reduce distress.

These findings at first stood as fascinating new discoveries, then as core facts in the growing body of research. After it became clear that these are robust and replicable findings, the focus of research switched from *demonstrating* the facts to *explaining* them. Just as astronomers were once driven by the desire to explain the recorded motions of the sun, moon, and planets, research on psychological distress is currently based on the desire to explain the recorded association with gender, marriage, events, and status. In this chapter we describe the established social patterns of distress. In Part IV we will discuss some of the discoveries of the past ten years that may explain these patterns.

First we need to clarify the nature of the facts. To begin with, they are probabilistic. When we say that women are more distressed than men we do not mean that all women are more distressed than all men. We mean that, on average, women are more distressed than men, and that a randomly chosen woman is more likely to be distressed than a randomly chosen man. Second, social facts are hard facts, but not eternal ones. The facts about distress can change as society changes. In particular, the difference in distress between men and women could disappear if certain trends continue. The reasons social differences in distress exist are also reasons the differences might disappear.

The Four Basic Patterns

Gender

Gove and his colleagues were among the first sociologists to examine why women are more distressed than men. While biologists might think to scrutinize hormones or patterns of sex-typed behavior among primates, sociologists have a different perspective. For heuristic purposes they think of people as essentially interchangeable at birth. It is clear that by adulthood there are many important differences in the things people prefer, value, believe, and do. Many of these differences are shaped by individual situations and personal histories; perhaps the same is true of differences in emotions. Perhaps women are more distressed than men because of differences in the lives that men and women live. Fifteen years ago the majority of adult women were exclusively housewives and men were the breadwinners and job holders. Gove reasoned that if women are more distressed than men because of something different in their lives, then women who are employed will be less distressed than women who are exclusively housewives. This is exactly what he found in his sample of 2248 respondents (chosen by stratified random sampling) throughout the United States. A number of follow-up studies replicated the finding (Gove and Tudor, 1973; Gove and Geerken, 1977b; Richman, 1979; Rosenfield, 1980; Ross, Mirowsky, and Ulbrich, 1983; Kessler and McRae, 1982). It was an important discovery. Freud argued that women are born to be housewives and mothers and cannot be happy in the competitive world outside the home. Parsons (1949), an influential social theorist of the 1950's and 1960's, argued that society and the people in it function most smoothly when women specialize in the loving, nurturing family realm and men specialize in the competitive, acquisitive job-holding realm. The discovery that women with jobs are less distressed than women without them overturned a century of armchair theorizing.

Gove's research shook certain preconceptions about women, but did not explain everything. Although employed women are less distressed than housewives, employed women are *more* distressed than employed men. Having a job is not the whole story. What explains the difference in distress between employed men and women? A clue turned up in a study by Kessler and McRae (1982), using data from 2440 randomly sampled American adults interviewed in 1976. They found that employment is associated with less distress among women whose husbands help with housework and child care, but that there is little advantage to employment among women whose husbands do not help. Surprisingly, they also found that the housework and child care contributed by husbands of employed women does not increase the husband's distress. Researchers had been comparing different types of women; perhaps it was time to compare different types of couples.

American marriages are changing, from arrangements in which the husband has a job and the wife stays home caring for the children and doing housework to arrangements in which the husband and wife both have jobs and share the housework and child care (Oppenheimer, 1982). Although many today may believe this a positive change, not many would have thought so in 1900. The change did not happen because of preferences and values, but because the logic of social arrangements in 1900 undermined itself as the economy grew and changed from one based on manufacturing to one based on services.

At the beginning of the century, women only took jobs in the period between graduating school and getting married. A married woman worked outside the home only if her husband could not support the family. Women could be paid much less than men with equivalent education and skills because the women's jobs were temporary or supplemental. Many jobs quickly became "women's work," particularly services such as waiting on tables, operating telephone switchboards, elementary schoolteaching, nursing, and secretarial work. The economic incentive for employers to hire women, combined with economic growth and the shift from manufacturing to services, increased the demand for female employees. Eventually there were not enough unmarried or childless women to fill the demand, and employers began reducing the barriers to employment for married women and encouraging those whose children were grown to return to work. Still the demand for labor in female occupations continued to grow faster than the supply of women in accepted social categories, and by the 1950's growth in female employment reached the sanctum sanctorum—married women with young children (Oppenheimer, 1973). Throughout the century individual women were drawn into the labor force by contingencies: economic need, the availability of work, and the freedom to work (Waite, 1976). Despite the low pay and limited opportunities, many women came to prefer working and earning money, and many husbands began to realize the benefits of two paychecks instead of one. But who was taking care of the house and children? This brings us back to the question of why employed women are more distressed than employed men.

In 1978, Huber surveyed a national probability sample of 680 married couples (Huber and Spitze, 1983). Respondents, chosen by random digit dialing, were interviewed by telephone. If the respondent was married, his or her spouse was also interviewed, making it one of the first surveys of a large, representative sample of married persons throughout the United States to interview both the husband and wife in each couple. With Huber, we compared the husband's and wife's distress in four types of marriages. (Ross, Mirowsky, and Huber, 1983). Distress was measured by a modified form of the Center for Epidemiological Studies' depression scale. Further details on sampling and measurement in the Women and Work Study appear in the Appendix to the book.

In the first type of marriage the wife does not have a job, she and her husband believe her place is in the home, and she does all the housework and child care. This is the traditional marriage and in 1978 accounted for roughly 44% of all couples. Because this type of marriage is internally consistent—preferences match behavior—it may be psychologically beneficial, but more so for the husband. He is head of the household and has the power and prestige associated with economic resources. The wife, on the other hand, is typically dependent and subordinate. We found that the wife in this type of marriage has a higher level of depression than her husband.

In the second type of marriage the wife has a job but neither she nor her husband want her to, and she does all the housework and child care. This accounted for roughly 19% of the couples. Both of them believe that he should provide for the family while she cares for the home and children, but she has taken a job because they need the money. Psychologically, this is the worst type of marriage for both partners, and their distress is greater than in any

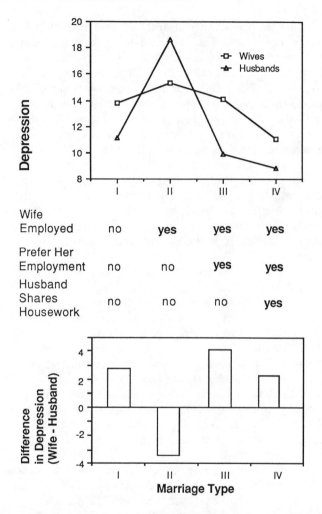

Figure 4.2. Depression levels of wife and husband in four types of marriages
(top), and the differences in depression levels between wife and
husband in each type (bottom). Data are from 680 couples in the
Women and Work Study (see Appendix). Depression levels are
measured by a ten-item depression scale described in the
Appendix to this book. Marriage types are based on the wife's
employment status, preferences for her employment, and the
household division of labor. Measurement of these characteristics is described in the Appendix also. The results are shown
adjusting for income, education, age, religion, and race.

other marriage type. The wife may feel that it is not right that she has to work, that her choice of husband was a poor one, that she cannot do all the things a "good" mother should; and she carries a double burden of paid and unpaid work. To the extent that the husband has internalized the role of breadwinner, he may feel that his wife's employment reflects unfavorably on him, indicating that he is not able to support his family. He may feel guilty and ashamed that she has a job, worry about his loss of authority, and suffer self-doubt and low self-esteem. This is the only type of marriage in which the husband is more distressed than his wife.

Although adjustment may come slowly, people do not long sustain tension between the way they live and the way they think they should live. As economic, demographic, and historical changes nudge lives into new patterns, husbands and wives come to view her employment more positively, particularly as more of their friends and neighbors become two paycheck families. Thus, in the third type of marriage the wife has a job and she and her husband favor her employment, but she remains responsible for the home. About 27% of all couples fell into this category. The husband is better off than ever before. He has adjusted psychologically, his standard of living is higher, and the flow of family income is more secure. He has even lower distress than men in the first type of marriage. However, things are not quite as good for his wife. She is better off than in the second type of marriage, but still carries a double burden. In a system in which the wife stays home and the husband goes out to work it makes sense for her to do the most time-consuming household chores. When she also works outside the home, and particularly when she stops thinking of her job as temporary, it becomes clear to her that the traditional division of the chores is no longer sensible or fair. Typically she assigns tasks to the children, mechanizes tasks like dishwashing, uses frozen foods and eats out more often, cuts down on optional events like dinner parties, and does not clean as often. Even so, the demands on her time are likely to be much greater than those on her husband's (Robinson, 1980). The wife's level of distress in this type of marriage is about the same as in the first type, and the gap between her distress and her husband's is greater than in any other type of marriage.

Once the wife accepts the permanence of her new role as employed worker, she may begin pressing for greater equality in the division of household labor. Although the husband may initially resist, once he has grown accustomed to the economic benefits of two paychecks he is likely to be open to negotiation. If his wife presses the issue, he often makes concessions rather than lose her earnings. In the fourth type of marriage the wife has a job, she and her husband approve of her employment, and they share housework and child care *equally*. This accounted for about 11% of the couples. Both the husband and the wife are less distressed in this type of marriage than in any other, and the gap between them is smaller than in any other type of marriage.

The gap that remains is probably due to two things: First, the large majority of wives in type IV marriages still earn less than their husbands. Second, the category contains a small minority of wives who are very distressed because they are employed mothers of young children and have difficulty arranging child care (see Chapter 5).

In adapting to the wife's employment, the central problem for husbands seems to be one of self-esteem—of overcoming any embarrassment, guilt, or apprehension associated with the wife's employment. For wives the central problem is getting the husband to share the housework.

We began with the unexpected discovery that women are more distressed than men, and housewives are more distressed than women with jobs. We conclude that couples who share both the economic responsibilities and the household responsibilities also share much the same level of psychological well-being, and are less distressed than other couples. The difference in distress between men and women does not appear to be innate. The difference is there because men and women lead different lives, and as their lives converge the difference begins to disappear.

About 20% of the employed wives surveyed were in marriages in which the husband shares the housework and child care. An analysis of the factors that increase the husband's share of the housework shows that husbands with higher levels of education do more. Husbands also do more the higher the wife's earnings, and they do *less* the more their own earnings exceed the wife's. Thus, equality in the division of labor at home, which provides psychological benefits to both husband and wife, depends on their economic equality in the workplace.

Marriage

We now come to the second major social pattern of psychological distress: Married people are less distressed than unmarried ones. Most of us are not surprised that widowed, divorced, and separated people are more distressed than married people, but it is surprising to find that adults who are single are almost as distressed as those who are divorced or separated.

What is it about marriage that improves emotional well-being? At first researchers thought it might be simply the presence of another adult in the household. A person who lives alone may be isolated from an important network of social and economic ties: the privileges and obligations centered on the home and family. These ties help create a stabilizing sense of security, belonging, and direction. Without them a person may feel lonely, adrift, and unprotected. Since unmarried people often live alone but married people almost always live together (often with children), this might explain why unmarried people are more distressed. Hughes and Gove subdivided three types of unmarried persons (never married, divorced or separated, widowed) according to whether they lived alone (1981). Contrary to what they expected, Hughes and Gove found that unmarried people are not more distressed if they live alone. The big difference is between married people and others, not between people who live alone and others.

One fact about marriages is that some are better than others. Is it better to be in a bad marriage than to be unmarried? Gove and his colleagues surveyed married people about happiness with marriage (Gove, Hughes, and Style, 1983). The 62% who report being very happy with their marriage are less distressed than unmarrieds, but the 34% who only say they are pretty happy with their marriage are no less distressed than the unmarrieds, and the 4% who say they are not too happy or not at all happy with their marriage are more distressed than unmarrieds of all types.

A good marriage provides something very important: the sense of being cared for, loved, esteemed, and valued as a person. Pearlin interviewed a representative sample of 2300 Chicago-area adults in 1972, and interviewed the same people again in 1976. He asked them if they could talk to their wives (or husbands) about things they felt were important to them, and count on their spouses for understanding and advice. Those who said "yes" were much less distressed by job disruptions such as being laid off, fired, or sick than those who said "no" (Pearlin et al., 1981). A close, confiding relationship actually protected the men and women against these stressful events. On the other hand, in situations when a spouse expects more than he or she is willing to give back, acts like the only important person in the family, and cannot be counted on for esteem and advice, men and women feel demoralized, tense, worried, neglected, unhappy, and frustrated (Pearlin, 1975a,b). Thus, it is not enough merely to have someone around. It is better to live alone than in a marriage characterized by a lack of consideration, caring, and equity.

It is easy to imagine that the victim of an unfair marriage is distressed by the situation, but what about the exploiter? Does a person gain or lose psychologically by taking unfair advantage of a spouse? The cynical view is that spouses are less depressed the more they get things their own way. Because one partner's dominance depends upon the other's submission, it follows that one partner's well-being results in the other's depression. The optimistic view is that exploiters, as well as victims, are more distressed than they would be in an equitable relationship. According to equity theory, exploiters face the disapproval of others, worry about retaliation and punishment, feel guilty, and must live with the obstruction and hostility of the victim (Mirowsky, 1985). In their hearts the husband and wife both know what is fair; if they do what is right they will both lead happier and more productive lives (Walster, Walster, and Berscheid, 1978).

Using the data on 680 married couples described earlier, we found some truth in both the cynical and the optimistic views (Mirowsky, 1985). The respondents were asked who decides what house or apartment to live in, where to go on vacation, whether the wife should have a job, and whether to move if the husband gets a job offer in another city. The responses ranged from the wife deciding to sharing the decisions equally to the husband deciding. Mapping the average levels of depression across this range revealed U-shaped patterns for wives and for husbands. Each spouse is least depressed if, to some extent, decisions are shared. However, the balance of influence associated with the lowest average depression is different for husbands and wives: each is least depressed having somewhat more influence than the other. The actual influence in these major decisions is typically closer to the balance that would minimize the husband's depression than it is to the balance that would minimize his wife's depression. This is one reason wives tend to be more depressed than their husbands. In one out of ten marriages, the wives are so far from their ideal balance of influence they are about 50% more depressed than would otherwise be the case.

We know why some marriages are worse than others or worse than no marriage at all, but the question of why unmarried persons are more distressed than marrieds is still not completely answered. The hypothesis is that unmarried persons are less likely to have a close, confiding relationship— someone they talk to about personal things and count on for understanding, help, and advice. If this explanation is correct, future research should find that unmarried persons with high levels of social support have levels of psychological well-being comparable to those of married persons.

Undesirable Life Events

So far we have been discussing the amount of distress people feel in different ongoing situations, such as being married, divorced, or widowed. Distress may also be associated with *changing* from one situation to another. The third major fact revealed in community surveys is that undesirable changes are distressing. At first, researchers believed that all major changes, good and bad, are distressing. As research progressed it became clear that only undesirable life events produce distress.

In the 1960's medical researchers noticed that major changes in a person's life seemed to increase susceptibility to disease. How could changes have this effect? Reasoning from laboratory experiments on regulatory mechanisms, the researchers concluded that every person's behavior tends to settle into an optimal pattern that minimizes the energy and resources expended to meet daily needs. Habits are easy, efficient solutions to everyday problems. Big changes in a person's life (such as getting married or taking a new job) disrupt habits and force the person to use mental and physical energy to adapt—that is, to develop a new set of habits that are optimal in the new situation.

To study the impact of change, Holmes and Rahe asked a group of people to judge the amount of change produced by each of a number of events (1967). Each event was assigned a value, called a life-change unit. The researchers then asked another group to name the changes that had happened in their lives in the past year, counted up the life-change units for each person, and found that people with more units of change suffered more illness and psychological distress. This finding initiated a wave of research that spilled across scientific and national boundaries. Researchers around the world began counting life-change units and correlating them with all kinds of physical and mental problems. Wherever they looked they seemed to find a devastating effect of change.

Although it was never the intent of the researchers involved, an image of the healthy, happy life emerged: a placid existence of undisturbed routines. Should we each withdraw to an asylum of our own making? The studies correlating change with sickness and distress seemed to say we should. In fact, the change theory of distress was so well-accepted that for years researchers never examined the impact of negative and positive events separately. When they did the evidence was clear: study after study found that undesirable events—not desirable ones—cause distress (Gersten et al., 1974; Mueller, Edwards, and Yarvis, 1977; Myers, Lindenthal, and Pepper, 1971; Vinokur and Selzer, 1975; Ross and Mirowsky, 1979; Williams, Ware, and Donald, 1981).

We analyzed data from the New Haven Study headed by J.K. Myers (Ross and Mirowsky, 1979). The project collected information on life events and distress of 720 randomly chosen adults in New Haven, Connecticut, interviewed in 1967 and again in 1969 (Myers, Lindenthal, and Pepper, 1971, 1974) We found that the more negative events people experienced the greater their distress. Positive events did *not* increase distress—change per se is not distressing. Subsequent research further refined this conclusion. Undesirable events over which a person has no control are most detrimental to psychological well-being (McFarlane et al., 1983). Controllable events—those in which the person has played some part and shared some responsibility—are less distressing. Some people had speculated that uncontrollable negative events are less distressing than controllable ones because fate, rather than oneself, can be blamed. Events outside the person's control suggest less personal inadequacy and thus protect self-esteem. This argument, while plausible, is not supported by research. Negative events over which a person has no control are more distressing than ones in which the person has played a part. Uncontrollable negative events increase feelings of helplessness and powerlessness. They leave people with the demoralizing sense that they are at the mercy of the environment; that no action will be effective in preventing bad things from happening in the future; and that they are not in control of their lives.

There is a postscript to this research. Not only is positive change not distressing, but people who view change as a challenge, who are instrumental, who set new goals and struggle to achieve them, have *low* levels of psychological distress (Kobassa, Maddi, and Courington, 1981). Change is not a useful explanation for the social patterns of distress while feelings of instrumentalism and control (as opposed to powerlessness and lack of control) are.

Socioeconomic Status

Events are brief periods that mark a transition. If undesirable events take their toll, ongoing situations are worse. If you lose your job, the event itself is distressing. Being unemployed for a prolonged period of time is more distressing. The problems that are always there can wear at the nerves and demoralize the spirit.

Some people have more problems and fewer resources with which to solve them. They are the poor and uneducated, working at menial jobs or living on welfare in rundown neighborhoods where crime is a constant threat. Others have fewer problems and more resources to help them cope. They are the well-to-do and educated, working at challenging and fulfilling jobs, and living in pleasant neighborhoods. The difference between these two groups is remarkable. It dwarfs the difference between men and women or between the married and unmarried, bringing us to the fourth fact: High socioeconomic status improves psychological well-being and low status increases psychological distress.

Although the impact of social status and achievement on distress seems obvious, there is a cultural myth of the successful person as driven by a sense of inadequacy, loneliness, or neurotic anxiety. This myth is not accurate. In fact, the typical successful person is active, inquisitive, open, and self-assured. If ever there was a formula for psychological well-being, this is it. How do some people get there, and others find themselves so far away?

The reasons for the vast difference in distress between the upper and lower ranks of society are intimately linked to the reasons those ranks exist. It is a self-amplifying process. Some people begin with fewer advantages, resources, and opportunities; this makes them less able to achieve and more likely to fail. Failure in the face of effort increases cognitive and motivational deficits, which, in turn, produce more failure and distress. These forces have been examined by Kohn and his colleagues (Kohn, 1972; Kohn and Schooler, 1982), Pearlin and his colleagues (Pearlin and Schooler, 1978; Pearlin et al., 1981), Wheaton (1978, 1980, 1983), and by us (Mirowsky and Ross, 1983, 1984).

There are two things that combine to produce psychological distress: one is a problem, the other is the inability to cope with the problem. A person who can solve his or her problems is, in the long run, happier than a person with no problems at all. There are two crucial characteristics of people who cope with problems successfully. The first is *instrumentalism*, which is the belief that you control your own life, that outcomes depend on your own choices and actions, and that you are not at the mercy of powerful people, luck, fate, or chance. When a problem arises, the instrumental person takes action. He or she does not ignore the problem or passively wait for it to go away. Furthermore, he or she takes action before problems occur, shaping the environment to his or her advantage. A second crucial characteristic is cognitive *flexibility*. The flexible person can imagine complex and/or multiple solutions to a problem and sees many sides to an issue. He or she does not cling to habit and tradition. When necessary, the flexible person can negotiate and innovate. Instrumentalism and flexibility together eliminate the impact of undesirable events and of chronic stressful situations on distress (Wheaton, 1983).

These characteristics are needed most where they are found least. Instrumentalism is learned through a long history of success in solving increasingly difficult problems, and flexibility is learned in solving complex problems. Instrumentalism and flexibility are mostly learned in college and on the job, but only jobs that are complex, unsupervised, and not routine have the desired effect (Kohn and Schooler, 1982). Kohn and his colleagues interviewed a representative sample of 3101 employed men in the United States in 1964 and again in 1974. They found that jobs that are simple, closely supervised, and routine reduce cognitive flexibility.

The people at the bottom of society are the most burdened with chronic hardship, barriers to achievement, inequity, victimization, and exploitation. Their instrumentalism is reduced by demoralizing personal histories. Their cognitive flexibility is reduced by limited horizons and constraining jobs in which they are told what to do rather than allowed to make their own decisions. Wheaton noted the important distinction between coping ability and coping effort: Low flexibility reduces the *ability* to cope with problems (1980). Low instrumentalism reduces the *motivation* to use whatever energy and resources are available. Without the will or ability to cope with the overwhelming stressors present at the bottom of the social hierarchy, the unsolved problems of the poor and poorly educated accumulate. This combination of more problems and fewer resources to cope with them increases the psychological distress of the disadvantaged. (See Fig. 4.3.)

A Note on Race

In the United States, blacks are disproportionately disadvantaged. On average, blacks have lower levels of education and income than whites, in large part due to a long history of discrimination. Thus, blacks have higher levels of psychological distress than whites because they tend to have low socioeconomic status (Mirowsky and Ross, 1980). Even at the same income level, blacks may be worse off than whites: recent evidence indicates that poor blacks have higher levels of distress than poor whites (Kessler and Neighbors, 1986). This may be because discrimination and blocked opportunity interfere with the upward mobility of this group. Perceptions of blocked goals are especially likely to make a person feel helpless, powerless, and unable to control life.

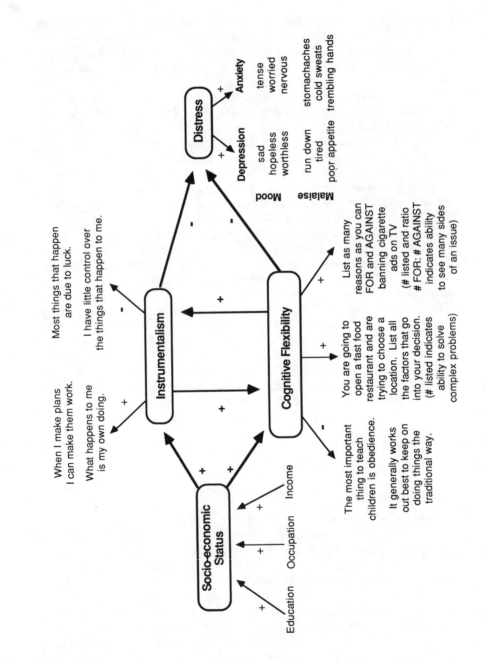

A Preview of Explanations

Instrumentalism and cognitive flexibility are important elements in the explanation of social patterns of distress. While we discuss our explanations in detail in Part IV, we summarize them here.

Although there is great diversity in the specific models proposed as explanations, most share a single abstract form: status, sex, marriage, events, and other sociodemographic variables mark the objective conditions of social life; based on socially patterned experiences, people develop beliefs, interpretations, and assumptions about the nature of society, human relations, themselves, and their relationship to others and to society; the level of distress depends on the nature of these beliefs. Three themes in the individual's understanding of self and society stand out as explanations of the known social patterns of distress: alienation, authoritarianism, and inequity. (A fourth theme—change—received a great deal of attention but, in our opinion, is probably not a major cause of psychological distress.) These themes are the link between the external reality of objective social conditions and the internal reality of subjective distress. (See Fig. 4.4.)

←——————————————————————————————————

Figure 4.3. Path diagram showing instrumentalism and cognitive flexibility as mechanisms through which socioeconomic status affects distress. Path diagrams are a graphic technique for representing systems of equations. The path diagram shows two types of variables: theoretical constructs and observed measurements. It also shows two types of relationships. The first is between constructs and their measured observations, shown by thin lines. For example, instrumentalism is measured by the tendency to agree (+) with the statements, "When I make plans I can make them work" and "What happens to me is my own doing" and to disagree (−) with the statements, "Most things that happen are due to luck" and "I have little control over the things that happen to me." The second is a relationship between constructs, shown by bold lines. For example, socioeconomic status tends to increase (+) instrumentalism, and instrumentalism tends to decrease (−) distress. The path model also shows the self-amplifying relationship between instrumentalism and cognitive flexibility. A path is formed by tracing arrows between constructs, following the normal rules for multiplying signs, so that the total causal effect of high socioeconomic status on distress is negative.

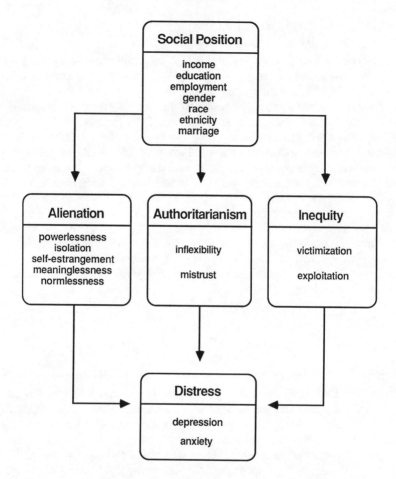

Figure 4.4. Theoretical model showing alienation, authoritarianism, and inequity as the links between social position and psychological distress.

Discussion

Patterns of psychological distress tell us about the quality of life in various social positions. Misery is an inherently meaningful yardstick in social research, serving much the same function as mortality in medical research. Although community surveys of the social patterns of distress only began in the 1960's, they have already corrected some erroneous preconceptions. In particular, the observed patterns of distress challenge the idea that emotional well-being results from a placid life of dependency, protection, and freedom from responsibility. Instead, the surveys show that responsibility, commitment, achievement, and a sense of control in one's own life, and reciprocity, consideration, and equity in personal relationships, are the sources of well-being.

The United States is in the middle of far-reaching historical changes. As forms of production become outmoded, the skills associated with them become obsolete. As families get smaller and more women are employed, traditional household arrangements also become obsolete. In the aggregate, people make these changes. As individuals, people are made over by them. They adapt in one of two ways. Individuals can be overwhelmed, demoralized, discouraged, and distressed or they can be creative, curious, openminded, active, and distressed.

CHAPTER FIVE

New Patterns: Questioning Cultural Myths

In the previous chapter we said there are four well-established social patterns of distress: (1) women are more distressed than men; (2) married persons are less distressed than unmarried persons; (3) the greater the number of undesirable life events the greater one's level of distress; (4) the higher one's socioeconomic status the lower one's level of distress. Because these findings are now well established they may seem obvious, but in fact all were uncovered by sociological research in the community. Our newest research in the community is uncovering new patterns. Possibly, in 10 years, these findings will also seem obvious. Today, many seem to contradict our cultural myths, assumptions, and beliefs.

Children: Blessing or Burden?

In this culture there are strong values about children. People believe that children bring joy and happiness. Without them, women in particular are said to feel empty, lonely, and unfulfilled. Those who decide not to have children are often viewed as selfish or immature. Although the strict sanctions against the decision to stay childless have abated somewhat, norms concerning the value of married couples having children are still strong, as partly seen in the fact that almost all married persons have children. Having children is considered good and valuable—an occasion for celebration.

What about the research evidence on the effect of children on parents' psychological well-being and distress? Does it support our myths? We have not included having children in our list of established findings in community mental health research because the findings are less conclusive than those on socioeconomic status, gender, undesirable events, and marriage. We are still demonstrating the facts about having children. But the picture is beginning to emerge, and some tentative conclusions can be drawn, conclusions which would surprise many. They do not support our myths.

One finding is clear. Children do not improve the psychological well-being of parents (Gove and Geerken, 1977b; Pearlin, 1975a; Cleary and Mechanic, 1983; Ross, Mirowsky and Huber, 1983; Radloff, 1975; Lovell-Troy, 1983; Gore and Mangione, 1983; Kessler and McRae, 1982; Brown and Harris, 1978; McLanahan and Adams, 1987). When the presence of children in the home is correlated with psychological well-being of mothers and fathers, in no case are parents found to be better off than nonparents. Furthermore, there are many instances in which parents—especially mothers—are more psychologically distressed than nonparents (Gove and Geerkin, 1977b; Pearlin, 1975a). The very group for whom children are believed to be most positive show the most negative effects.

Children are most detrimental to the mental health of single and divorced mothers (Brown and Harris, 1978; Pearlin, 1975a; Aneshenshel *et al.*, 1981; Alwin, Converse, and Martin, 1984; Kandel, Davies, and Raveis, 1985). Although most people would not be surprised that children increase depression and anxiety among mothers who are single, divorced, or separated, some evidence indicates that children also increase distress among married mothers. On the other hand, children do not seem to affect the mental health of fathers as much, except by increasing economic strains.

Why would children increase psychological distress? They tend to be valued and loved (although the disturbing facts about the prevalence of child abuse undermine this assumption somewhat). How could children be loved and valued and still increase distress levels among mothers?

The first explanation is that children increase economic strains on the family. At the same level of income, a family without children feels fewer economic pressures than one with children (Ross and Huber, 1985). In the latter, each dollar must go further, must buy more food, clothes, and medical care. Furthermore, the presence of young children is likely to increase pressures to buy or rent a larger place to live. An apartment may seem too small or the couple may prefer a house with a yard in which to raise children. At the same time that young children increase the need for a larger home and thus increase economic difficulties, their presence often means the mother does not work outside the home. She may quit her job while the children are young, thus decreasing the family's income. If she continues to be employed, funds are often needed for day care. Economic hardship is associated with increased depression for both men and women. The chronic strain of struggling to pay the bills and feed and clothe the children often results in nagging worries, restless sleep, and feelings of depression, such as feeling run down, feeling that everything is an effort, that the future is hopeless, and that there is not much to enjoy in life.

Economic hardship largely explains the negative effect of children on the psychological well-being of single and divorced mothers, who, with their children, are the new poor in the United States. In 1980, 18% of all births were out of wedlock; and another 43% of all children born in wedlock in 1980 will experience parental separation before they are 16 years old (Preston, 1984). By 1982, 23% of all children under age 14 were living in poverty—most in households headed by females (Preston, 1984). If these mothers can find work, it tends to be poorly paid, and it means that they must struggle to find and pay for child care. Both the children and their mothers are in extremely disadvantaged positions; for the mothers this often has psychological consequences of depression and anxiety.

Single and divorced mothers are poorer, on average, than married mothers, but many intact families also feel economic hardship. In addition to the chronically unemployed, many families above the poverty level also feel economic strain. In these families the husband is usually employed, unless temporarily laid off or sick. The wife may be employed as well, just to make ends meet. Many people in the working and lower middle classes live with their resources pushed to the breaking point. Furthermore, parents with low levels of education (and thus jobs that do not pay well) tend to have the most children. College-educated women have fewer children, on average, than women with high school educations or less. Thus, families that can least afford to have children often have the most, increasing the economic strain already present.

Children may also have negative effects on the quality of the marriage. Satisfaction with marriage decreases with the birth of the first child, and does not return to prechildren levels until all the children have left home. Both husbands and wives are most satisfied with their marriage when there are no children at home, whether because they are childless or because their children are grown and gone. As the number of children, especially young children, increases, marital satisfaction decreases (Campbell, Converse, and Rodgers, 1976; Pleck, 1983; Rollins and Feldman, 1970; Glenn and Weaver, 1978; Veroff, Douvan, and Kulka, 1981; Renne, 1970). The quality of one's marriage significantly affects psychological well-being. People who are satisfied with their marriage, who feel that the marriage is characterized by consideration, caring, love, and equity, who feel that they can really talk to their spouse about things they feel are important to them, are much less depressed and anxious than those in marriages characterized by conflict, inequity, and a lack of consideration and caring.

Children could worsen the quality of the marriage indirectly through the economic strain they may be causing. A couple with economic difficulties is living in a stressful environment in which failures are likely to be blamed on the other spouse. Furthermore, marital conflicts about money are more likely to occur when there is not enough.

Children affect the quality of the marriage directly, too. Husbands and wives spend less time together when they have young children, and the time they do have together is spent with (and focused on) the youngsters. Husbands feel they are getting less emotional support from their wives, whose energies now go into child care. Wives, too, feel they get less support from husbands, who often distance themselves (sometimes literally) from the difficult task of caring for young children. Women, especially those in the working class, report that their husbands are less likely to be confidants—to be there to talk to when needed—after the birth of the first child (Brown and Harris, 1978).

Apart from the quality of marriage, young children put constant demands on mothers who are home all day with them. They separate mothers from other adults and make them feel they are "stuck" in the house, and at the same time decrease their privacy and time alone (Gove and Geerken, 1977b). Housewives who are not employed are much more likely to feel that others are making demands on them than are employed mothers or fathers (Gove and Geerken, 1977b). The traditional female role of housewife and mother who is not employed outside the home is stressful (Gove and Tudor, 1973). These women have higher distress levels than employed women because housework and child care are generally menial, low prestige, invisible, powerless, tiring, and economically unrewarded tasks; and women in this role are economically dependent on their husbands. This implies that children are most stressful for women in the traditional role—those who are home all day (Brown and Harris, 1978; Gove and Geerken, 1977b).

The opposite argument, that children are bad for the psychological well-being of employed mothers because of role overload and conflict, is also plausible. Marriages are shifting from an arrangement in which the husband is employed and the wife does the domestic work to one in which both spouses are employed and both are responsible for child care and housework. But the transition is far from complete. Many employed wives are still solely or largely responsible for child care. The result is role strain—overload from the sheer amount of effort it takes to perform in both arenas, and conflict from meeting the expectations of people who do not take each other into account (i.e. one's boss and one's children).

Many women face incompatibilities between their roles of mother and employee because the institutional and family support necessary to fulfill both roles often does not exist. Possibly the major area of concern is that of child care. Readily available, affordable, child care may ease the strain on employed mothers.

To examine some of these issues, we used the data on 680 husbands and wives throughout the United States, described earlier. We examined depression levels of husbands and wives according to whether or not there are young children (under the age of 12) at home, whether or not the wife is employed, whether the husband shares child care responsibilities with his wife or whether the wife has the major responsibility for child care, and whether child care arrangements for working parents are readily available or whether arranging child care while the parents are at work is difficult.

Figure 5.1 shows the deviations from the overal mean depression level for wives. (We focus on wives because regression analyses indicated that caring for children does not significantly affect husbands' well-being.) It shows mean differences, which the regression analyses indicated are not merely spurious consequences of differences in age, education, income, or number of children.

Nonemployed wives with young children have significantly higher levels of depression than those without children. For employed wives, it is not children per se, but the difficulty in arranging child care and the husband's participation in the child care that affects psychological well-being. Employed wives with no children have lower than average depression levels. Many

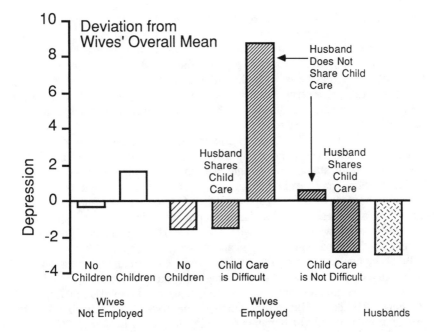

Figure 5.1. Deviations from the mean depression level for all wives, depending on employment status, children, difficulty of child care, and the husband's participation in the child care. Data are from 680 couples in the Women and Work Study. See the Appendix to this book for the measurement of depression and the description of the sample.

employed wives with children also have lower than average depression, most notably employed mothers whose husbands share the child care responsibilities with them and for whom arranging child care while the parents are at work presents no difficulties. These wives have depression levels as low as husbands. On the other hand, employed mothers whose husbands do not share the child care responsibilities with them and who have difficulty arranging child care have much higher than average depression levels.

In terms of the wives mental health, the best arrangement appears to be employment and motherhood, coupled with easily arranged and shared participation by the husband in care for the young children. The next best arrangement is employment and no children. The third best is employment, motherhood, and shared participation by husbands in child care, even if the couple has difficulty arranging child care. (The husband's participation in child care has more of an impact on wives than does the difficulty of arranging child care, possibly because it indicates two things: actual help with child care, and an equitable and fair relationship.) Women in these three situations have lower than average depression levels. In the best case, the average depression is as low as that of husbands, and in all three cases the difference in average depression compared to husbands is small enough to be explained by chance. Staying home with the children is significantly more stressful. However, the most stressful situation for wives is one in which they are employed, have young children, and have difficulty arranging and have sole responsibility for child care.

When social roles of husbands and wives are similar, their depression levels are similar. The gender gap in psychological well-being closes due to lower depression among wives and not due to greater depression among husbands. Some have argued that employment among wives puts a strain on husbands because of added responsibility for child care. We find no evidence that this is the case. *If* the wife's employment increases her husband's depression *at all* when he helps with child care, the increase in his depression is very small compared to the decrease in hers.

What we now think of as a traditional family pattern (in which the husband is employed and the wife stays home and cares for the household and children) is actually a consequence of the Industrial Revolution (Tilly, 1983). Parsons (1949) claimed it is functionally imperative that the husband be the provider and the wife the homemaker and child rearer. Becker (1976) claimed that, from the perspective of maximizing household efficiency, it was economically rational for the wife to stay home caring for children because her market wages were typically lower than those of her husband. Parsons' and Becker's theories of marital roles seem timebound. The massive entry into the labor force of married women with children has reduced the credibility of both theories. A pattern that appeared with industrialization may disappear in a postindustrial period.

It is understandable, however, that scholars writing in a transitional period should see a shift away from the complementary marriage pattern in which the husband is employed and the wife stays home as stressful, disturbing, and threatening to the marriage. What is stressful is the transition in which one aspect of family roles has changed (such as employment of mothers of young children) but other family roles (such as the husband's participation in the child care) or the family's links to other institutions (such as the availability of child care) have not caught up.

A return to the traditional family of the 1950's would return wives and mothers to a psychologically disadvantaged position, wherein husbands have much better mental health than wives. A shared family pattern in which both spouses are employed and both are responsible for home and child care, and in which there are supportive institutions for child care outside the nuclear family, is one in which both husbands and wives have low levels of depression. The well-being of husbands is not taxed by these changes. In fact, increased responsibilities for child care on the part of husbands may strengthen families by bringing fathers closer to their children.

Since 1970, married women with young children, as a group, had the greatest increase in the percentage employed, and there is no reason to think the trend will be reversed. It is unrealistic to think that Americans can care for their children by returning to a time when mothers were not engaged in productive labor and child care and homemaking were full-time jobs (a short period of time, historically). As the number of working couples increases, the need for child care increases.

There are three things society can do about the high depression levels caused by the stress on employed mothers of not having available, affordable child care. The first is nothing. This is unacceptable because it ignores individual suffering and demoralization, as well as the fact that depression may interfere with the ability to work and care for the children. The second option is to treat the depression and leave the social problem unsolved. This is the usual response. The third option is to provide affordable child care for everyone who needs it.

Compare the second and third alternatives in terms of cost. If an employed mother receives treatment from a psychiatrist for her depression, the psychiatrist might prescribe medication, monitor her for side effects, listen to her, interpret her dreams, hypnotize her, send her to a hospital, and so on. The one thing a psychiatrist cannot do is solve her child-care problem. How much money would have to be spent on psychiatrists, drugs, therapies, and hospitals to get this woman's depressive symptoms down to a tolerable and humane level? Let us estimate that it costs about $4000 a year for child care for one child (Kamerman and Kahn, 1979). And let us estimate that psychiatric care for a woman with high levels of depression who sees a psychiatrist once a week costs $4800 a year (48 × 100). (This does not include the costs of prescription drugs.) The costs of treating this woman's depression are at least as high as providing care for her child. Furthermore, the child care could prevent the depression in the first place, instead of exposing her to the stress, frustration, and demoralization that leads her to seek help.

This century has been characterized by increases in educational levels, increases in women's labor force participation, and decreases in fertility. The three trends are closely related, since women with more education are more likely to be in the labor force and are less likely to have many children. There is no evidence that these trends will be reversed. The association between employment and fewer children is in part due to the fact that the institutional and family arrangements necessary to be employed and be a mother often do not exist. Providing this support reduces the strain on employed mothers and is associated with very high levels of psychological well-being on their part, higher than that of mothers who are not employed. There is nothing necessarily antifamily or antinatalist about the employment of women. It is the lack of readily available child care and the lack of shared responsibility for children that puts stress on the mothers and their families.

Religion: Comforting Belief?

Most people believe that religion comforts and heals; reduces pain and suffering; and provides meaning, hope, and security to one's life. Religion is thought to help people cope with the existential problems of life. Even theorists, such as Freud and Marx, with very negative views of religion, describe it as providing (false) comfort, security, and escape from painful reality (an opiate).

According to William James, in turning to religion, "the time for tension in our soul is over, and that of happy relaxation, of calm deep breathing, of an eternal present, with no discordant future to be anxious about, has arrived. Fear is . . . expunged and washed away" (1978, p. 63). Religion can bring inner peace and happiness; it can reduce depression, demoralization, and misery.

The emotional function of religion is well accepted and typically unquestioned and unexamined. The research that does exist examines the effect of religious belief on psychological well-being only among those who profess a religion. People who report that they do not have a religion are typically excluded. Thus, the crucial comparison is not made.

The few studies on the association between religious belief and psychological well-being that do exist tend to support the view that, among people with a religion, those with strong beliefs or those that attend church frequently (another indicator of religiousness) have lower levels of psychological distress and worry, and are better adjusted and happier than those whose beliefs are weaker (Gurin, Veroff, and Feld, 1960; Lindenthal et al., 1970).

What about those who say they have no religion? If the claim is made that religion improves psychological well-being, it seems crucial to compare the believers with those who reject religion altogether, yet no one has. People who say they have no religion are a very small minority in the United States. We are perhaps the most religious of all western societies. Although the percentage has been declining somewhat, about 90% of Americans have a religious affiliation, attend services, pray, and believe in God (Herberg, 1960; Alwin, 1988). We are a religiously heterogeneous society, in contrast to France, for example, which is a religiously homogeneous one (the large majority are Catholic), though the French are not very religious (as measured by church attendance or belief in God). According to Herberg (1960), to be an American is to belong to one of the three dominant faiths—Protestant, Catholic, Jew. To reject religion in this country sets a person apart and puts him or her in a minority, deviant position, clearly outside the dominant

American culture. Those who claim no religion may face rejection and prejudice. They are thought to be un-American.

Because it is clearly a minority position, lack of religious affiliation is not a choice that is made lightly. According to Hadaway and Roof (1979), those who say they have no religion have made a conscious decision to reject it as well as many of the dominant values that religion and religious institutions symbolize. Americans who say they have no religion are *not* indifferent. They have made a choice that is quite different from saying one is Protestant, for example, but does not believe very strongly. If we compare this group to those who have a religion, where do they stand? Are they miserable, demoralized, and depressed, as theory predicts?

In order to examine this question—which had not been examined before—we used data collected by telephone in 1984 from a representative sample of 400 people in Illinois. (The Health Behavior study is described in the Appendix to this book.) People with any religious affiliation (such as Protestant, Catholic, Jewish, and others) were compared to those who report having no religion. Those with a religion were also differentiated according to how religious they were (strong belief, moderate, or weak). Distress levels of four groups (those who rejected religion, those with weak religious belief, moderate belief, and strong religious belief) were compared. Distress was measured by symptoms of depression and anxiety. In addition, we adjusted for sociodemographic characteristics, including income, education, race, gender, age, and marital status. It is important to statistically adjust for these potentially confounding variables when examining the effect of religion on well-being. For example, women, people with low incomes, and older people are more religious than men, the well-to-do, and younger people. In order to make sure that effects are really due to religion and not to age, gender, income, and so on, they must be adjusted. When these adjusted comparisons are made, the findings might surprise some.

Figure 5.2 shows the distress levels of the four groups as deviations from the average. Two groups have lower than average distress levels: those with strong religious beliefs and those with no religion. The people with the highest distress level are those who claim a religious affiliation but say they have only a weak belief in their religion. Those with moderate religious beliefs have about average levels of distress. Thus, there is a U-shaped effect of religious belief on distress. People who do not believe in religion—who have made a conscious decision to reject religious affiliation in a country where over 90% of the population (95% in Illinois in 1984) claims a religious affiliation—have very low distress levels. At the other end, people who believe strongly in their religion also have low distress levels. It is those who have not made a commitment, who belong to a religion, not out of choice but out of indifference, who have the highest distress levels.

Commitment may be the explanation for these results. People in this country who reject all religion are not indifferent or uncommitted. They have

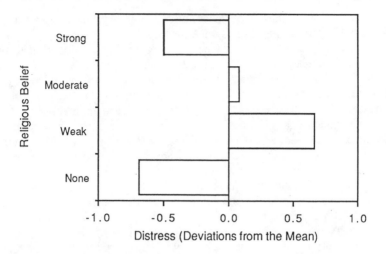

Figure 5.2. Religious belief and psychological distress shown as deviations from the mean. Data are from the Health Behavior Study, which is described in the Appendix, as is the measurement of distress. The graph shows the results adjusting for age, gender, marital status, education, income, and race.

likely made a conscious, difficult decision and are likely to have other strong commitments. On the other hand, those with strong religious beliefs also have strong commitments—in their case, to religion. Neither group appears to be self-estranged. It is the group that claims a religious affiliation without much belief that may be most self-estranged. They belong to an organization they do not much believe in. Affiliation may be imposed or taken for granted rather than a voluntary choice. Possibly they grew up Protestant, or Catholic, and still identify themselves as such, but do not really believe in the church, do not find fulfillment in it, and do not see their affiliation as an expression of themselves. (See Chapter 7 for a discussion of self-estrangement.)

Statistically there are no differences among religious groups in the percentage of persons who say they have only a weak belief. Strong beliefs and weak beliefs are found among all religious groups. Yet recently, the American Catholic church has been concerned with estrangement (in part because Catholics now give much less money to the church than do Protestants). Between 1968 and 1975 church attendance rates fell among Catholics, possibly because Catholics became disaffected with the church's teaching on birth control (Hout and Greeley, 1987). However, very few Catholics left the church: most continued to identify themselves as Catholic (Hout and Greeley,

1987). Instead, they became less committed; more estranged. If our results are correct, this group, like any other group that belongs to an organization they see as separate from themselves rather than an expression of themselves—has high levels of distress.

Ours is the first study to explicitly compare those with and without religion. Past exclusion of those who said they had no religion led to results that were only partially true, and that were not correct in their implications for those with no religion. Although it is true that persons who believe strongly have lower distress levels than those with weak beliefs, the extrapolation that those with no beliefs would have the highest distress is not correct; the opposite is true. Commitment to religion is only one of many possible commitments a person can make. Any commitment improves psychological well-being. It is those who have not made a commitment, who belong to a religion, not out of choice but out of inertia, who have the highest distress levels.

Overweight: Internalized Stigma?

Sociological, psychological, and psychiatric theories predict that the overweight and obese have lower levels of psychological well-being than those who are normal in weight or thin. Popular beliefs reinforce this view.

In the United States today, overweight and obesity are viewed negatively. Fat is bad; trim is good. We have such strong norms against being overweight that by the time girls graduate from high school, the majority have been on a diet to lose weight (Dwyer, Feldman, and Mayer, 1970). Our society does not consider fat attractive (although other cultures have), and the negative attitudes toward the overweight are generalized beyond the level of appearance. Researchers find that overweight individuals are ranked last or next to last in friendship preferences. Not only are overweight persons disliked, but they are considered lazy, sloppy, mean, and stupid by both adults and children (Maddox, Back, and Liederman, 1968; Richardson, 1970). Overweight is a stigma—something that leads others to evaluate a person negatively: to reject, hate, or ridicule the person (Goffman, 1963; Maddox, Back, and Liederman, 1968; Dejong, 1980). Self-image is a reflection seen in the opinions of others that are expressed through their words or actions of acceptance or rejection, esteem or disrespect, liking or hate (Cooley, 1964). If our feelings about ourselves are shaped by the attitudes of others, overweight persons may suffer low self-esteem, have negative images of themselves, and think others dislike them. This could lead to high levels of psychological distress.

This may be especially true for the groups for whom it is least acceptable to be fat—women, the well-to-do and well-educated, the young, and those who are single. Overweight and obesity are uncommon and thus more of a deviation from the norm in these groups, but may be more acceptable and carry less personal blame among men, those in the lower social classes, older persons, and those who are married. It is hard to imagine a young, well-educated, successful businesswoman who is obese because it is so uncommon—norms against overweight in certain groups are very strong.

With Hayes, we examined the association between overweight and psychological distress, as measured by symptoms of depression and anxiety, using a representative community sample of 400 persons in Illinois, interviewed by telephone in 1984 (Hayes and Ross, 1986). Relative overweight is measured on a continuum of weight relative to height (weight/height^2, sometimes called the Quetelet index after the epidemiologist who developed it in the nineteenth century). Weight and height are reported by respondents. Self-reported weight and height are highly correlated with scale weights, although the very heavy tend to underestimate their weight a little. In community studies, degree of overweight is best measured by weight with reference to height, since it is not possible to use skinfold thickness or water displacement measures. Weight divided by height squared is highly correlated with skinfold thickness and is an excellent indicator of total body fat for most persons. (The rare exceptions in a community study would be athletes whose weight comes from muscle. Most people's weight comes from fat.) We measure degree of overweight two ways: (1) as a continuum from the very thin to the very fat, and (2) as a dichotomous measure of obese versus not obese, based on an agreed cutoff on the Quetelet index. Of the sample, 21% is classified as obese. The average woman in the sample is 5'4" and weighs 140 pounds. The average man is 5'8" and weighs 176 pounds. Americans are very concerned with thinness, but are not, on average, thin.

We looked at the association between overweight and obesity and psychological distress, controlling for confounding factors such as socioeconomic status. We found no association. The overweight are not more distressed than those of normal weight. The obese are not more distressed than the nonobese. People who are slender do not have higher levels of psychological well-being than the overweight and obese. There is no association between overweight and psychological distress even among people for whom overweight is least acceptable—women, young people, single people, the well-educated, and the well-to-do. Given these surprising findings, we went back to the literature to reassess past research.

We found study after study that supported our results. In neither the community nor the clinic did the obese and overweight have higher levels of psychological distress than those of normal weight or those who were thin, even in cases in which the obesity was severe enough to have led the person to seek help. (See Moore, Stunkard, and Srole, 1962; Silverstone and Solomon, 1966; Crisp and McGuiness, 1976; Kittel et al., 1978; Holland, Masling, and Copley, 1970.) It seemed to be another instance (like life change) in which theory had blinded us to the facts. Some researchers, more convinced by theory than by their own results, speculated that the obese were denying their depression. [This is very unlikely given that depression is *not* measured by asking people, "Are you depressed because you are overweight?" or even "Are you depressed?" but by a series of indicators, many of which (such as sleep disturbances and lack of energy) may not even be recognized as depression.] Simply because the theory is convincing does not mean it is true.

Why is overweight not detrimental to psychological well-being, even for people in subgroups where it is not considered acceptable to be fat? Possibly, the overweight and obese have friendship networks that insulate them from the negative evaluations of society as a whole. There is some evidence that people who are overweight themselves do not respond negatively to others who are overweight (Young and Powell, 1985). Alternatively, the idea that psychological well-being depends heavily on the evaluations of others (Cooley, 1964) may be overstated. Our self-evaluations may be based more on objective factors such as socioeconomic success—a good job that pays well; or on qualities of marriage or support networks. The fact that our culture evaluates overweight negatively—models are never fat and we are bombarded with messages to lose weight—may, in fact, have little impact on day-to-day life.

Theory predicted that overweight people internalize the negative evaluations of others, leading to low self-esteem, devaluation of themselves, and depression. This theory has little factual support. Being overweight will likely be bad for mental health only if it impedes someone from getting ahead: if the person faces discrimination on the basis of weight and is refused a job or a promotion. Although at first it seemed as if the lack of an association between overweight and obesity and poor mental health was surprising, similar results have turned up in reference to the mental health of minority groups such as blacks. It was once thought that blacks have higher levels of psychological distress than whites because blacks internalize the negative evaluations of whites. In fact, negative evaluations and prejudice are not the problem; discrimination and disadvantage are. Blacks are more depressed and anxious than whites because they are a disadvantaged group; they have lower levels of education and income than whites. Blacks are disproportionately poor in this country, and it is poverty, not the evaluations of whites, that put them at a disadvantage in terms of psychological well-being (Mirowsky and Ross, 1980).

There are two postscripts to this research. First, although overweight is not associated with depression and anxiety, dieting is. People who are currently on a diet to lose weight (whether they would be considered overweight or not) are more depressed and anxious than those who are not on a diet (Stunkard and Rush, 1974). This may be due to feelings of deprivation that have a physiological, psychological, or social basis. Trying to fit norms of attractiveness may be more stressful than not fitting them. Second, exercise is associated with lower levels of depression and anxiety. People who engage in physical activities, exercise, or sports have higher levels of psychological well-being than those who do not (Hayes and Ross, 1986). The effect of exercise on psychological well-being may be internally mediated: increased levels of endorphins improve mood, and better norepinephrine regulation improves mood and decreases physiological symptoms of depression such as feeling rundown and having trouble sleeping. The effect may also be socially mediated: doing activities with others or feeling more in control improves well-being. It is better for psychological well-being to exercise (whether one is overweight or not) than to diet.

Age: The Best Years of Your Life

Many believe that youth is the best time of life. We live in a society in which beauty, vigor, health, and well-being are practically synonymous with youth. Many assume the young are happy and carefree. Our data show that this is not the case. Depression is high in the younger age groups, decreases until age 55, and then increases. We interviewed a representative sample of 800 Illinois residents in 1985. Our sample contains people ranging from 18 to 85 years of age. We find that as people age, their depression levels decrease until age 55, start rising a little, and then increase steeply as people retire and age into their 70s and 80s. The optimum age is 55.

Anxiety is very high among the young and decreases in a linear fashion with age. It never rises again as does depression. Although it is usually the case that the same people who have high levels of depression also have high levels of anxiety (as among the young), it is not the case among the elderly, who have high levels of depression and low levels of anxiety.

Economic well-being may partially explain why depression is high among the young, low among the middle-aged, and high again among the elderly. Family income increases with age. The average annual family income among 22- to 29-year-olds is $29,171. It increases, on average, to $37,579 among 40- to 50-year group, stays at that level until retirement, and then decreases by over $10,000. Persons in their 70s and 80s have family incomes of $18,000 and $17,000, respectively—amounts just above poverty level. These incomes are averaged across socioeconomic classes. People in the lower and working classes start with lower incomes during their employment years, see less of an increase, and see their earnings peak much earlier, often when they are in their 30s. When they retire, their benefits are lower and they may have very little money saved. Figure 5.5 shows that depression and family income are mirror images of one another. Family income is highest in the middle years, when depression is lowest. Family income is lowest among the elderly, when depression is highest.

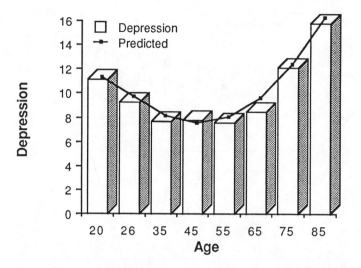

Figure 5.3. Depression levels as a function of age. The bars show the mean depression levels in various age groups, and the line shows the prediction based on the regression equation with a parabolic effect of age (age + age^2). The parabolic effect of age is significant adjusting for marital status, gender, race, education, and income. Data are from the Illinois Survey of Well-Being, described in the Appendix.

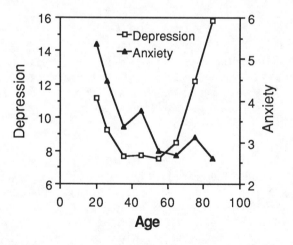

Figure 5.4. Depression and anxiety as functions of age. Data are from the Illinois Survey of Well-Being, described in the Appendix. Also described are the measures of depression and anxiety.

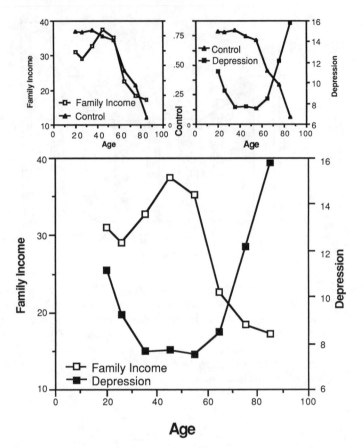

Figure 5.5. The relationships among perceived control, family, income, and depression as functions of age. Data are from the Illinois Survey of Well-Being. The measures of depression, family income, and control are described in the Appendix.

Income affects depression in part by way of perceived control. People holding jobs in which they earn high incomes tend to feel in control of their lives. These feelings of control—as opposed to those of powerlessness—decrease depression. Even more important than the amount of money a person earns is the fact of having a job and earning money. Retirement marks a status change, from an employed person to an unemployed one. Without a job people feel less worthwhile, less respected, and, most importantly, less in control of their lives. Figure 5.5 graphs family income and perceived control as functions of age. Perceived control is high among the young, whose incomes are rising. Even though young people have low incomes when they first leave their parents' homes and go out on their own (in their 20s), their perceptions of control are high. This is likely because they perceive that their incomes will increase with age, that they will get promotions and raises, that things will improve. A sense of control stays fairly high until retirement. With retirement and the sharp drop in income comes a sharp decrease in feelings of control. A low income at the end of life means something very different than a low income at the beginning of life. The figure shows a convergence of income and control after age 60. With retirement comes a

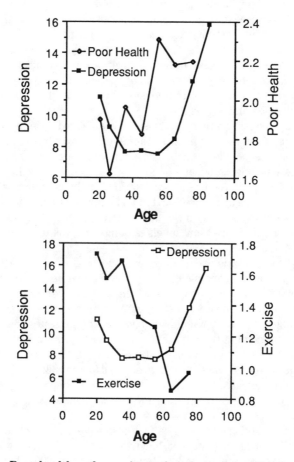

Figure 5.6. Poor health and exercise as functions of age. Data are from the Health Behavior Study. Measures are described in the Appendix to this volume.

decrease in family income, a decrease in the perception that one is in control of life, and an increase in depression.

Other factors may increase feelings of powerlessness among the elderly, most notably poor health. Although health does tend to decline with age, many elderly are not in ill health. This relationship is not as relevant to depression as are work and earnings. Figure 5.6 maps the relationships among poor health and depression as functions of age. Poor health increases with age, but the relationship is not striking. In fact, in the oldest groups, where the deaths of those in poor health may have left a residue of those in good health still alive, subjective health is slightly better than for those in their 60s. Another physical factor that may affect depression among the elderly is lack of physical activity. Figure 5.6 also maps the relationships among age, exercise, and depression. Exercise decreases with age. Since exercise and physical activity are associated with psychological well-being, lack of physical activity may be part of the explanation for increasing levels of depression after age 55. Like ill health, lack of physical activity may affect depression in part by way of decreasing perceived control over life. If a person is unable to get out of the house and be somewhat active, he or she may feel powerless and depressed.

With old age comes an increased risk of widowhood. Having a spouse die increases depression more than any other event. Apart from the event itself, the change leaves people without the support levels they had previously. Relatively few people under age 55 are widowed, but once they reach their 80s, almost 70% are. As friends and other family members also die, the person may feel more and more isolated and deprived of emotional support.

Thus far we have focused on the upturn in depression at older ages. What explains the high depression levels among the young? They have low incomes, but that does not seem to increase perceptions of powerlessness because of the expectation that things will improve. It may affect depression more directly though economic hardship. Young married people need to buy goods to set up a household, goods which increase debt and the bills that arrive every month. They often struggle to feed a family on an inadequate income. Young couples with children may feel the pressure to buy or rent a larger place, which puts them further in debt, or they may continue to live in crowded conditions, which increases stress. Economic hardships may exacerbate feelings of being worn down, tired, and demoralized. They may also increase feelings of anxiety. Thus, young married people, especially those with children, may feel the pressure of a low income, which may increase depression.

On the other hand, young singles may also have high levels of depression and anxiety because they do not have the emotional support available to married persons. In the 18- to 22-year-old age group, 86% of the sample is single; 42% of the 23- to 29-year-olds are single; and 18% of the 30- to 35-year-olds are single. After that, few people are single (see Fig. 5.7).

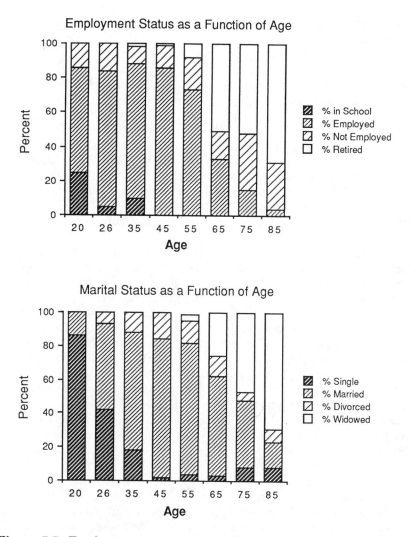

Figure 5.7. Employment status and marital status as functions of age. Data are from the Illinois Survey of Well-Being, described in the Appendix.

Anxiety levels of young people, whether married or single, may be high because of uncertainty. Young people are not secure or settled in jobs, families, or living arrangements. They may be anxious about whether they will succeed or fail. Those still in school have especially high levels of depression and anxiety. Of the group under age 22 in our sample, 25% are still in school.

As we age, life becomes more certain, more settled, and more secure. People get settled in jobs, incomes rise; people get married and buy homes. All this decreases depression according to multiple regressions we ran to test our explanations for the effect of age on depression. In these regressions, age is modeled as a parabola (age + age^2) which is superimposed over the actual average depression of each age group, as shown in Figure 5.3. The parabola fits the data well. Multiple regressions that statistically adjust for other variables (Tufte, 1974) in predicting depression levels show that employment, higher income, and home ownership decrease depression. People in school have high levels of depression (and very high levels of anxiety), while married people have lower levels of depression. These factors largely account for the decrease in depression that occurs as people age from 18 to about 55.

After age 55 depression begins to rise slowly; it rises precipitously after age 65. Two explanations—marriage and work—are similar for both young and old. Like young people, older people are less likely to be married. Widowhood greatly increases depression; in fact, its effect on depression is much stronger than the effect of being single. The meaning of being unmarried, like the meaning of low income, is different at the end of life. Being young and single may be stressful, but the young anticipate someday getting married. Being widowed is also stressful because one is alone; in addition, there is usually little anticipation of being married again. Like the young, the old are less likely to work. Being retired is associated with even higher levels of depression in our sample than being in school.

In sum, the young and the old are both less likely to be employed, less likely to earn good incomes, and less likely to be married than are those in their middle years. But the meaning of these statuses differs for the two groups. This is evidenced by the fact that the young feel in control of their lives in spite of objective circumstances such as low incomes. The elderly are likely to feel powerless. Feelings of powerlessness, as opposed to control, increase depression. Remember that everyone in our sample lives in the community. Elderly in nursing homes or other institutions likely feel much more powerless than those in the community, some of whom, nevertheless, may not be as independent and autonomous as they once were. We find that about 80% of people between the ages of 45 and 65 own their own homes, whereas less than 50% of those in their 80s own the home they live in. Either poverty has forced them to sell their homes, or they are no longer able to live on their own and must live with relatives. This may decrease feelings of being in control of life. Perceptions of powerlessness are the strongest explanation in our data for the upturn in depression among the elderly; such perceptions do not explain the high levels of depression among the young.

Given that two of the social statuses most important to mental health —marriage and socioeconomic position—are stratified by age, and that the elderly are likely to experience negative life events like retirement and widowhood that mark transitions to conditions of less support, fewer resources, and less control, it would be surprising if age were not associated with mental health. Yet the cultural myth that the young are the happiest of all age groups is not correct, and the scientific research results to date have not been consistent.

Many researchers study community samples in which persons over age 65 are not interviewed. They generally conclude that depression decreases with age. On the other hand, gerontologists often study samples that contain *only* older people. They often conclude that the elderly have high levels of depression. As previously noted, our sample includes people 18 to 85 years of age. We do not limit it to certain adult groups. Thus, some inconsistencies in past research are resolved. Both the young and the old have high levels of depression, in part for similar reasons (like work and marriage) and in part for different reasons (powerlessness, on the one hand, and anxiety, on the other).

Other inconsistencies arise from the psychiatric approach to diagnosing major depression. Weissman concludes that major depression is most prevalent in the 18- to 44-year-old age group, followed by those 45 to 64 years of age, and least prevalent in the group over age 65 (1987, Fig. 4). This conclusion—that the elderly are least likely to be depressed—could be due to the fact that persons are excluded from receiving a diagnosis of depression if they are grieving the death of a loved one, are physically ill, or are functioning well enough for their roles. The elderly, more than any other age group, are likely to be recently widowed or sick. Limited social roles may mean their functioning is not impaired, because not much is expected of them. As the community sample shows, the elderly do feel more depressed, even though they are least likely to qualify for a psychiatric diagnosis of depression.

Because our sample was collected at one point in time, everyone who is the same age was born in the same year. Some might argue that what we are seeing is not an effect of aging over the life cycle, but a period or cohort effect. For example, perhaps everyone born in 1920 went through similar experiences, and it is these experiences, not aging, that is producing different depression levels in different age groups. Or maybe changes occur with each successive cohort that are affecting depression levels.

With regard to the latter theory, there have been a number of changes occurring over this century, the most important for mental health being increases in educational levels, increases in income and home ownership, decreases in number of children per family, increases in divorce, and increases in women's employment. These macrolevel social changes mean that in every successive cohort, any one individual is more likely to be well educated, have a higher income, and so on than in the previous cohort. To take these changes into account, we use multiple regression to control for these factors on the individual level: education, income, employment, home ownership, number of children, and marital status. Thus, we adjust for these long-term trends, or cohort effects, as they affect individuals.

Second, we take period effects into account by also looking at the effect of age in the national sample of husbands and wives collected in 1978 (described earlier). By looking at the effect of age in two data sets, one collected in 1985 and one in 1978, we can see the effect of aging apart from the effect of the year in which a person was born. For example, people who are 70 in the 1985 sample were born in 1915, whereas people who are 70 in the 1978 sample were born in 1908, and the Great Depression may have affected these groups differently. We find the same parabolic effect of age on depression in the 1978 sample as in the 1985 sample. Thus, the conclusion that aging over the life cycle affects depression seems warranted. The effects of age on psychological well-being do not appear to be due simply to period or cohort effects.

In sum, with old age comes losses—of loved ones and of status and control. The elderly may feel powerless, isolated, self-estranged; they may feel that life does not have the meaning it used to. The young also have high levels of depression and anxiety; youth is not the best time of life, according to our data—middle age is. Youth is associated with uncertainty, lack of stability, low income, and lack of the kind of support that marriage provides. Being in school is stressful. However, the meaning of earning a low income, not being married, not owning a home, and so on are different at the beginning of life and at the end. The young have high levels of anxiety, but low levels of powerlessness. The elderly have low levels of anxiety, but their high levels of powerlessness increase depression to levels that are greater than at any other time of life.

A Preview of Explanations

Like the established patterns, the new patterns can also be explained in terms of alienation, authoritarianism, and inequity. Age, children, and religion mark objective conditions of social life; these conditions shape people's experiences which, in turn, affect beliefs, interpretations, and assumptions about themselves and the world; the nature of these beliefs affects distress. Powerlessness versus control; self-estrangement versus commitment; isolation versus support; lack of meaning versus meaning; and other types of alienation, authoritarianism, and inequity may be important explanations for the new patterns relating to children, religion, and age, as well as for gender, marriage, socioeconomic status, and undesirable events.

IV

Explaining the Patterns

CHAPTER SIX

Life Change

Not long after the results of the first community survey were published, *life change* became widely accepted as the main explanation for the social patterns of distress. Its popularity was phenomenal, despite weak supporting evidence. It was so well accepted that, for years, researchers thought of life change and social stress as synonymous. After a decade or more of accumulating counterevidence the explanation was put to rest in scientific circles. No doubt there are many in the general public who still believe it.

Most, if not all, of the current research projects trying to explain social patterns of distress trace their ancestry to studies of life-change events. Although life change eventually was rejected as a unifying explanation, the process of discovering its inadequacy was the gestation of our current science. Three maxims can be derived from the story of that discovery:

1. Inferences from physiological process to social patterns are often leaps from substantial knowledge to unsubstantiated interpretation. The solidity of the ground from which a leap is taken does nothing to verify an interpretation.

2. The relevant attribute captured by an index may not be the one it was constructed to represent.

3. A causal chain is only a chain if none of the links are broken.

A Scientific Myth

Life-change events mark major alterations in a person's daily activities. They include transitions such as the death of a spouse, birth of a child, move to a new home, loss of a job, marriage, graduation from school, and so on. Each event is relatively uncommon in any one person's life, but likely within the lifetime and common in the community as a whole. Life-change events require adaptation and readjustment of a person's habitual activities and social relations. They typically require a renegotiation or redefinition of the individual's social identity, due to the loss or gain of social roles and networks. Big changes in daily life force a person to use mental and physical energy developing habits and an identity that are suited to the new situation.

To a large extent, life change became the paramount explanation by working backward, from the symptoms of distress, to the endocrine and autonomic activity that produce such symptoms, to the environmental conditions that seemed likely to produce such biological activity. Much of the inspiration came from Hans Selye's discovery in 1936 of the General Adaptation Syndrome, as well as related studies in psychosomatic medicine (Selye, 1976). Selye was a physician studying the endocrine system, particularly the hormones of the adrenal cortex. Almost all medical research prior to Selye's was concentrated on the body's specific response to specific organisms, toxins, or damage. In experiments on rats, Selye discovered a nonspecific response to a variety of injected toxins: enlargement of the adrenal cortex, indicating hyperactivation; shrinking of the thymus, spleen, lymph nodes, and all other lymphatic structures in the body, plus the disappearance of eosinophil cells in the blood; and deep ulcers in the stomach and duodenum (Selye, 1976). The instigation of these changes eventually was traced to secretions of the pituitary gland, which in turn is stimulated by secretions of the hypothalamus—a small structure in the brain that bridges that organ and the endocrine system. Selye and his colleagues discovered that the same changes produced by the injection of toxins could be produced by the injection of hormones such as adrenaline and insulin, by purely physical stressors such as extreme heat or cold, by behavioral stressors such as forced exercise or restriction of movement, and by psychological stressors such as noise or crowding.

Physicians, such as Selye, were interested in the somatic response to stressors rather than the emotional response. Their research focused on diseases that result directly from the body's response to stressors, such as stomach or duodenal ulcers, and on increased susceptibility to infections, toxins, and autoimmune problems resulting from overtaxed adaptive mechanisms. It was believed that the body's adaptive mechanisms could be triggered by mental and emotional states, which were the link to external stressors such as noise or crowding. For example, the brain can directly stimulate the adrenal medulla, which releases adrenaline (epinephrine) into the blood, which in turn can produce Selye's general adaptation syndrome. In theory, the chronic stimulation of this "fight or flight" mechanism results from prolonged or repeated fear and anxiety, which in turn results from threatening conditions such as life in the slums, from tense jobs such as air traffic control, or from conflict-ridden relationships such as a bad marriage. Although some mental or emotional connection between social conditions and somatic response was assumed, the initial focus was on the somatic response and the ways it produces or allows disease.

Two physicians, Holmes and Rahe, set out to demonstrate the connection between social-psychological stressors and somatic illness in humans. To do so, they needed to adapt the concepts and findings of laboratory rat studies to research on people out in the world. Generalizing from the somatic concepts of homeostasis and adaptation, and from Adolf Meyer's clinical "life chart," they decided to look for things that disrupt habitual activities and that demand adjustment to a new state (Holmes and Rahe, 1967; Holmes and Masuda, 1974). This was the first leap away from the solid ground of the laboratory rat studies. Nothing in the actual methods or results of rat studies indicated that events and change, rather than ongoing conditions and noxious stimuli, were the culprit. Nevertheless, the *concepts* of homeostasis and adaptation suggest a system temporarily destabilized and expending its energy to regain equilibrium, much like a spinning top righting itself.

Holmes and Rahe needed a general and universal measure of each person's exposure to demand for readjustment. To obtain it, they had subjects rate the amount of readjustment demanded by each of 43 events (Holmes and Rahe, 1967). Holmes, Rahe, and their colleagues found that subsequent physical illness increased with the sum readjustment weight of a person's events in the previous year (Holmes and Masuda, 1974). It was not long before popular magazines published do-it-yourself checklists for assessing one's own Social Readjustment Units (SRUs). If you experienced a lot of changes last year, magazines warned, you might need help to deal with the stress.

Holmes, Rahe, and their colleagues asserted the importance of change itself. They specifically rejected the importance of the psychological and social meaning of events. Speaking of the events listed in the Social Readjustment Rating Scale, Holmes and Masuda (1974) note the following:

> . . .only some of the events are negative or "stressful" in the conventional sense, that is, are socially undesirable. Many are socially desirable and consonant with the American values of achievement, success, materialism, practicality, efficiency, future orientation, conformism, and self-reliance. . . . The emphasis is on change from the existing steady state and not on psychological meaning, emotion, or social desirability (p. 46).

The emphasis on change per se, apart from its meaning and valence, was purely theoretical. The Social Readjustment Rating Scale was constructed on the assumption that change is the stressful aspect of events. In all their research constructing and using the scale, Holmes and Rahe never tested this assumption. They simply proceeded as if it were true. Many other researchers in psychosomatic medicine, epidemiology, psychiatry, sociology, and psychology did the same.

The second leap away from the solid group of Selye's rat studies was the switch from somatic disease to emotional distress as the outcome of interest. Selye, Holmes, and Rahe were interested in somatic disease. Whatever strengths or weaknesses their ideas might have as explanations of somatic disease, they were not meant to explain emotional distress. Nevertheless, most researchers studying distress were quick to see a connection. If things such as noise, crowding, or the death of a spouse can produce somatic illness, there must be a mental or nervous-system link. The clear involvement of psychoactive hormones, such as adrenaline, imply a connection to emotional state. Probably the most suggestive fact, though, is the strong and consistent correlation between depressed or anxious mood and physiological malaise, such as headaches, sour stomach, palpitations, breathlessness, trouble sleeping, loss of appetite, and lethargy. Anything that causes psychosomatic illness is likely to also cause emotional distress.

Despite the impressive rationales based on endocrinology and biological equilibrium, there never was much evidence that life change, itself, is emotionally distressing. On the contrary, there were always good reasons to suspect that the valence of an event, more than just the amount of change it demands, is the emotionally salient factor. Even rats distinguish between rewards and punishments. Research by Osgood and his colleagues (Snider and Osgood, 1969) shows that a good–bad, desirable–undesirable evaluation is the most powerful semantic dimension in human thought. Strong–weak is the second most powerful semantic dimension, and static–active is a distant third. Judgments of the change demanded by events are highly influenced by their desirability or undesirability (Ruch, 1977). For example, Hough, Fairbank, and Garcia (1976) found that Anglos in Texas rate the change demanded by abortion on a level with that demanded by marriage, retirement, and birth of the first child. Although the latter three events mark substantial changes in ongoing, everyday habits and behavior, abortion does not. It is an undesirable event, and an unpleasant one, but it does not demand a major rearrangement of daily life. The desirability or undesirability of events is far more salient than degree of readjustment required.

Undesirability, not change, is the distressing characteristic of life events (Gersten et al., 1974; Mueller, Edwards, and Yarvis, 1977; Ross and Mirowsky, 1979; Vinokur and Selzer, 1975). Holmes and Rahe published their Social Readjustment Rating Scale in 1967 (Holmes and Rahe, 1967). As early as 1969, there were indications from clinical studies that only undesirable events are distressing. Patients admitted to treatment for depression, attempted suicide, and schizophrenia all reported higher rates of undesirable events than a comparison group of normal controls, but there was no difference in the rate of desirable events (Paykel, 1974). A decade later, we systematically compared the impact of various aspects of life events in a random community sample. We found that distress increases with the number of undesirable events. Events weighted by Holmes and Rahe's Social Readjustment Units were not associated with distress once their undesirability was taken into account (Ross and Mirowsky, 1979). When we compared undesirable events with high change scores, undesirable events with low change scores, and desirable events with high change scores, only the undesirable events affected distress (whether or not they had high change scores). Even the desirable events that require a lot of readjustment, such as getting married, starting school, graduating, getting one's first job, and getting promoted, do not increase psychological distress.

Undesirability is highly salient to respondents because it is an evaluation of consequences. *Undesirable events mark transitions to worse positions.* Dohrenwend (1973) called them "status loss" events, which may be a better term. Undesirable, or status loss, events mark transitions to positions of lower status: from employed to unemployed, from married to divorced, from wife to widow. Some of these represent losses of income, power, or prestige. Compared to an employed head of household, an unemployed head receives less money and esteem, and has less authority. Nevertheless, the demands of other statuses such as parenthood remain constant, resulting in a gap between means and obligations and a higher level of distress. Some of these losses involve emotional support. After divorce or death of a spouse the person is left without anyone to come home to, talk to, or to provide support and comfort. The result, again, is a higher level of distress. In each case, it is not the event, per se, that is important, but what the event signifies in terms of ongoing social position. Undesirable events mark transitions to social positions associated with higher levels of distress—unemployment, poverty, role overload, being divorced or widowed, and so on.

Ongoing social positions and all that they indicate in terms of hardships versus successes, helplessness and powerlessness versus mastery and control, role overload and conflict versus compatibility of roles, and so on, are critical to psychological well-being (Belle, 1982). It is time to give up life events as a measure of social stressors and concentrate on ongoing stressors. Many of the things respondents report as life events are actually ongoing troubles. Often, they have been present for a long time. The person may be adjusted to the troubles, even resigned to them, but the troubles are still distressing. So-called events in this category include serious physical illness (of respondent or family member), trouble with in-laws, trouble with the boss, frequent minor illness, declining financial status, lack of work for over a month, problems in school, and so on.

Many things such as death of a spouse, the most stressful event, seem to be events but are actually part of a prolonged situation. There are cases in which it is a pure event—the person left for work in the morning and was killed in a car accident. In most cases, however, it is not. Typically, the respondent had been caring for an ill husband or wife for a long time. They knew their spouse was dying. The spouse had been sick and in and out of the hospital. What had been interpreted as an event—a death that must be adjusted to—is actually much more. It reflects the ongoing stress of caring for a loved one, of having resources depleted by expensive medical care, of not being able to get out of the house to do enjoyable things, of adjusting psychologically over weeks and months to the fact that the spouse is dying while the healthy one is helpless to stop it. This is not an event; it is a prolonged stressor.

One of the problems with indexes of life events is that they add together things that may be quite different in their origins or routes to distress. This is true even if the index contains only undesirable events. Information on the characteristic causes and consequences of a specific event is lost if they are all combined in one index. The impact of getting divorced on psychological well-being is an important issue. How do people adjust to divorce and what are the long-term implications for mental health of being divorced? The impact of getting married or fired is important too. We do not increase our understanding of any of these by lumping them together. For years, social stressors have been measured by indexes of life events—indexes that are at best conceptually vague and at worst refer to incorrect concepts, such as change. Conceptual clarity in the measurement of social stressors is decreased by adding up unrelated events.

It is unfortunate that, just as sociologists are finally abandoning life change events as the explanation for social patterns of distress, Lazarus and other psychologists have developed a similar inventory of "daily hassles." (Lazarus and Folkman, 1984; DeLongis et al., 1982). Like life-events lists, this inventory adds up unrelated things. The approach takes one step forward by including daily problems rather than large changes, but takes two steps backward. First, it confounds cause and effect. Instead of asking people if they get stuck in traffic a lot and then correlating it with distress, people are asked whether being stuck in traffic is a hassle for them (Dohrenwend and Shrout, 1985).

Worse than the confounding of cause and effect, the daily-hassles approach trivializes the social causes of distress. Being stuck in traffic, losing something, having unexpected company, or missing your bus is a hassle. Poverty is not a hassle. Having a job that does not pay well, being told what to do instead of making decisions, and being economically dependent are not hassles. Inequity and conflict in marriage is not a hassle. Living alone, without friends or support is not a hassle. Ongoing social positions that increase feelings of powerlessness, dependency, inequity, and isolation are not hassles. They are serious problems.

Both the idea of daily hassles and that of life change trivialize the social causes of psychological distress. They deny stratification as causes of distress—things like inequality, poverty, injustice, and lack of opportunity. Just as everyone has daily hassles to put up with, everyone's life changes. Life change is not disproportionately associated with lack of education, poverty, minority status, being female, or being unmarried. Change per se cannot explain the social patterns of distress because it is not linked to social position or to distress. The link is the undesirable events, losses, failures, and ongoing stressors that flow from inequality, inequity, and lack of opportunity.

CHAPTER SEVEN

Alienation

Our explanations of the social patterns of distress refer first to alienation in one or more of its forms. On the most general level, alienation is any kind of social detachment or separation. Although it may be possible to define types of alienation in terms of objective social conditions, studies of distress more commonly follow Seeman's (1959) classic definition in terms of expectations and beliefs. Seeman described five major types of alienation: powerlessness, self-estrangement, isolation, meaninglessness, and normlessness. He expressed his hope that subsequent research would uncover their consequences and the social conditions that produce them. As the material that follows will show, distress is one of the major consequences. In this chapter, we will describe each type of alienation, its social causes, and its emotional consequences.

Although Seeman's descriptions of the five types of alienation provide a core set of concepts, 25 years of research have broadened the topics being considered (Seeman, 1983). We will discuss five issues that incorporate Seeman's original ideas, their variations, and related concepts: control, commitment, support, meaning, and normality.

Control

Of all the beliefs about self and society that might increase or reduce distress, one's sense of control over one's own life may be the most important. Seeman placed the sense of powerlessness at the top of his list of types of alienation, defining it as "the expectancy or probability, held by the individual, that his own behavior cannot determine the occurrence of the outcomes, or reinforcements, he seeks" (Seeman, 1959, p. 784). He was careful to point out that powerlessness, as a social-psychological variable, is distinct from the objective conditions that may produce it and the frustration an individual may feel as a consequence of it. Thus, Seeman clearly stated the central position of powerlessness in a three-part model of conditions, understandings, and feelings, while calling for an end to the practice, which was common at the time, of measuring alienation as a jumble of causes and effects.

---

*Parts of this chapter are reproduced, with permission, from the *Ann. Rev. Sociol.*, Vol. 12 © 1986 by Annual Reviews, Inc.

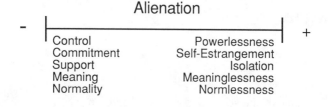

Figure 7.1. Five types of subjective alienation, each scored from low (−) to high (+).

The Faces and Names of Powerlessness

The importance of powerlessness is recognized in social and behavioral sciences other than sociology, where it appears in a number of forms with various labels. In psychology the concept of powerlessness appears in two major forms, depending on whether the psychologist has a behavioral or cognitive orientation. Behaviorists speak of learned helplessness, which results from exposure to inescapable, uncontrollable negative stimuli and is characterized by a low rate of voluntary response and limited ability to learn successful behaviors (Seligman, 1975). Even the purist has difficulty refraining from attributing unpleasant feelings to the whimpering, passive animal that has been exposed to uncontrollable punishment, the clear purpose of which is to produce an analog of human depression. It is important to remember, though, that learned helplessness refers to the behavior and not the imputed emotion. [This is the original theory of learned helplessness based on behavioral conditioning experiments, not the revised theory based on the Attributional Style Questionnaire (Peterson and Seligman, 1984).] Cognitive psychologists speak of an external versus internal locus of control (Rotter, 1966). Belief in an external locus of control is a learned, generalized expectation that outcomes of situations are determined by forces external to one's self such as powerful others, luck, fate, or chance. The individual believes that he or she is powerless and at the mercy of the environment. Belief in an internal locus of control is a learned, generalized expectation that outcomes are contingent on one's own choices and actions. The individual believes that he or she can master, control, or effectively alter the environment. In anthropology the concept appears as the "man-nature orientation" (Kluckhohn and Strodtbeck, 1961), or "fatalism" (e.g., Madsen, 1973). In sociology beliefs about control appear under a number of different names in addition to powerlessness, notably the sense of personal efficacy (Kohn, 1972), self-directedness (Kohn and Schooler, 1982), mastery (Pearlin *et al.*, 1981), and fatalism versus instrumentalism (Wheaton, 1980). These concepts are not precisely the same but, as with the various types of distress, they are roughly interchangeable in a wide range of instances.

Conditions that Generate a Sense of Powerlessness

An individual learns through social interaction and personal experience that his or her choices and efforts are usually likely or unlikely to affect the outcome of a situation. Failure in the face of effort leads to a sense of powerlessness, fatalism, or belief in external control, which can in turn increase passivity and the likelihood of giving up. Success leads to a sense of mastery, efficacy, or belief in internal control, characterized by an active, problem-solving approach to life (Wheaton, 1980, 1983; Mirowsky and Ross, 1983a, 1984).

Sociological theory points to several conditions likely to produce a belief in external control. Powerlessness, defined as an objective condition rather than a belief, is the inability to achieve one's ends, or, alternatively, the inability to achieve one's ends when they are in opposition to those of others. Structural inconsistency is a situation in which society defines certain goals, purposes, and interests as legitimate and desirable and also defines the allowable procedures for moving toward the objectives, but does not provide adequate resources and opportunities for achieving the objectives through legitimate means. Alienated labor is a condition under which the worker does not decide what to produce, does not design and schedule the production process, and does not own the product. Dependency is a situation in which one partner in an exchange relationship has fewer alternative sources of sustenance and gratification than the other. In looking for the correlates of a sense of powerlessness and belief in external control, the researcher looks for variables associated with conditions of powerlessness, structural inconsistency, alienated labor, and dependency.

Sociodemographic Correlates of Powerlessness

Surveys find six major sociodemographic correlates of powerlessness and belief in external control: general socioeconomic status, education, occupation, job disruption and unemployment, sex, and minority status.

We find that a high socioeconomic status, as indicated by family income, educational level, occupational prestige of the respondent or breadwinner, and interviewer ratings of the social class of the neighborhood, home, and respondent, decreases the sense of powerlessness and thus increases the sense of mastery and control (Mirowsky and Ross, 1983a). Jobs are important for a number of reasons. Low-status jobs produce a sense of powerlessness because the job, and the opportunities and income it provides, are seen as barriers to the achievement of life goals (Wheaton, 1980). Jobs that are substantively complex (work primarily with data and people rather than with things) increase the sense of personal responsibility, control, and self-directedness (Kohn and Schooler, 1982). Job disruptions such as being laid off, demoted, or fired, and leaving work because of illness, all decrease the worker's sense of mastery, partly by lowering income and increasing difficulties in acquiring necessities such as food, clothing, housing, and medical care, or optional but useful items such as furniture, automobiles, and recreation (Pearlin et al., 1981).

In addition, we find that women have a greater sense of powerlessness than men (Mirowsky and Ross, 1983a, 1984). Although the reason women feel more powerless has not been fully established, it may be due to economic dependency, restricted opportunities, role overload, or the menial nature of housework and many women's jobs.

Finally, minority status is associated with belief in external control after taking into account lower levels of education, income, and occupational status (Mirowsky and Ross, 1983a; 1984; Ross and Mirowsky, 1989). For Mexican-Americans, this is partly due to an emphasis on subordination to the family, but mostly due to restricted opportunity in the Anglo-dominated economic system. For blacks, it is due to restricted opportunities.

Powerlessness and Distress: Demoralization versus Instrumental Coping

The sense of powerlessness can have two effects on distress. It can be demoralizing in itself and it can hamper effective coping with difficult events or situations. People who believe they have little influence over the things that happen to them, that what is going to happen will happen, that we might as well decide what to do by flipping a coin, and that success is mostly a matter of getting good breaks, tend to be more distressed; whereas those who believe that when they make plans they can make them work, that people's misfortunes result from the mistakes they make, that there is really no such thing as luck, and that what happens to them is their own doing, tend to be less distressed (Wheaton, 1980). Similarly, increasing belief that "There is really no way I can solve some of the problems I have," or that "I have little control over the things that happen to me" increases distress over time, whereas increasing belief that "I can do just about anything I really set my mind to," or that "What happens to me in the future mostly depends on me" decreases distress over time (Pearlin et al., 1981). A self-directed orientation plays a central role in a three-way relationship with problem-solving flexibility and distress. Greater self-directedness increases problem-solving flexibility and decreases distress. In turn, the greater flexibility and lower distress boost self-directedness. The result is a self-amplifying feedback that magnifies the impact of occupational routinization, closeness of supervision, and substantive complexity on distress (Kohn and Schooler, 1982). (The impact of self-direction on distress is much larger than the "rebound" effect of distress on self-direction, so the cross-sectional analyses that assume one-way causation are probably not seriously biased.)

In addition to its direct, demoralizing impact, the sense of not being in control of one's own life can diminish the will and motivation to cope actively with problems. Wheaton (1983) argues that fatalism decreases coping effort. Belief in the efficacy of environmental rather than personal forces makes active attempts to solve problems seem pointless. The result is less motivation and less persistence in coping and, thus, less success in solving problems and adapting. Taking Wheaton's arguments a step further, the fatalist has a reactive, passive orientation whereas the instrumentalist has a proactive one. Instrumental persons are likely to search the environment for potentially distressing events and conditions, to take preventive steps, and to accumulate resources or develop skills and habits that will reduce the impact of unavoidable problems. (For example, driving carefully, wearing a seatbelt, and carrying accident insurance.) When undesired events and situations occur, the instrumental person is better prepared and less threatened. In contrast, the reactive, passive person ignores potential problems until they actually happen. The result is that problems are more likely to happen and the person is less prepared when they do. Furthermore, passive coping—such as trying to ignore a problem until it goes away—fails to limit the consequences of problems. Thus, the instrumentalist is constantly getting ahead of problems whereas the fatalist is constantly falling behind. The theoretical result is a magnification of differences, with the fatalists suffering more and more problems that simply reinforce the sense of powerlessness and lack of control and thus produce greater passivity in the face of difficulties.

The idea of instrumental coping implies an interaction between belief in internal control and stressful events or situations. In interaction models, "two or more conditions must be present; together they set off a process that neither alone could produce, and literally, the resultant whole is greater than the sum of its parts" (Wheaton, 1983, p. 221). Research on the interactive effects of instrumental, active coping with stressful events and conditions is still relatively undeveloped. There is an intriguing table in a report by Murphy (1978) in which he compares Montreal women with unusually low levels of distress to those with unusually high levels. When faced with the need for a decision, 87% of the women with unusually low distress say they decide on their own or consult with others, and only 13% say they have no strategy, wait for others to decide, or leave the matter to time, chance, or God. The comparable breakdown for women with unusually high distress is 50% and 50%, respectively. When feeling irritated or dissatisfied, 74% of the women with unusually low levels of distress start doing something different or seek compensation in company, and only 26% turn to religion or seek passive distraction such as television, bingo, or gambling. The comparable breakdown for women with unusually high distress is 44 and 56%, respectively. When troubled by a disease symptom, 76% of the women with high distress seek rest or distraction or wait for it to go away, and only 24%

attempt to track down and treat the cause. The comparable breakdown for women with low distress is 48 and 52%, respectively. Although these percentages suggest some interesting possibilities, they are not adjusted for differences in socioeconomic status between high- and low-distress women, and they do not explicitly model the interaction of instrumental coping with difficult events or situations.

Some studies engaged in trying to explain social class differences in distress have looked at interactions explicitly. Kessler and Cleary (1980) found that lower-status persons are more likely than middle- and upper-status people to develop symptoms of distress when exposed to undesirable events or physical health problems. Furthermore, the differences in distress between social strata are attributable to differences in emotional response more than to differences in the level of undesirable events and health problems (although differences in the level of problems do exist and do account for some of the differences in distress). Further analysis shows that the protective effect of higher status is actually due to the presence of upwardly mobile persons in the high-status groups. Kessler and Cleary speculate that "the experience of success associated with upward mobility creates the sort of assertive coping skills needed to avoid the psychological damage that can result from undesirable life events. . . . Success in overcoming adversity—one important instance of which is rising above one's disadvantaged social origins—can help create in an individual the sort of personal characteristics—feelings of self-esteem, confidence, perserverance—that are the stuff of competent problem management" (Kessler and Cleary, 1980, p. 472). In support of this idea, Kessler and Cleary argue that the use of tranquilizing drugs is a form of passive coping. They find there is no association between exposure to undesirable events and the use of tranquilizers among the upwardly mobile; whereas among people in the same social class who are not upwardly mobile, exposure to undesirable events increases the probability of tranquilizer use.

In a study of women in southwestern Ontario who recently gave birth, Turner and Noh (1983) replicated the finding that the same events are more distressing to lower-class persons than to middle- or upper-class persons. Turner and Noh also went a step further and measured perceptions of control. Women who express a sense of powerlessness and fatalism are distressed by low socioeconomic status, but women who express a sense of efficacy and instrumentalism and are members of a network in which they feel valued and esteemed are not. However, lower-status women are more likely than middle- and upper-status women to lack a sense of control, which in part accounts for the greater impact of events and thus the higher level of distress among lower-status women.

Wheaton (1983) developed the theory of instrumental coping further, extended the model to include chronic stressors in addition to acute events, and distinguished among three psychological outcomes. He defines chronic stress as the perception of barriers to the achievement of one's goals, or stagnation in the improvement of one's condition; the perception of inequity (inadequate rewards in comparison to one's effort or qualifications); excessive or inadequate demand in the environment relative to the capacity of the individual; frustration of role expectations; and the absence of necessary objective resources. Wheaton looks at three psychological consequences of acute and chronic stressors: (1) depression, such as feeling moody, unhappy, useless, lethargic, or low in spirits; (2) anxiety, such as rapid heartbeat or shortness of breath when not exercising, cold sweats, trembling hands, restlessness, irritability, and worrying; (3) schizophreniform hallucinations and delusions, such as hearing voices, seeing things, thinking your mind is dominated by forces beyond your control, or believing you are being plotted against. He finds that instrumentalism reduces or eliminates the impact of acute and chronic stressors on depression and schizophrenia, but does not modify the impact of stressors on anxiety. Stated another way, a fatalistic orientation is a necessary condition for a depressed or schizophrenic response to stressful events and situations, but it is not necessary for an anxious response. Wheaton speculates that anxiety in response to stressors does not depend on a passive coping style because much of anxiety is psychophysiologic arousal, which may be a natural response to stressors and not necessarily dysfunctional (although uncomfortable).

Wheaton's findings suggest that studies of the interaction between stressors and fatalism can achieve different results depending on whether they measure distress as depression or as anxiety. This may account for the fact that McFarlane et al. (1983) find no interaction between events and fatalism in their effect on distress. They measure distress using the Langner index, which is composed primarily of items indicating anxiety and psychophysiologic arousal. Paralleling Wheaton's findings concerning depression and schizophrenia are our findings, which suggest that the threat of victimization and exploitation posed by life in lower socioeconomic positions is associated with mistrust and suspiciousness among people who believe in external control. Among those with a strong sense of mastery and instrumentalism, low socioeconomic status is not associated with a lack of trust (Mirowsky and Ross, 1983a). This suggests that people who feel in control of their own lives and take an active approach to problems feel they can generally deal with (and benefit from) their relationships and interactions with other people, even in situations where the threat of exploitation is present.

To reiterate, instrumentalism and a sense of mastery are associated with achievement, status, education, wealth, and work that is complex, variable, and unsupervised; whereas fatalism and a sense of powerlessness are associated with failure, stagnation, dependency, poverty, economic strain, and work that is simple, routine, and closely supervised. People in higher socioeconomic positions tend to have a sense of personal control, and people in lower socioeconomic positions tend to have a sense of personal powerlessness. This produces socioeconomic differences in levels of distress (particularly depression, mistrust, and schizophrenia). The sense of powerlessness can be depressing and demoralizing in itself, but worse, it can undermine the will to seek and take effective action in response to problems. As a result, people in lower socioeconomic positions have a triple burden: first, they have more problems to deal with; second, their personal histories are likely to have left them with a deep sense of powerlessness; and third, that sense of powerlessness discourages them from martialing whatever energy and resources they do have in order to solve their problems. The result for many is a multiplication of despair.

Commitment

It is impossible to find an English word that is an unambiguous label for the second concept of alienation. We have chosen to refer to the absence of this form of alienation as commitment, but words such as freedom, self-expression, involvement, identification, and pride each tap a part of the concept.

Self-Estrangement and Alienated Labor

The issue of commitment is probably best known from Marx's discussion of alienated labor. Marx was concerned about the impact of wage labor and factories on the quality of life. He argued that in working for someone else the laborer belongs to another person and not to himself. The work is a means of satisfying certain needs rather than being satisfying in itself; it is external rather than part of the worker's nature, imposed rather than voluntary. Workers deny themselves in work rather than fulfill themselves. Marx argued that alienated labor exhausts the worker physically and debases him mentally as opposed to developing his or her mental and physical energies. Thus, alienated labor produces a sense of misery rather than well-being (Kohn, 1976). The orientation thought to result from alienated labor is called self-estrangement (Seeman, 1959). Alienated labor is the condition in which the worker does not decide what to produce, does not design the production process, and does not own the product. Self-estrangement is the sense of being separate from that part of one's thoughts, actions, and experiences given over to the control of others; of work being foreign to oneself rather than an expression of oneself (Mirowsky and Ross, 1983a). Work is seen as drudgery; it has no intrinsic value; there is no pride in it. Any rewards lie outside the activity itself. At best one is compensated for it, at worst one is forced by circumstances to submit to it.

Although the idea of self-estrangement is clear, measures of it are often ambiguous or mixed with indicators of other concepts. Some researchers ask people if they are satisfied or dissatisfied with their work, and interpret the response as an indication of self-estrangement. However, many workers may think of satisfaction as a question of adequate compensation and good relations with co-workers and the boss. A worker could claim to be completely satisfied and yet find the idea of intrinsic gratification from work utterly incomprehensible and a contradiction in terms. To many, work seems to be, by definition, that which you would not do if no one was paying you to do it. To the alienated worker, financial compensation is the only reason for working. To the committed worker, on the other hand, pay makes it possible to work and signifies recognition of the quality and value of one's work. Thus, measures of self-estrangement often include statements about intrinsic gratification and the meaning of remuneration: "I can put up with a lot on my job as long as the pay is good" (Pearlin and Schooler, 1978, p. 21); "I find it difficult to imagine enthusiasm for my work," or "I find it hard to believe people who actually feel that the work they perform is of value to society" (Kobasa, Maddi, and Courington, 1981, p. 372). Our discussion of self-estrangement suggests several other items that might be useful to include in indexes: "I feel lucky because I get paid to do work I like to do anyway," "My job is like a hobby to me," "My job gives me a chance to do things I enjoy doing," "Work is a grind," "If it wasn't for the pay, I'd never do the things I do at work."

Based on the existing research, occupational self-estrangement is more common among workers who are older, have lower incomes, are less educated, and come from lower-status backgrounds (Schooler, 1972; Pearlin and Schooler, 1978). It is also correlated with a sense of external control and powerlessness, and with a focus on the goals of security and freedom from want (Kobasa, Maddi, and Courington, 1981). Studies of distress have examined its association with conditions of alienated labor, but have not yet addressed the issue of whether or not self-estrangement is the mental link between the objective working conditions and the emotional response. Kohn (1976) argues cogently that closeness of supervision, routinization, and the substantive complexity of work are the crucial characteristics of jobs, more than ownership of the means of production, position in the hierarchy, status, income, or co-worker relationships. Kohn and Schooler (1982) show that work requiring initiative, thought, and independent judgment instills habits of self-direction and an openminded, flexible approach to solving problems, both of which reduce distress. Gove and Tudor (1973) note that much housework is routine, uncomplex drudgery, which could partly explain why married women are more distressed than married men. [However, we find evidence that the husband's depression does not increase if he takes on a larger share of the housework, possibly because the strain of additional work is counterbalanced by the gain in equity and fairness (Ross, Mirowsky, and Huber, 1983).] Overall, there are surprisingly few studies of the impact that alienated labor and self-estrangement have on distress. Those that do exist suggest that the impact of alienated labor is much as Marx said it would be.

Voluntary Participation in Community Activities

Commitment is an issue in the wider social arena as well as in the workplace. Many people are deeply involved in churches, political parties, civic or charitable organizations, clubs, and hobbies. Because participation in these activities is voluntary and without pay, it is self-expressive rather than self-estranged. Mutran and Reitzes (1984) studied the social patterns and consequences of participation in voluntary organizations and cultural activities among persons age 65 and over. They find that the amount of time spent in clubs, volunteer groups, political activities, or hobbies, and the frequency of attendance at movies, museums, concerts, and sports increase with education and income and decrease with age and poor health. These community activities are, in turn, associated with feelings of being excited or interested in something, a greater sense of pride and pleasure in having accomplished something, and a feeling of being on top of the world. Community activities are also associated with fewer feelings of upset, loneliness, boredom, and depression among the elderly, controlling for family social support. Using over-time data on adult heads of households in rural Illinois, Wheaton (1980) found that the number of voluntary organizational memberships a person claims is increased by socioeconomic status and by the number of major changes in one's life in preceding years; the number is decreased by fatalism and by the sense that one's income, present job, and job opportunities are barriers to achievement. Membership in voluntary organizations is negatively correlated with psychological and psychophysiological distress. However, when fatalism is controlled there is no significant association between the number of memberships and the level of distress, which appears to contradict the results of Mutran and Reitzes. The different results could be due to the fact that Wheaton measured the number of memberships rather than the frequency and amount of participation, or to the fact that Mutran and Reitzes did not adjust for fatalism in their analysis, or to differences between the samples in age, location, and so on. As it stands now, participation in voluntary organizations and social activities may itself reduce distress, or it may simply indicate an instrumental orientation that reduces distress.

Support

In all forms of alienation the individual sees himself or herself as detached from society in some way. Powerlessness is a sense of detachment from effective social influence, and self-estrangement is a sense of detachment from productive activities. Powerlessness and self-estrangement have to do with the individual's sense of place in the macrosocial order—the system of stratification and production. A third type of alienation has to do with the individual's sense of detachment in the microsocial order of personal relationships. Social isolation is the sense of not having anyone who is someone to you and not being someone to anyone. The opposite of isolation is commonly called social support, which is the sense of being cared for and loved, esteemed and valued as a person, and part of a network of communication and obligation (Kaplan, Robbins, and Martin, 1983). This concept of isolation and support differs radically from the classic definition of isolation as the individual's tendency to, "assign low reward value to goals or beliefs that are typically highly valued in the given society" (Seeman 1959, p. 789), which is sometimes called "cultural estrangement" to distinguish it from social isolation of the sort discussed here. Although Seeman (1959, p. 789) originally excluded "the warmth, security, or intensity of an individual's social contacts" from his definition of isolation, it is precisely this meaning that has greatest currency today, and that is most important in research on the social patterns of distress (Seeman, 1983).

Social Embeddedness: Benefits and Costs

Studies of the relationship between distress and support fall into two categories: those looking at objective social conditions indicative of more or less isolation, and those looking at the individual's sense of having fulfilling personal relationships. Those of the first type are actually studies of social integration rather than of social support. Presumably the structural density of a person's network, the number of relationships, the frequency of contact, and the number and types of social roles a person performs increase the probability of his or her having fulfilling personal relationships, but they do not guarantee it. For example, marital status is generally considered an important indicator of social integration. As noted earlier, studies consistently find that married persons are less distressed than people who are divorced, separated, widowed, or those who have never been married. We find that married people have a greater sense of support that decreases their distress, but it does not account for all of the psychological benefits of marriage (Ross and Mirowsky, 1989). Marriage is not the only source of support, and it is also not a guarantee. Unmarried persons can have supportive relationships with their parents, children, other relatives, and friends, and many married persons report a lack of reciprocity, affection, and communication that is strongly associated with distress (Pearlin, 1975b; Gove, Hughes, and Style, 1983).

Results concerning the impact of social integration on distress are mixed. Williams, Ware, and Donald (1981) found that increases in psychological well-being over time are associated with an index of social integration that includes contact with neighbors, friends, and relatives, as well as participation in religious and social groups. However, it is not clear whether integration into personal networks or participation in community groups is the active factor.

Hughes and Gove (1981) have looked at the impact of living alone on distress. They note that, according to theory, the density of social interaction strengthens common sentiments, and intensifies or fortifies the meaning of life, social regulation, and constraint. It is assumed that those who live alone typically experience less social interaction. Hours spent sleeping, cleaning house, preparing and eating meals, watching television, and so on, are less likely to be spent with others. Relationships are less likely to build to the same level of closeness and intensity, and are less likely to be characterized by primary mutual obligations and mutual reinforcement. The person who lives alone is presumably isolated from a network of social and economic ties—the privileges, duties, and obligations centered on the dwelling place and typically associated with family. Counter to theoretical expectation, Hughes and Gove found that within categories of marital status (never married, separated or divorced, widowed) there is no difference in distress between those who live alone and those who live with relatives or friends. The difference in distress is between married persons and everyone else rather than between those who live alone and everyone else. Hughes and Gove speculate that social integration may involve a psychological trade-off: ". . . just as persons may gain substantial satisfaction and personal gratification from family relations, they may also suffer frustration, aggravation, hostility, and repressed anger from being constrained to conform to the obligations necessary to meet socially legitimated demands of others in the household" (Hughes and Gove 1981, p. 71). This speculation is given credence by the results of three other studies. In an analysis of data from the nationwide Health and Nutrition Examination Survey, Eaton and Kessler (1981) find that depression is lower in two-person households than in households with only one person or with three or more persons (adjusting for marital status, age, sex, education, income, employment, race, and urban versus rural residence). This suggests that the trade-off between social support and social demands is typically optimized in two-person households.

We find costs and benefits of social integration in Mexican culture, which emphasizes the mutual obligations of family and friends. Responsibility to the group places constraints on the individual, who must take into account the expectations, desires, and well-being of family and friends. These constraints produce a sense of not being in control of one's own destiny, which increases depression. However, the group is also responsible to the individual, which decreases anxiety (Mirowsky and Ross, 1984).

Similarly, Mutran and Reitzes (1984) found that among widowed persons age 65 and over, receiving financial help, personal services, and practical advice from relatives is associated with lower distress, but giving similar forms of help to relatives is associated with greater distress. It appears that integration into personal networks may have costs as well as benefits.

Social integration can also be viewed as a question of identity rather than a question of mutual obligation and help. Thoits (1983) views social integration from the perspective of symbolic interactionism, which argues that a normal personality and appropriate social conduct develop when the individual recognizes and adopts the roles associated with his or her social position. According to Thoits' identity-accumulation hypothesis, "Role requirements give purpose, meaning, direction, and guidance to one's life. The greater the number of identities held, the stronger one's sense of meaningful, guided existence. The more identities, the more 'existential security,' so to speak" (Thoits, 1983, p. 175). Stated another way, the fewer one's social roles the greater one's quandary, and, thus, the greater one's distress. To test this hypothesis, Thoits counted the respondent's number of identities, adding one point if the person is married, has children, is employed, is in school, attends organizational meetings, attends church services, visits neighbors, and has two or more friends. In an over-time analysis she found that the initial number of identities and increases in the number of identities are both associated with lower distress. She also found an interaction between the initial state and changes over time: the more identities lost the less good it does to have had them; the more identities gained the less damage it does not to have had them. This implies that one's present situation tends to eliminate the impact of one's past. Thoits also found some evidence of an equilibrating or floor-and-ceiling effect: The greater the initial number of identities, the more one tends to lose identities over time; and the lower the initial number of identities, the more one tends to gain identities over time. (This effect could be driven by trade-offs of the sort discussed earlier, although it may also simply reflect a life-cycle trajectory of gains and losses.) These results provide circumstantial support for the identity-accumulation hypothesis. It would be worthwhile to invest in the development of direct evidence by measuring the individual's sense of a meaningful, guided existence; by showing that the association between the number of identities and the level of distress vanishes with adjustment for the individual's sense of existential security; and by showing that the vanishing association is not actually attributable to a sense of control or commitment related to the number of identities.

Emotional Support

Discussions of social integration often assume that embeddedness in a social network indicates the availability of social support. However, Pearlin et al. (1981) argue that support in times of trouble is not automatic simply because one has family, friends, and associates. "Support comes when people's engagement with one another extends to a level of involvement and concern, not when they merely touch at the surface of each other's lives. . . . The qualities that seem to be especially critical involve the exchange of intimate communications and the presence of solidarity and trust" (Pearlin et al., 1981, p. 340). Social support in this sense is emotional intimacy, which Pearlin et al.

measure by asking if the respondent feels his or her spouse is someone "I can really talk with about things that are important to me," and by asking if the respondent has a friend or relative (other than the spouse) he or she can tell just about anything to and count on for understanding and advice. In an over-time study of the impact of job disruptions such as being laid off, fired, or put on sick leave, Pearlin and his colleagues found that emotional support indirectly reduces the impact of the disruption on depression. Job disruption typically decreases the sense of self-esteem and mastery, which in turn increases depression. However, emotional support reduces the impact of job disruption on self-esteem by as much as 30% and reduces the impact of job disruption on the sense of mastery by as much as 50%.

In a study of job stress among employed men, LaRocco, House, and French (1980) found that overwork, conflicting demands, uncertainty, insecurity, lack of opportunity to use one's skills, abilities, and training, and lack of influence on the decisions that affect you increase depression, irritation, anxiety, and malaise. However, social support from one's supervisor, co-workers, wife, family, or friends tend to reduce the psychological impact of job pressures. Similarly, Turner and Noh (1983) found that the absence of emotional support is a necessary condition for the association of low socioeconomic status with distress among women who have recently given birth. The women who feel loved, wanted, valued, and esteemed, who feel that others in their networks can be counted on, and who have a sense of mastery are not more distressed in lower-status positions than in higher-status ones, but women who lack either a sense of support or a sense of mastery are much more distressed in low socioeconomic positions.

Although some studies, such as the ones described above, find that support acts as a buffer which reduces the impact of potentially stressful events and situations, others do not find an interaction between stressors and support. For example, Kaplan, Robbins, and Martin (1983) found that undesirable events increase distress among young adults regardless of whether they feel loved and esteemed by peers and family. The presence of social support reduces distress but does not reduce the impact of undesirable events on distress. In a review of 22 studies that tested the possible interaction of stressors and social support, Wheaton (1985a) reports that seven found some evidence of interaction but the other 15 did not. However, the types of stressors investigated and the definitions and measures of social support vary considerably across studies. In four of the seven that found interactions, the evidence pertains to job-related stressors, and in two of the other three studies the central indicator of support is marital status, which is an ambiguous indicator (as discussed above). This is not strong evidence for a general interaction between social support and stressors, but neither is it strong evidence against such an interaction. In a review of 23 studies, Kessler and McLeod (1985) found that the largest studies with the most reliable and valid measures of social support tend to find a significant buffering effect, presumably because the power of the significance test is better. Variation in the reliability or validity of support measures, as well as variation in sample size, can produce variation in the ability to detect a significant interaction. Also, as Wheaton's comparisons suggest, we may eventually find that only specific types of support reduce the impact of specific types of stressors in specific populations. Finally, Thoits (1982) makes a convincing argument that the importance of social support does not rest solely on whether it reduces the effect of stressors on well-being. Love, understanding, appreciation, mutual commitment, and clear expectations may reduce distress in and of themselves, aside from any value they may have as protection against stressful events and situations.

Meaning

In addition to a sense of control, commitment, and support, people may also require a sense of meaning in their lives. An unintelligible world can be disturbing for a number of reasons. Clearly, a world that cannot be understood also cannot be controlled (or, more precisely, a sense of mastery implies a sense of understanding about how things work). If a person cannot choose among conflicting explanations or cannot predict with confidence the results of acting on a given belief, then he or she cannot logically expect to act effectively unless it is by sheer luck or instinct (Seeman, 1959). Thus, a sense of meaninglessness implies a sense of powerlessness, which increases distress. However, the importance of meaninglessness may go beyond its implications for the sense of control. People may require a sense of purpose in their lives—of knowing where they want to go as well as believing they know how to get there. Furthermore, people may require a sense of the inherent significance and value of their existence. This is what Thoits (1983) speaks of as existential security. It is the self-assurance of believing that you know what is and what is right.

The concept of meaninglessness has a prominent place in some explanations of the social patterns of distress. This prominence is based on a respect for the thoughts of Durkheim and Mead and on the convenience of meaninglessness as an interpretive concept, rather than on empirical validation. None of the studies we reviewed developed or used an index of meaninglessness, and only one used an index that reasonably might be interpreted as a measure of it. Kobasa, Maddi, and Courington (1981) measured "alienation from self," defined as the belief that trying to know yourself is a waste of time, the belief that life is empty and meaningless; and a preference for a simple life with no decisions. The index is highly correlated with a sense that most of one's activities are determined by what society demands and that it doesn't matter if people work hard because only a few bosses profit. The index is also moderately correlated with belief in external control. Measures of self-esteem often contain items that might be considered indirect measures of meaninglessness, such as the feeling that one is a person of worth and that one is not useless. Measures of depression also may contain items that could be interpreted as indications of a sense of meaninglessness, such as wondering if anything is worthwhile.

Several things are necessary to transform the concept of meaninglessness from a plausible explanation of distress to a valid one: a definition of meaninglessness that makes clear both its essence and its distinction from other concepts such as self-esteem, depression, powerlessness, and so on; a reliable index of beliefs that have validity as indicators of meaninglessness and that are not indicators of self-esteem, depression, and so on (this may require purging indicators of meaninglessness from indexes measuring other concepts); and tested models showing that variations in the sense of meaninglessness account for social patterns of distress. As noted earlier, theory and circumstantial evidence strongly suggest that this would be a productive effort.

Normality

Detachment from the rules and standards of social life constitutes the fifth and final type of alienation that links social conditions to distress. In addition to a sense of control, commitment, support, and meaning, people may also need a set of reliable expectations, which can be violated if actions do not follow normal, usual, discernible, or socially desirable patterns. The failure of others, society, or one's own life to conform to expectations can be distressing. Research on normality and distress has developed around four topics, each of which is discussed below: normlessness, labeling, role stress, and the life cycle.

Normlessness

Normlessness is the belief that socially unapproved behaviors are required to achieve one's goals (Seeman, 1959). If the community fails to convince the individual of the legitimacy of its standards for behavior, the individual may choose the most efficient means toward ends, whether legitimate or not. The principle of efficiency displaces that of social desirability as a behavioral guide. A pattern that is related to normlessness, and that can be discussed under the same heading for our purposes, is the displacement of community values such as prestige and respect with that of elementary pleasures. Instead of wanting to own a nice home, earn a good salary from a respectable job, and raise a family that is liked and esteemed by the community, the individual prefers to seek basic, personal pleasure in sex, drugs, and other thrills. The essence of normlessness, as broadly defined, is the rejection of the community as a source of behavioral standards. Good advice and exemplary behavior are seen as invalid guides. In rejecting standards that arise from the expressed needs, preferences, and rights of others, the individual falls back on biologically intrinsic satisfactions and pragmatic efficiency as guides that do not require faith in others.

Next to powerlessness, normlessness is the form of alienation with the most developed measures and indexes. Some of these focus on insensitivity to anything but crude enforcement, as indicated by the belief that if something works it does not matter whether it is right or wrong, that it is all right to do anything you want as long as you stay out of trouble, that it is all right to get around the law as long as you do not actually break it, and that nothing is wrong if it is legal (Kohn, 1976). Others focus on more extreme antisocial attitudes, such as the belief that people are honest only out of fear of getting caught if they are dishonest, that you can get around the law, and that people should take everything they can get, and antisocial behaviors such as ignoring people who are upset by your behavior or scaring people just for fun (Ross and Mirowsky, 1987). Although excellent measures are available, the causes and consequences of normlessness have not been widely explored in research on social patterns of distress. Theory suggests that normlessness is most common under conditions of structural inconsistency, where access to effective legitimate means is limited. However, in a study of the effects of occupation, Kohn (1976) found that normlessness actually increases with position in the organizational hierarchy or ownership of the means of production, controlling for the level of occupational self-direction (complex, unsupervised, nonroutine work). Self-direction is negatively associated with normlessness, controlling for hierarchical position and ownership, but about half the correlation is attributable to higher education among self-directed workers. Because ownership and hierarchical position are highly correlated with education and self-direction, normlessness tends to be most common among nonowners in low-ranked positions, even though ownership and rank by themselves create some pressure toward normlessness.

The theoretical consequences of normlessness are mistrust and anxiety. In the extreme, a person who is despised by the community and wanted by the law is one person against the world. Other people exist to be manipulated, cheated, robbed, or used. The normless person must disguise his or her actions and purposes, or otherwise protect against preemption and retaliation. As a result, normlessness is correlated with signs of mistrust and paranoia, such as believing you are being plotted against, feeling it is safer to trust no one, feeling alone or apart even among friends, hearing voices without knowing where they're coming from, and believing that people talk about you behind your back, as well as with symptoms of distress such as brooding, worrying, feeling nothing is worthwhile anymore, and being afraid of closed places (Mirowsky and Ross, 1983b). In rejecting the community as a source of guidance, the normless person sets himself or herself against everyone else. If all human contact is a potential invasion or infiltration, then others can provide gratification but not comfort.

Labeling

The second link between normality and distress is the social process of labeling. People who are thought of as mentally ill, insane, disturbed, disordered, schizophrenic, psychotic, neurotic, depressed, manic, anxious, suicidal, obsessive-compulsive, paranoid, hysterical, demented, addicted, alcoholic, antisocial, maladjusted, psychosomatic, Type A, and so on, are being placed in a mental pigeonhole by the person thinking of them in these terms. Each word suggests an idea, and each idea represents a grouping of phenomena treated as if they have an existence and essence that transcends the individual being considered. Putting aside the philosophical question about whether this style of thought is logically defensible, it is widely used in both science and everyday life, and for practical purposes it may be a useful way of thinking. However, labeling theorists note that there are potential pitfalls associated with it. One of these is the possibility of "secondary deviance": if I think someone is mentally ill, then I will tend to act as if they are mentally ill, and their reaction to being treated as mentally ill will be interpreted as a sign of mental illness because such behavior is common among persons considered mentally ill.

For our purposes, the question is whether psychiatric diagnosis and treatment might actually increase distress. So far, the existing evidence is sketchy and indirect. In a follow-up study of a group of mental patients mostly hospitalized with the diagnosis of schizophrenia, Greenley (1979) found that whether the family expected the patient to be better, the same, or worse after release did not affect the returned patient's actual level of symptoms. However, the family's expectation that the patient would not be able to help with household chores, dress and groom himself or herself, manage finances, help with shopping, or perform the usual duties of breadwinner, housewife, or student actually decreased the returned patient's performance of these tasks, controlling for the patient's level of symptoms and level of performance before hospitalization. Greenley's data suggest that social functioning is influenced by expectations but symptoms are not. However, Greenley's subjects were primarily classified as schizophrenics, so their symptoms were mostly hallucinations, delusions, and bizarre behavior rather than sadness, anxiety, and malaise. The results might have been different if the patients were largely classified as depressed. Also, the research on powerlessness strongly implies that poor social functioning and dependence on one's family among returned patients will increase their distress. Perhaps future studies building on Greenley's will distinguish anxiety and depression from the cognitive and behavioral symptoms.

Role Stress

The third link between normality and distress has to do with disjunctions in the system of roles. Each role involves a set of expectations concerning the behavior of the person in the role and of people in complementary roles (e.g., husband and wife, mother and child, employee and employer). The expectations are standards or norms in two senses. First, they are understandings and assumptions about the usual behavior of people in particular social categories or situations. As such, they are like maps or guidebooks that represent the behavioral topography and provide handy information for the social traveler. The planning and coordination of action is greatly enhanced by knowing what to expect of others and knowing what others expect of you.

Second, role expectations are standards or norms in that they are required and enforced. If sociology had a set of propositions akin to the laws of thermodynamic in physics, one surely would be that the usual is required and the unusual is prohibited. By demanding the usual of one another we simplify decisions and plans, minimize the amount of negotiation necessary to coordinate our lives, and create a workable social order. Because the violation of expectations disturbs this order, it carries an onus that threatens both self-evaluations and one's relationships with others. Role stress arises when expectations are not met. Aside from the situation in which the individual chooses not to meet expectations, which was discussed in the section on normlessness, there are three types of role stress: (1) Role conflict, which exists when two legitimate expectations produce incompatible or mutually exclusive demands, such as when a man's family expects him to be at his child's birthday party at the same time that his boss expects him to be at work. (2) Role ambiguity, which exists when what is expected is unclear, such as when grandparents are planning a holiday family gathering and do not know whether to invite the father of their grandchildren who has divorced their daughter. (3) Role overload, which exists when expectations imply demands that overwhelm the resources and capabilities of the individual, such as when an employee is expected to work double shifts to meet a crash order.

Most studies of role stress have focused on jobs and the workplace. For example, LaRocco, House, and French (1980) found that an excessive amount of work and conflicting demands on the job are associated with depression, irritation, anxiety, and somatic complaints. However, the impact of role conflict and overload on distress can be reduced by emotional and instrumental support from the worker's family, friends, co-workers, and supervisor. In other words, openminded understanding and a willingness on the part of significant others to adjust to the worker's plight can reduce the distress produced by conflicting or excessive demands. This makes perfect sense. If our expectations put somebody on the spot, readjustment of our expectations can ease the tension.

Although studies of the workplace tend to support the role-stress hypothesis, studies of employment among married women may appear to contradict it. Since the turn of the century there has been a trend toward higher rates of employment among married women. However, the trend toward general approval of such employment tended to lag over much of the period, and the trend toward readjustment of household and family roles was even slower—really only getting underway in the last decade (Ross, Mirowsky, and Huber, 1983). One would expect overwhelming role stress and sharply elevated levels of distress among employed wives and their families, due to conflict between the demands of the job versus those of home and family, ambiguity and uncertainty concerning the proper obligations and rights of an employed wife and mother, and overload among women struggling to do all the things a good mother and wife should do while simultaneously holding a job. However, research results either did not confirm this prediction or flatly contradicted it. Studies comparing the husbands of employed wives to the husbands of women who were exclusively homemakers sometimes found greater distress (e.g., Kessler and McRae, 1982), sometimes found less (e.g., Booth, 1976), and sometimes found no difference (e.g., Roberts and O'Keefe, 1981). Studies comparing wives who were employed to those who were exclusively housewives either found no difference (e.g., Radloff, 1975) or found that the employed wives were actually less distressed than the housewives (e.g., Kessler and McRae, 1982). However, further research showed that the apparent inconsistencies were due to the fact that marital and family roles are in transition. Some couples are living according to the traditional norms, some according to new egalitarian norms, and many are in between. Husband and wife are less distressed if the wife's (un)employment matches the couple's role preferences and are more distressed if her (un)employment contradicts their preferences. The pattern of differences in distress suggests that, in the transition from traditional to egalitarian roles, the central problem for husbands is one of self-esteem—of overcoming any embarrassment, guilt, or apprehension associated with their wives' employment. For the wives the central problem is getting their husbands to share the housework (Ross, Mirowsky, and Huber, 1983).

Life Cycle

The fourth and last link between normality and distress is the standard or normal sequence of roles, statuses, and transitions over the life cycle. For example, a man usually finishes school, gets a job, gets married, has children, raises his children and sends them off on their own, retires, and dies—in that order. Transitions that happen out of their usual sequence create practical and moral dilemmas, and may also threaten one's sense of the meaningful, predictable, and secure social reality. Even highly undesirable events, such as the death of a parent, can have very different effects depending on when in

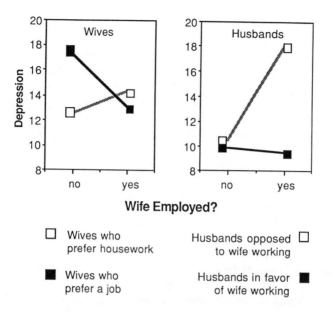

Figure 7.2. The effect of the match between roles and role preferences on depression. Data are from 680 couples in the Women and Work Study, described in the Appendix to this book, where the measure of depression is also described. The effects of employment and preferences for employment on depression are shown controlling for income, education, age, religion, and race.

one's life they occur. For example, Brown and Harris (1978) found that the loss of her mother before a girl reaches age 11 greatly increases her vulnerability to stressful events and situations in adulthood. Such a loss in childhood disrupts the usual cultural and social arrangements for the child's training and care, puts the child's relationships with other relatives and the outside world in flux, and undermines the child's assumption that social support is secure and continuous. In contrast, the loss of one's mother in middle age may bring grief, but rarely directly disrupts one's job, friendships, daily home and family life, or community ties.

Research on the life course of men provides indirect evidence that deviations from usual patterns are distressing. Hogan (1978) found that men typically finish school first, then get a job, and then get married. Deviations from this order result in a 17–29% increase in the probability that the first marriage will end in divorce or separation, controlling for ethnicity, level of education, military service, age at marriage, and cohort. As noted earlier, being divorced or separated is associated with distress (e.g., Hughes and Gove, 1981).

Many of the effects of expectations on distress can be thought of as *contextual effects*. Expectations are mental representations of normal social conditions. The higher the prevalence of certain events or sequence of events among others in the same social category, the less unusual they are and the greater the cultural, social, and mental preparation for them. For example, Lennon (1982) examined the impact of menopause on distress. Although it is commonly believed that menopause represents a natural period of distress for women, Lennon argues that the appropriate timing of life course change is socially defined and that individuals are aware of these age expectations and evaluate their own experience against the normative standard. Life course changes are not ordinarily traumatic if they occur on time because they have been anticipated and rehearsed. Major distress is caused by events that upset the normal expected sequence and rhythm of life. Menopause marks midlife: the median age of menopause is 49.7 years, and three-quarters of natural menopauses happen between ages 45 and 54. Using data from the Health and Nutrition Examination Survey on 3886 women, Lennon found that women experiencing menopause between the ages of 25 and 43 have 72% more symptoms of depression than premenopausal women of the same age, and women going through menopause between the ages of 54 and 74 have 78% more depression than postmenopausal women of the same age. Among women ages 44 through 53, there is no difference in depression between those who are premenopausal, currently menopausal, and postmenopausal (controlling for race, marital status, education, income, and number of children). Thus, the impact of menopause on distress depends entirely on whether it happens inside or outside the usual age range. This illustrates the effect that sociodemographic variations in prevalence can have on the emotional consequences of events. In the coming decade we may see many more studies of the effects of contextual expectations. To the extent possible, researchers should try to demonstrate two things: first, that the amount of distress associated with the event or situation in question is lowest in the sociodemographic groups where it is most common, or, alternatively, that the most common pattern or sequence in a group is the least distressing one; second, that the prevalence of the event or situation in a person's sociodemographic group increases his or her preparation or even preference for it, or increases the availability of institutional and personal support, and that these are the proximate factors which modify the impact of events and situations on distress and thus explain the role of prevalence.

Summary

Sociological theory about the forms, causes, and consequences of alienation has inspired much of the recent research on social patterns of distress.

Perceptions of control, commitment, support, meaning, and normality can reduce distress either by inherently meeting basic psychological needs or by reducing the impact of potentially threatening or disturbing events and situations. Although social variations in alienation are a major source of social variations in distress, other factors such as authoritarianism and inequity, discussed next, also play a part.

CHAPTER EIGHT

Authoritarianism and Inequity

Authoritarianism

Authoritarianism is a complex world view with a number of thematically related elements. Chief among these is a sense that tradition and authority are compelling guides to behavior, and a belief that ethical conduct and compliance with the dictates of tradition and authority are identical. Other beliefs and habits of thought associated with this concept are: the belief that there is one and only one legitimate perspective; stereotyped ideas about people in other social categories, including a tendency to disregard variations among individuals within the stereotyped categories; the belief that differences in opinions and behaviors arise either because others perversely refuse to acknowledge the truth and conform or because others are ignorant of the truth due to misfortune or the machinations of diabolical forces; rejection of negotiation and compromise and the glorification of righteous indignation, hostility, and aggression as the proper response to opinions, preferences, and behaviors that are different from one's own; the belief that human suffering is the consequence of failure to conform to traditional ways, and is therefore just punishment that should not and cannot be alleviated except by reforming the sufferers; the belief that mankind's unrestrained nature is evil; and the belief that familiar social institutions, traditions, and roles are facts of nature, results of cosmic laws, or manifestations of divine will and not simply the aggregate product of human interactions over a period of time (Gabennesch, 1972; Meissner, 1978). Theoretically, authoritarianism has many consequences, including racism, jingoism, and popular support for repressive and dictatorial regimes. Two others are particularly important in explaining social patterns of distress: (1) inflexibility in dealing with practical and interpersonal problems, and (2) suspiciousness and mistrust.

Inflexibility

Cognitive flexibility is an open-ended, open-minded approach to solving problems; it is characterized by the ability to elaborate upon and weigh arguments and evidence both for and against a proposition, by the ability to imagine a complex set of actions necessary to solve a practical problem, and by the ability to imagine and compare multiple solutions to a single problem. Inflexibility is characterized by a tendency to favor particular modes of coping in all stressful situations, by a dearth of strategies for solving problems, by reliance on conformity and obedience as coping strategies, by the rigid application of rules and standards, by an inability to imagine contradictory views and complex solutions, and by dedication to tradition as a means of adaptation (e.g., Kohn and Schooler, 1982; Wheaton, 1983).

According to theory, inflexibility is learned as a habitual style of thought and action in social situations that limit the individual's horizons and demand conformity and obedience. Insular personal networks and a lack of exposure to the views of other cultures, historical periods and sectors of society can create a sense that the familiar, traditional order has a universal and unique validity that transcends time, place, and situation. Low-status jobs often require unreflecting compliance with rules and plans the individual did not have a part in making. Studies find that education increases intellectual flexibility, and that the characteristic demands of one's occupation also have an effect. Jobs that are routine, closely supervised, simple, and that involve things rather than people or data tend to reduce the individual's flexibility in solving cognitive and social problems. Furthermore, educational and occupational experiences shape the values and beliefs that parents pass on to their children (e.g. Kohn and Schooler, 1982; Schooler, 1972). The result is that inflexibility is associated with low current socioeconomic status and with a low status of origin.

Wheaton (1983) compares the theoretical effect of inflexibility on distress with that of fatalism. As discussed earlier, the belief that outcomes are determined by external forces beyond one's control implies a lack of coping effort. If luck, fate, chance, and powerful others are the controlling forces in your life, then there is no point in trying. By comparison, inflexibility reduces coping ability. The individual who lacks the mental skill to imagine all aspects of a problem or multiple solutions to a problem, who cannot understand other points of view, and who thus finds it difficult to negotiate and compromise, will have trouble solving personal, interpersonal, and social problems. Both theory and laboratory studies of animals suggest an intimate link between fatalism and inflexibility, with the two reinforcing each other. Recall that learned helplessness is created by exposing animals to inescapable electric shock. It is characterized by subsequent failure to attempt escape when an avenue of escape is available and by a diminished ability to learn escape behaviors even when forcibly and repeatedly demonstrated (Seligman, 1975). It is as if the animal learns inattention to the connections between signs, actions, and outcomes. Similarly, fatalism may produce inflexibility by reducing the individual's efforts to understand events and situations. Not only will this tend to produce a rigid, habitual response to any given problem, but it will also limit the development of intellectual problem-solving skills. This inflexibility, in turn, reduces the ability to cope with problems, and the consequent failures increase the sense of not being in control. Thus, there could be a vicious circle, with low coping effort producing low coping ability, which in turn produces low coping effort.

Kohn and Schooler (1982) found evidence of this pattern in their study of the cognitive and emotional impact of job characteristics. They found that a self-directed orientation increases problem-solving flexibility, which in turn increases self-directedness; thus the two are mutually reinforcing. Furthermore, in the long run flexibility and self-directedness leads the individual into jobs that are less routine, less closely supervised, and more complex substantively, which reinforces the individual's flexibility and self-directedness. Kohn and Schooler did not find a direct effect of flexibility on distress. However, they did find that self-directedness decreases distress. Because flexibility reinforces self-directedness, boosts the impact of job characteristics on self-directedness, and leads to jobs with characteristics that produce self-directedness, problem-solving flexibility has a substantial indirect impact on distress.

Wheaton (1983) examined the effect of flexibility on distress in a somewhat different but complementary way. If flexibility increases coping ability, then the impact of acute and chronic stressors on distress will decrease as the level of flexibility increases. Wheaton looked at three outcomes: depression, anxiety, and schizophreniform hallucinations and delusions. He found that flexibility reduces the amount of depression associated with acute and chronic stressors and that flexibility eliminates the association between stressors and schizophrenic symptoms. He also found that flexibility decreases anxiety, although it does not reduce the impact of stressors on anxiety. Overall, it appears that flexibility improves the individual's ability to cope, reinforces coping effort, and eventually leads the individual into situations that demand and produce greater flexibility and instrumentalism—all of which reduces distress.

Mistrust

The second characteristic of authoritarianism associated with distress is mistrust, which is the habit of interpreting the intentions and behaviors of others as unsupportive, self-seeking, and devious. Mistrust is an absence of faith in other people based on a belief that they are out for their own good and will exploit or victimize you in pursuit of their goals. It is a logical corollary of the authoritarian belief that mankind's unrestrained nature is evil. Theory points to three related causes of mistrust: (1) awareness that one's internal impulses are frustrated and controlled by external authority, which means that others also have selfish motives which must be restrained; (2) belief that there is an inherent scarcity of wealth, power, and prestige, so that one person's gain is always another person's loss; and (3) belief that victimization and exploitation are common and have dire consequences for the victim. Theory thus implies that mistrust is most common where control is external, resources and opportunities are scarce, and crime and exploitation are common. Research shows that mistrust is greatest among persons with low levels of education, who have low family income, live in low-status neighbor-hoods, have low prestige jobs, and believe in external control. Furthermore, there is an interaction between low socioeconomic status and belief in external control, so that the combination of the two greatly increases mistrust. Stated alternatively, the threatening conditions of life in low-status positions only increase mistrust among persons who feel they do not control their own lives. Instrumental individuals with a sense of internal control are not suspicious and mistrusting in low-status positions (Mirowsky and Ross, 1983a).

The consequences of mistrust can be farreaching and severe. According to theory, mistrust can interfere with the development, maintenance, and use of social support networks. Trust allows pairs of individuals to establish cooperative relationships whenever doing so is mutually beneficial. In contrast, the mistrusting individual may not seek social support when in need, may reject offers of such support, and may be uncomfortable with any support that is given. Furthermore, suspicious individuals can help create and maintain the very conditions that seem to justify their beliefs. Their preemptive actions may elicit hostile responses, and their diminished ability to participate in networks of reciprocity and mutual assistance may have several consequences: without allies they are easy targets of crime and exploitation, when victimized or exploited they cannot share their economic or emotional burden with others; and by not providing aid and assistance to others they weaken the community's power to forestall victimization and exploitation and to limit its consequences (e.g., Mirowsky and Ross, 1983a; Rotter, 1980). We find that mistrust tends to develop into paranoid beliefs about enemy conspiracies and that it is highly related to distress and demoralization (Mirowsky and Ross, 1983,a,b).

Inequity

The sense of right and wrong, feelings of guilt or grievance, and the relationship of exploiter and victim are concerns as old as the earliest stories and writings. Emotions are deeply related to a sense of fairness. Indignation and guilt are the marks and consequences of unfairness. They are the types of distress attributed to the sense of being either victim or exploiter.

Victims and Exploiters

People get angry when they see themselves giving more than they get (Walster, Walster, and Berscheid, 1978). It may seem, at first, that anger and depression are incompatible emotions. They are not. Anger about relationships within the family is far more common among severely depressed women than among women with similar social characteristics who are not distressed (Weissman and Paykel, 1974). Anger and depression are both reactions to situations that are frustrating and unfair. In part, depression results from the implicit lack of control. Some people choose to exploit, but few choose to be victims. The victim in an unfair relationship is constrained and directed in ways he or she does not desire, which produces depression. Outbursts of anger about the unfairness also lead to depression indirectly. Women often seek treatment for severe depression after finding themselves uncontrollably enraged at members of their family (Weissman and Paykel, 1974). The explosions make them feel as powerless to control themselves as they are powerless to control the situation. The rage can leave a deep sense of remorse and guilt, especially if the anger is directed at an innocent but powerless child rather than at a powerful spouse who is the source of the frustration.

If equity theory simply argued that the victim in an unfair relationship is distressed by the unfairness, then its predictions would not be unique. However, equity theory argues that the exploiter in an unfair relationship is also distressed, for several reasons. The exploiter may feel guilty about taking advantage of someone. Guilt and depression are correlated among students, and guilt is far more common in depressed patients than in nondepressed controls (Peterson, 1979; Prosen et al., 1983). Furthermore, flagrant unfairness is a violation of general norms and may meet with disapproval from others. Since a person's sense of self-worth reflects the approval or disapproval of others, violating the norms of fairness can lower the sense of self-worth or self-esteem necessary for emotional well-being (e.g., Prosen et al., 1983; Weissman and Paykel, 1974). The exploiter also may dread retaliation and punishment by the victim and by others who see the relationship as unjust (Walster, Walster, and Berscheid, 1978). Symptoms of anxiety such as nervousness, cold sweats, headaches, trembling hands, and acid stomach are correlated with depression to such a high extent that both are often combined in measures of general psychological distress (e.g., Wheaton, 1982; Mirowsky and Ross, 1983b). Finally, flagrant unfairness elicits hostility from the victim. It is unpleasant to be a target of hostility, and a hostile victim may obstruct the exploiter's actions. The difference between willing and grudging compliance represents a tremendous loss of efficiency and effectiveness. The victim's resistance limits the exploiter's personal control.

Marriage: Cynical and Optimistic Views

Most of the current work on equity and distress is concerned with marriage. The relationship between husband and wife is a particularly good laboratory for such a study. Marriages are long-term relationships that are meaningful to the couple and others in their social circle. The lives and fortunes of married partners are intertwined and they, their friends, and families have firm beliefs about proper marital conduct (Schafer and Keith, 1980; Pearlin, 1975b).

Pearlin (1975b) found that people feel distressed if their marriage partners act like the only important ones in the family, expect more than they are willing to give back, and demand more compliance than they are willing to give. How does the selfish partner feel? Schafer and Keith (1980) found that married persons are more depressed if their partners' efforts at cooking, housekeeping, earning income, companionship, and child care seem too small *or too great* compared to their own effort.

Equity theory presents an optimistic view of marital relations: In their hearts the husband and wife both know what is fair. If they do what is right they will both lead happier and more productive lives; there is no inherent conflict of interest. One can take a more cynical view. Getting what you want, doing what you choose, and directing your own life and actions increases mental well-being (e.g., Kohn and Schooler, 1982; Pearlin *et al.*, 1981; Wheaton, 1980). If it is better to dominate than to submit, to control than to be controlled, and to be the one who makes the decisions than the one who does not, then dominance in the family reduces depression. Since one partner's dominance is the other's submission, it follows that one partner's well-being is the other's depression.

The self-aggrandizement hypothesis is a cynical view of the balance of marital power. Well-being is achieved at the partner's expense. The psychological benefits of domination are unmitigated by fairness, sympathy, or mutual interest. Each partner feels best when dominating as much as the other will tolerate submitting, and submitting as little as possible in return.

The truth lies between the optimistic and cynical views. Husband and wife both find that sharing marital power is less depressing than usurping it. However, each is least depressed by a balance of power more in his or her own favor than the balance the other is least depressed by. Equity is partial in two senses of the word. First, an element of self-aggrandizement remains, so equity is incomplete. Second, each spouse is partial to his or her own influence.

A sense of equity reduces the tension between husband and wife over marital power, although the gap between their equity points allows some tension to remain. The existing balance of power cannot minimize both partners' depression if the two have different equity points. One can enjoy minimum depression at the other's expense, or each can compromise on a balance that is less than optimal for both. Compromise is typical, but it usually favors husbands. The actual balance of power in the average marriage is closer to one that minimizes husbands' depression than it is to one that minimizes wives'.

As Homans puts it, "Justice is a curious mixture of equality within inequality" (Homans, 1961, p. 244). Equal influence in major family decisions is not necessarily seen as fair. Not only are the equity points different for

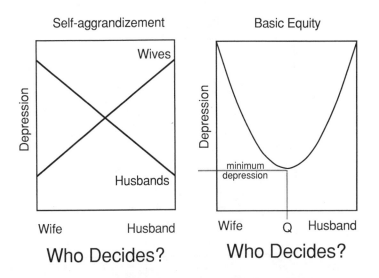

Figure 8.1. The self-aggrandizement hypothesis contrasted with the basic equity hypothesis. Each graph shows depression as a function of marital power. On the left side the wife makes all the important decisions and on the right side the husband makes them. According to the self-aggrandizement hypothesis, the husband's depression decreases and his wife's increases as his influence in the major decisions increases. According to the basic equity hypothesis, depression is high at the extremes, where one spouse makes all the decisions. Depression is lowest in the middle, where decisions are shared. The extent of the husband's predominance versus his wife's that is associated with the lowest depression is the equity point, labeled "Q".

husbands and wives, but they shift depending on the husband's earnings. The shift has more to do with norms than with the objective value of contributions to the marriage. A dollar earned by the wife buys the same things as a dollar earned by the husband, but only the husband's earnings shift the equity points. The more he earns the more his marital power is justified, in her eyes as well as his. The less he earns the less it is justified. Her earnings, or the absence of them, do not justify more or less of her influence.

The wife's sense of a just division of marital power also depends on her acceptance of a social philosophy that supports the husband's dominance. The husband's does not. The more traditional the wife's sex-role beliefs are, the greater the amount of her husband's marital power that is associated with her minimum depression. The husband's sex-role beliefs do not influence his

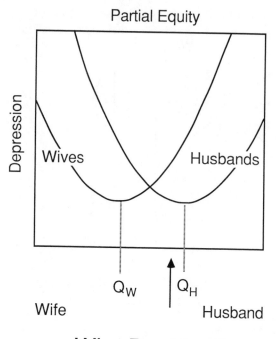

Who Decides?

Figure 8.2. Equity is partial. Based on data from 680 couples in the Women and Work Study, described in the Appendix, there are separate equity points, Q_H and Q_W, for husbands and wives. The husband's depression is lowest when the balance of marital power is far more in his favor than the balance at which his wife's depression is lowest, and vice versa. The arrow points to the actual balance of marital power in the average couple. It is closer to the husband's equity point than to the wives'. Results shown are adjusted for age, education, earnings, religion, and sex-role beliefs.

equity point. Regardless of whether his beliefs are traditional or nontraditional, the more the husband earns, the more he feels justified in making the major family decisions.

Income: Just Reward or Just Enough?

The sense of equity links the quality and nature of marital relationships to depression. Does equity also mediate the impact of larger, more impersonal social relationships? Are there people suffering from a sense of having far greater income and wealth than they deserve? The answer is simple: If there are such people, community social surveys have yet to find them. It appears that in our society, impersonal, competitive economic relationships free us from any sense of economically exploiting others (e.g., Kluegel and Smith, 1986).

The essence of equity theory is the assertion that getting more than you deserve is worse psychologically than getting exactly what you deserve. It is very difficult to test this assertion in regard to income and wealth, let alone demonstrate its truth, because so few believe that they have or get more than they deserve—about 2% in the United States, compared to 30 to 40% who believe they get substantially less then they deserve (Robinson and Bell, 1978; Kluegel and Smith, 1986; Shepelak and Alwin, 1986). The wealthiest and highest paid are not typically the ones who feel overbenefited. People who say the fair pay for their job is less than they earn tend to be in the middle-income brackets, and to be somewhat traditional wives whose earnings are approaching those of their husbands (Mirowsky, 1987). On the whole, excessive economic benefit is something that happens to others (Alves and Rossi, 1978; Jasso and Rossi, 1977). Top executives, physicians, and government officials are considered overpaid by 70% of Americans (Ross and Lauritsen, 1985), but very few of them consider themselves overpaid. Depression due to a sense of excessive income and wealth is moot.

On the other side—the down side—there are plenty of people who feel their pay is unfairly low. Using data from the Women and Work study (described in the Appendix to this book), we find that depression among husbands is proportional to the *percentage* raise needed to close the gap between what they get and what they feel they deserve. There is no association between depression and the dollar amount of the gap. In addition, there is no association between depression and perceived underpayment among employed wives, although this may change. It appears that a sense of underpayment is only distressing if it implies inadequate sex-role performance. Last, economic hardship, the sense of not having enough money to provide food, clothing, shelter, and medical care for one's family, is profoundly distressing for both husbands and wives. Dismay over not meeting family needs is far worse than discontent with one's pay. It is the hardship, not the injustice, that is most distressing.

V

Conclusion

CHAPTER NINE

Why Some People Are More Distressed Than Others

Control of One's Own Life

Of all the things that might explain the social patterns of distress, one stands out as central: the sense of control over one's own life. Many studies in many sciences find the sense of control associated with lower distress. This sense reflects the reality of the individual's experiences, opportunities, and resources. It implies an attentive, active, and proactive approach to problems. As we discuss below, the sense of control relates to most of the known patterns and to the other explanations of distress. However, there are limits to its psychological value. These limits are embodied in two facts: Psychologically beneficial control comes from the power to get things done, not from the power to win conflicts; and from power over your own life, not from power over the lives of others. Because the different forms of power are associated, they are easily confused, causing some people to go beyond the beneficial limits of control. For the large majority, though, a greater sense of control would be psychologically beneficial.

Control and the Patterns of Distress

All of the established and emerging social patterns of distress point to the sense of control as a critical link. The patterns of distress reflect the patterns of autonomy, opportunity, and achievement in America. The realities of class and status have a profound influence on the sense of control. Education, family income, unemployment, and economic hardship all affect the sense of control and, through it, depression, anxiety, malaise, and even paranoia and schizophrenia (Ross and Huber, 1985; Pearlin et al., 1981; Wheaton, 1985b; Mirowsky and Ross, 1983a; Kohn and Schooler, 1982; Link, Dohrenwend, and Skodol, 1986).

Minority status—being black, Hispanic, Asian American, or native American—is also associated with a reduced sense of control (Mirowsky and Ross, 1983a, 1984), partly due to generally lower education, income, and employment. Partly, though, it reflects the fact that any given level of achievement requires greater effort and provides fewer opportunities for members of minority groups. This is reflected in a lower sense of control, and consequent distress.

Undesirable events also decrease the sense of control (Pearlin *et al.*, 1981). By their very nature, undesirable events are unwanted. Their occurrence implies powerlessness to avoid them (Wheaton, 1980). Undesirable events also interact with a preexisting sense of powerlessness, each magnifying the other's demoralizing impact (Pearlin *et al.*, 1981; Wheaton, 1983). Many people are caught in a self-reproducing spiral of undesirable events that lead to difficult situations, both of which undermine the sense of control, which undermines attentive, active, and proactive problem-solving, which leads to more undesirable events and difficult situations (Hiroto, 1974; Pearlin *et al.*, 1981; Kohn and Schooler, 1982; Wheaton, 1980, 1983). Depression, and possibly schizophrenia, emerge from and add to such spirals.

Aging also decreases the sense of control, as was shown in Fig. 5.5. The early years of adulthood combine a moderate income with a strong sense of control, reflecting optimism about the future. Family income peaks in the mid-40s and drops precipitously after the 50s. The sense of control plummets with it, and depression shoots up. The elderly face a reality of shocking losses. Only a lucky few have jobs. Many have seen their lifelong friends and partners die. The future promises little more than sickness and death. As resources, networks, and powers decay, so does the sense of control and well-being.

The barriers of class and status, the misfortunes of life, and the losses of old age are impersonal oppressors. The personal worlds of family and faith hold out the hope of an alternative source of power and succor. It seems that the hope can be realized, but it can also be undermined. Marriage is psychologically beneficial for both men and women, but more so for men. Women are more distressed than men, particularly in marriage. The effect of marriage on the sense of control is uniformly positive for men, but there are some contradictory effects for women. On the one hand, marriage increases the sense of control of both men and women by increasing the average household income and by creating a partnership of mutual effort. On the other hand, if we compare married and unmarried with similar incomes and social support, the men have a greater sense of control if they are married, and the women have a greater sense of control if they are not married. To the extent that marriage represents an alliance of two partners, it gives both of them greater strength and effectiveness in their own lives. To the extent that marriage represents an unequal alliance, with one partner dominating the other, it benefits one at the expense of the other. For 2 to 4% of married persons, an unfair and unsatisfying marriage makes them more distressed than the average person who is separated or divorced (Gove, Hughes, and Style, 1983; Pearlin, 1975b).

For married women, employment also shapes the sense of control. In general, employment increases wives' sense of control, but for some it decreases it: employed mothers whose husbands do not share the child care responsibilities with them and who have difficulty arranging child care are under a lot of strain. These women, who are not getting help they desperately need, may feel overwhelmed—powerless to influence their employers and husbands, and powerless to provide proper care for their children. Religion also offers the hope of an alternative source of strength. Like marriage and family, religion's impact depends on specifics. It can bolster individuals' sense of control over their own lives by providing direction, purpose, and a network of like-minded people to call on. Prayer can bring forth strength and understanding in solving personal and social problems. On the other hand, religion can pressure the individual to submit to authority and communal will. Prayer can be used as a magical cure, as a substitute for facing problems. Religion can be a friend or oppressor; prayer, an inspiration or an opiate.

Control and Other Explanations of Distress

Control is not the only possible explanation for the social patterns of distress. Commitment, support, meaning, normality, flexibility, trust, and equity are other pertinent factors. Each may add something unique to the overall patterns, but much of what they imply is greater effectiveness, and thus a greater sense of control.

Commitment means that your actions and labors, the fulfillment of your obligations, are expressions of your own will and identity. Commitment is the opposite of self-estrangement, which is the sense of being the instrument of someone else's will. A slave can perform a task with more or less energy, skill, and insight, but the task is still imposed rather than chosen. While everyone is happier putting as much energy, skill, and insight into a task as it will allow, even the simplest and most tedious job is transformed if it is chosen and performed as a means to one's own ends. People stuffing envelopes for a charitable or political campaign voluntarily and happily perform a task that many could not be paid to do. Every job is a component in a system of behavior directed toward some end. If the goal expresses the will of the person performing the job, then doing it enhances the person's sense of control.

Support is the sense of being valued by others who are close, and being part of a network of communication and obligation. It is the opposite of isolation, the sense of detachment from personal relationships. Support can enhance the sense of control by bolstering confidence. Close family and friends are allies, helpers, boosters, and comforters. They may increase a person's sense of control directly by providing services, and indirectly by providing feedback and encouragement. Apparently, though, support can also undermine control. A person can be hemmed in by friends and family, overly constrained by a thicket of obligations. Helpers, boosters, and comforters may inadvertently foster dependency, defensive or unrealistic assessments, and emotional rather than instrumental responses. The large majority of Americans would benefit from a greater sense of support, but a substantial minority would benefit from greater independence.

Meaning is the sense that life is intelligible, purposeful, and valid. Meaninglessness is the sense that life has no rhyme or reason, that it is "a tale told by an idiot, full of sound and fury and signifying nothing" (Shakespeare's *Macbeth*, Act V, Scene v). Logically, a sense of meaning is necessary for a sense of control. Without knowledge, control is impossible; without purpose, control is moot. One must judge the value of events and outcomes, and the appropriateness of beliefs and actions. On some level, these judgments rest on conditioned intuition—like finding meaning in language or beauty in music.

Normality is the sense that things are going as expected. Normlessness is the opposite sense that social rules and standards do not exist, apply, or fit. Normality enhances the sense of control by making the future seem orderly and predictable. The middle-class student who graduates high school and goes to college acts out of habit, convention, and the belief that attending college will have the same consequences in the future as it had in the past. The young couple intending to finish school, get married, and have a baby can expect that things will go more smoothly if they do these things in the usual order than if they do not. Normality enhances the effectiveness of planning, and thus enhances active and proactive problem solving. If norms seem ambiguous, contradictory, or inapplicable, then the individual has no standard means with which he can achieve his ends.

Flexibility is a capacity for open-ended, open-minded problem solving. It is characterized by the ability to elaborate and weigh arguments, to consider two or more sides of an issue, to think of complex solutions to problems, and to imagine multiple or contingent solutions. Flexibility increases the sense of control by allowing the individual to find solutions to problems. In particular, flexibility allows the individual to negotiate with and among others. It also increases the psychological benefits of a sense of control, increases the effectiveness of effort, and reduces the trade-offs between personal control and social support.

Trust is the belief that people are basically benign, charitable, and sincere. Mistrust, on the other hand, is the belief that others are unsupportive, self-seeking, and devious, which is highly distressing. A sense of control greatly increases trust, particularly in circumstances which would otherwise be threatening. A firm sense of control eliminates the mistrust otherwise associated with life in low socioeconomic positions.

Equity is a sense of proportionality between contributions and rewards, and of fair exchange in relations with others. For the victims, inequity erodes the sense of control. Victims feel caught in unfair situations not of their choosing. For the exploiters, inequity erodes the emotional value of a greater sense of control. Resistance undermines the exploiter's effectiveness. Victims cannot be trusted. Retaliation or rebellion must be feared. The exploiter's sense of personal control may be enhanced, but its emotional value is canceled by mistrust and suspicion.

Limits on the Psychological Value of Control

As our discussions of social support and equity suggest, a greater sense of control is not always better, for several reasons. One is that there are realistic limits on how much control a person can exercise. The limits depend on resources and opportunities. Some people may hold themselves responsible for outcomes beyond their effective range. As evidence, Wheaton (1985b) discovered a U-shaped relationship between depression and the sense of control among Mexicans and Americans in El Paso and Juarez. We found the same relationship among the adult residents of Illinois, as illustrated in Fig. 9.1. The large majority would benefit from a greater sense of control, but a minority have a sense of control greater than that associated with the minimum expected depression.

There are other indications of limits on the emotional value of an increased sense of control—the findings regarding equity in marriage, described in Chapter 8, and preliminary findings from the Illinois Survey of Well-Being

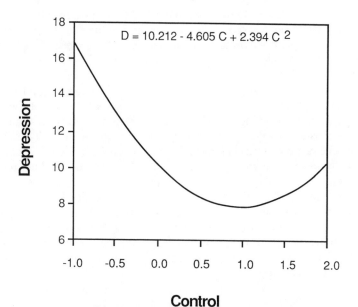

$$D = 10.212 - 4.605\,C + 2.394\,C^2$$

Control

Figure 9.1. Depression and the optimum sense of control: Wheaton (1985b) found that there is an optimum sense of control, associated with the lowest expected depression, among Mexicans and Americans in El Paso and Juarez. We found the same pattern in the Illinois Survey of Well-Being, as illustrated above.

among them. We find that autonomy on the job reduces depression, but authority does not. People who decide themselves what to do or when to do it, or who negotiate equally with their supervisor, feel more in control and less depressed. Those whose supervisors make all the decisions feel less in control and more depressed. Autonomy is beneficial in itself, and is also associated with increased earnings. In contrast, authority only increases the sense of control because it leads to higher earnings. People who supervise others have a greater sense of control because they earn more, not because they supervise others. In fact, people who supervise others are more likely to say that, when faced with a problem, they often feel helpless to do anything about it. The total effect of supervision on depression is beneficial, but only because higher pay compensates for the intrinsic frustrations.

Another indication of the limits of control is the interaction between social support and the sense of control. We find that the fact of having someone caring to call on in times of trouble is associated with decreased depression, but this is less so the greater one's sense of control. The opposite is also true. The benefits of increased control are smaller when one has greater social support. For the most part, this is because control and support are alternative psychosocial resources. More of one eliminates some of the need for more of the other. However, there are also diminishing returns to the sum of the two resources, to a point where it is only beneficial to have more of one if you also have less of the other. Very high levels of one psychosocial resource reduces the ideal level of the other.

The beneficial limits of control, actual and perceived, are an important focus of future research. We think the various manifestations of those limits reflect two underlying facts: (1) Emotionally beneficial power is the ability to achieve chosen outcomes, not the ability to win conflicts. (2) Emotionally beneficial control is control of one's own life, not control of the lives of others. Counterproductive levels of control exist because of socially patterned confusion. Principally, people often fail to see the distinction between beneficial and nonbeneficial forms of power and control because the two forms tend to go together. Many people may simply overshoot the mark. Having gotten some power was good, so it seems that getting even more will be that much better. Finally, society may have ways of enticing individuals into paths that wind up being counterproductive for some, as in the case of compensation for supervision.

Social Causes of Psychological Distress—How Important Are They?

How important are the social patterns of psychological distress? This question has two parts. First, how much of all distress is attributable to social factors? What fraction of the pool of misery would be drained if all social groups had things as good as the ones who have it best? Second, how serious is the distress that is socially patterned? Is it strictly minor psychological irritation, or does it include extreme states of profound distress? In this section we will show that, by both these standards, social factors are major sources of psychological distress.

The Proportion of Symptoms Attributable to Social Factors

Given what we know about the patterns, we can grade people according to their risk of distress based on social factors. We divided the 809 respondents in the 1985 Illinois Survey of Well-Being into ten groups of roughly equal size, based on their family income, education, minority status, gender, age, and senses of personal control and social support. There are more social factors that could be taken into account, but these are the most important. We defined the groups in a way that maximizes the differences among them in average distress. The first group is the 10% of the sample (the decile) with the social traits that indicate the lowest risk of distress. The second decile has the second lowest risk, and so on. [For simplicity, we will only show the depression results. The anxiety results are the same, the one exception (noted in Chapter 5) being that anxiety decreases with age.]

The social traits of the ten groups are illustrated in Fig. 9.2. The deciles are characterized by decreasing family income and education; by a decreasing sense of control and support; by decreasing percentages married, employed full time, and male; and by increasing percentages retired and in minority groups. It is interesting to compare the traits of the worst decile with those of the best: in the worst decile, the odds of being female are 21.7 times greater, the odds of being in a minority group are 49.8 times greater, the odds of not being married are 11.7 times greater; the odds of being retired are 40.1 times greater; the average family income is 59.1% lower; and the average number of years of education is 29.7% lower.

The collective impact of social factors on depression is illustrated in Fig. 9.3. The average number of symptoms increases as we go from the decile with the best social traits to the one with the worst. The bars represent the average level of symptoms in each social decile. Each average has two parts. The base represents the symptoms we would find if all ten segments of the sample had the same level of symptoms as the best tenth. The excess represents the symptoms attributable to not having the best social traits. Of all the symptoms reported, 48.6% are in the base, and 51.4% are excess. At least half of all the symptoms of depression are attributable to social factors. In the worst social decile, 72.0% of all symptoms are excess (above the base)—symptoms that people in the best social decile do not have.

There is a substantial base of depression. Even in the best of social circumstances, people get sick, loved ones die, accidents happen, relationships break up, ventures fail, and there are bad weeks. But there is an equally

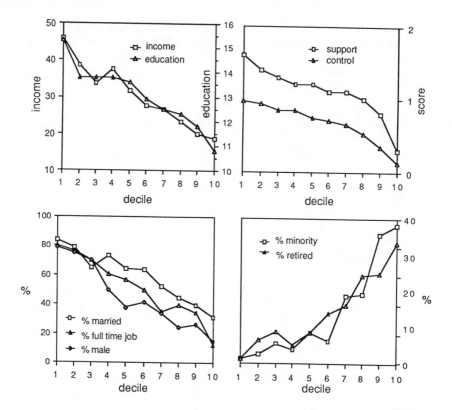

Figure 9.2. Social traits of the "best" to the "worst" deciles, defined in terms of their predicted levels of depression: Each person was given a score representing the depression predicted for someone of their gender, minority status, age, family income, education, sense of control, and sense of support. The first decile is the 10 percent of the Illinois sample with the lowest scores, the second decile is the 10 percent with the next lowest scores, and so on. Data are from the Illinois Survey of Well-Being.

substantial excess of depression that is attributable to social factors. If the most fortunate 10% of society avoids the excess depression suffered by others, then perhaps the others can avoid it too. The common strains of human life can be minimized, even if they can never be entirely eliminated.

Social Factors and Severe Psychological Problems

Social factors account for a lot of distress, but do they account for severe psychological problems? Some people believe that serious psychiatric disorder

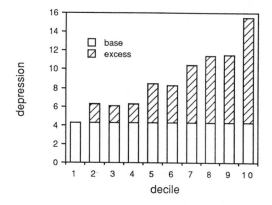

Figure 9.3. Base and excess depression in the best to worst social deciles: If the rest of society had as few symptoms as the best 10%, the total pool of symptoms would be reduced by 51.4%. Data are from the Illinois Survey of Well-Being.

is essentially genetic in origin, and has relatively little relationship to social factors (e.g., Weissman, 1987, as discussed in Chapter 2). According to this view, serious emotional problems are typically "endogenous" rather than "reactive." This means that they develop from a flaw in the organism, rather than from a normal response to environmental stress. Organic flaws are more or less random with respect to social traits, according to this theory, so *severe* psychological problems are largely uncorrelated with social traits, too. The alternative point of view, which we endorse, is that severe psychological problems are a normal response to very difficult situations. If this is the case, then extreme distress is a function of social factors, too.

In order to explore this issue, we define extreme distress as a level of symptoms greater than that found in 95% of the population. By this definition, the extremely distressed have at least four out of seven symptoms every day. This level of symptoms typically indicates a problem severe enough to get a psychiatric diagnosis. A community study shows that 61% of people with this level of symptoms meet the criteria for a psychiatric diagnosis (Boyd *et al.*, 1982). Of the severely distressed, 35% are eligible for a diagnosis of major depression, 4% for a diagnosis of minor depression, and 22% for other diagnoses such as anxiety, phobia, panic, somatization, or drug abuse. Thirty-seven percent would otherwise get a diagnosis, but are disqualified because they are grieving the death of someone close, because they have a major physical illness, or because their social functioning is not impaired and they have not sought help. Extreme distress is unusual in people who would not get a diagnosis. Of the people in the community who do not qualify for a psychiatric diagnosis, only 3% are severely distressed, according to our definition. Again, most of those who do not qualify for a

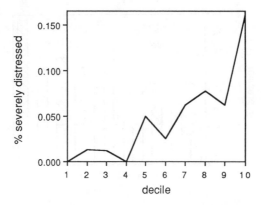

Figure 9.4. The probability of having more symptoms of depression than
95% of the sample, by decile: Sixty-one percent of people with
scores this extreme qualify for a psychiatric diagnosis. Among
people who do not qualify for a psychiatric diagnosis, only 3%
have symptoms this extreme. Data are from the Illinois Survey
of Well-Being.

diagnosis but are severely distressed are grieving, ill, or managing to
function despite their mood.

Severe distress is highly related to social factors, as illustrated in Fig. 9.4.
The pattern of severe distress by social decile is similar to the pattern of
mean depression. In fact, if we split society into two halves, better and
worse, the worse half of society has 83.8% of all severe distress. The better
half has only 16.2% of the severe distress. Stated another way, the odds
of being severely distressed is 5.9 times greater in the worse half than in
the better half. Severe distress is particularly concentrated in the worst
10% of society. In the worst decile, 16.1% are severely distressed (compared
to 4.6% in the total sample). This means that the 10% of society with the
worst profile of traits has 35% of all the severely distressed in the entire
population.

What About Genetics and Biochemistry
as Alternative Explanations?

Currently, the most popular alternatives to social-psychological explanations
of distress are biochemical and genetic. The popularity of biochemical
explanations stems from the advances in psychopharmacology of recent
decades. The popularity of genetic arguments comes from the advances in
genetic theory over recent decades, coupled with studies of twins. Despite

the impressive body of research in both these areas, neither biochemical nor genetic factors have been shown to account for any substantial part of the differences in levels of distress found in our society. More to the point, they have not been shown to account for the social patterns of distress, either as common causes that render the social patterns spurious or as mechanisms through which social factors take effect.

Of the two alternatives, the genetic explanations have a stronger base of findings in community research, and fewer logical weaknesses. In order to show that genetic factors cause distress, it is necessary to show that they are associated with it, that the association is not spurious, and that genotype is not the consequence of distress (see Chapter 3). Evidence of association comes from studies which show that identical twins are more like each other in their symptoms than nonidentical twins (particularly symptoms of manic-depression)(Baldessarini, 1983; Winokur, 1981). Fetal exposure to lead, alcohol, or other chemicals in maternal blood, or to infectious microorganisms, cannot account for this greater similarity among identical twins, so the association is not spurious. There is no way that distress could be the cause, rather than the consequence, of genotype, because genotype is fixed at conception. On the whole, there is reason to believe that genetic heritage is a cause of psychological symptoms.

There are two logical weaknesses of genetic explanations of distress. The first is that twin studies cannot tell us what portion of the pool of symptoms is attributable to genetic heritage. Samples of twins, and of their biological and social families, are not representative of the population as a whole. Even if we believe that genetic heritage is a cause of adult symptoms, we do not know if it accounts for 60% of the pool of symptoms, or 40 or 4, or .0004%.

We think that a small fraction of the population may be genetically more susceptible to depression than everyone else. The depression of the genetically susceptible is indistinguishable from the depression of others, except for a greater probability of manic episodes. The genetic trait is neither necessary nor sufficient to make a person depressed. It magnifies the likelihood and extent of depression by magnifying the impact of social and environmental stressors. An analogy comes from research on the causes of heart disease. One of the chief proximate causes is hypercholesterolemia, which is high levels of circulating cholesterol. A small fraction of the population is genetically susceptible to this problem because of a shortage of receptors that sweep cholesterol out of circulation and signal the body to suppress its own cholesterol production. The most common cause, though, is too much animal fat in the diet and too little exercise. People with the genetic trait have to be especially careful about diet and exercise, but it is a difference of degree rather than of kind. Habits that kill the genetically susceptible at age 40 kill others at age 60. Similarly, a small fraction of the population may be genetically more susceptible to depression, particularly manic-depression.

They would constitute a larger fraction of the people psychiatrists consider clinically depressed, but probably still a minority.

The second logical weakness of genetic studies is they they tell us nothing of the mechanisms by which genetic heritage has its effect. It is possible that genetic heritage causes distress through ascribed status or traits that give a competitive advantage or disadvantage in the context of a particular society. For example, genetic heritage determines skin color, which largely determines racial status, which influences opportunity, which influences achievement, which shapes the sense of control, which affects symptoms of depression, anxiety, and schizophrenia. In this causal chain, the link between race and opportunity is conventional and social, so the link between genetic heritage and symptoms is as well. We do not know of any evidence that genetic factors per se cause depression, over and above their social consequences.

The two weaknesses of genetic explanations stem from the fact that geneticists have not isolated the DNA profile that distinguishes depressed people from others. Imagine sociologists trying to demonstrate and unravel the effects of income on depression without ever measuring income. That is the situation geneticists are in. They are only now developing the ability to measure the attributes they talk about.

There are two studies that have tried to correlate specific DNA markers with diagnoses of manic-depression in families with unusually high concentrations of the disorder. One found an association in a single large Amish family, but the other failed to find an association in three Icelandic families (Hodgkinson et al., 1987). There are many studies which show that patients' families have high rates of similar problems, but which provide no evidence that the cause is genetic or that the mechanism is a biochemical disorder (e.g., Weissman, Kidd, and Prusoff, 1982; Weissman et al., 1984; Blehar et al., 1988).

Genetic heritage will remain a weak explanation of why some people are more distressed than others until geneticists measure a depressive DNA profile directly, and distinguish it from its presumed "phenotypic" consequences. To demonstrate the relevance and importance of genetic heritage, the following needs to be done: take a random sample of people in the community; measure genotype, symptoms, demographic traits, and social status; show that genotype accounts for a substantial part of the total pool of symptoms; show that a substantial part of the association between genotype and symptoms cannot be explained by social conventions such as ascribed status or attractiveness.

The biochemical alternative to social explanations of distress has a weaker base of findings in community research, and more logical problems, than the genetic alternative. The links between nervous response, endocrine activity, and symptoms of distress are well established. Most would agree that these systems, functioning normally, are the mechanism through which events, conditions, perceptions, and beliefs produce the subjective sensation of emotion. The question is whether or not defects in the endocrine and nervous systems are a major reason that some people are more distressed than others. There are reasons to think that the defects, if they exist, are a consequence of persistent problems rather than their ultimate cause (Gold, Goodwin, and Chrousos 1988a,b; Selye, 1976).

To extend the example used above, genetic heritage determines skin color, which largely determines racial status, which influences opportunity, which influences achievement, which shapes the sense of control, which arouses nervous response and endocrine activity, which is manifest in symptoms of depression, anxiety, and schizophrenia. The presence of a biochemical link elaborates the causal chain but does not alter the basic story.

Unlike the glucose tolerance test for diabetes, there are no definitive biological tests for emotional disorders. However, there are some candidates. The two most important ones are the dexamethasone suppression test for hypercortisolism, and 3-methoxy-4-hydroxyphenylglycol test for norepinephrine metabolism. Research shows that the results of both these tests are correlated with the presence or absence of a diagnosis of depression. All the studies we have read comparing the test results of depressed and nondepressed people share certain characteristics that are worth mentioning. The results are correlations at one point in time between the diagnosis and the biochemical value. The correlations are not adjusted for likely sources of spurious association such as occupation, poverty, unemployment, education, chronic strain, undesirable life events, or slum living, but occasionally they are adjusted for age or sex. The samples, which are not selected at random from any known or stated population, are grossly unrepresentative. These facts make interpretations and inferences based on the results highly speculative. Although the methods of sampling and statistical comparison are unacceptably crude by the standards of social science, the results are given a great deal of currency in biological circles.

The dexamethasone suppression test (DST) can reveal a dysfunction in cortisol regulation that appears in about half of patients with melancholia, which is depression accompanied by agitation, early morning rising, and disturbances of circadian rhythm (Carroll et al., 1981). Cortisol is an anti-inflammatory hormone released as part of the "fight or flight" response. The apparent dysfunction is uncommon in patients with other mental problems or no mental problems (about 3%). The underlying trait appears to be categorical. It is as if there are two types of people: suppressors have lower average amounts of cortisol in the blood the evening after a nighttime dose of dexamethasone, and nonsuppressors have higher average amounts. Even though there are a lot of differences *within* each group in the amount of cortisol in the blood, the differences *between* groups is so great that the range of cortisol levels in suppressors hardly overlaps at all with the range in nonsuppressors. The nonsuppressors are concentrated among people with melancholia, although only about half of those who qualify for the diagnosis are nonsuppressors.

There is little reason to think that cortisol dysregulation causes depression. On the contrary, both are probably consequences of prolonged stress (Gold, Goodwin, and Chrousos, 1988b). Among people with a diagnosis of major depression, there is little or no difference in mood or personal and social functioning between those diagnosed as melancholic and others (Carroll et al., 1981). Among the melancholic patients there is only a small correlation of cortisol levels with mood and personal and social functioning. Among the melancholics, suppressors and nonsuppressors do not differ in mood, length of treatment, or response to treatment (Greden et al., 1983). Patients treated for melancholy get better at the same rate, whether or not they had cortisol dysregulation (Greden et al., 1983). Even though there are great differences in cortisol levels among nonsuppressors, those differences are not associated with worse mood or personal and social functioning (Carroll et al., 1981). Cortisol dysregulation appears to be an additional or secondary consequence of the same things that cause depressed mood: chronic personal, social, economic, and environmental stressors.

Other important tests measure blood or urine concentrations of 3-methoxy-4-hydroxyphenylglycol (MHPG). The chemical is a product of the metabolism of norepinephrine (noradrenaline) in the brain (Gold, Goodwin, and Chrousos, 1988a). Widespread acceptance of the urinary MHPG test may be inhibited due to the fact that, in the early 1980's, experts said *low* MHPG levels indicate depression (e.g., Baldessarini, 1983), but now they say *high* levels indicate depression (Gold, Goodwin, and Chrousos, 1988a). The old theory was that depression is caused by a shortage of norepinephrine at critical receptors (called the "catecholamine-depletion hypothesis"). The new theory is that depression is marked by excess activity of neurons that synthesize norepinephrine and release it at the synapse. While the old data showed relatively low levels of MHPG in the blood and urine of depressed people, the new data show relatively high levels to be present.

It is tempting to see the MHPG reversal as one more example of life imitating art. To be fair, though, the difference between old and new findings could be real in a sense, but a consequence of unrepresentative sampling. Chronic strain may produce both the feeling of depression and a cycle of activity in nerves that produce norepinephrine, with hyperactivity followed by depletion of chemical resources and a phase of low activity. The change from old to new findings may represent a change in sampling biases introduced by drifting diagnostic standards. Old studies may have favored selecting patients with depressed mood combined with forms of inactivation, such as trouble thinking, sleeping too much, and feeling run down. New studies may favor selecting patients with the same depressed mood, but combined with forms of arousal, such as anger, restlessness, early waking, and poor appetite. Note that the mood is the same. Only the nerve activity has changed. The feelings of depression are equally correlated with inactivation and arousal, as the results in Chapter 2 show (Fig. 2.3). Whether MHPG is higher or lower in depressed patients compared to nondepressed controls may depend on whether the sampling bias favors the selection of patients in an aroused phase or a depleted phase. The fact that the mood is the same in either case contradicts the idea that the mood results from either arousal or depletion in nerves that synthesize norepinephrine. It suggests that the mood and the cycle have the same causes: chronic personal, social, economic, and environmental stressors.

We think the correlation of depression and other forms of distress with cortisol dysregulation and with the cycle of arousal and enervation is spurious. It exists because all three have common causes in the world outside the body. For the sake of those who do not believe our interpretation of the research on biochemistry and emotional disorder, several questions are worth asking. What part of the total pool of symptoms may be attributable to biochemical dysfunction? Is it 60, 40, 4, or .004%? Is biochemical dysfunction a cause or a consequence of employment status, marital status, level of earnings, family income, the sense of control, and the sense of support? To demonstrate the relevance and importance of biochemical dysfunction, researchers must do the following: take a random sample of people in the community; measure biochemical dysfunction, symptoms, demographic traits, social status, and beliefs; show that biochemical dysfunction accounts for a substantial part of the total pool of symptoms; show that a substantial part of the association between symptoms and demographic, social, and cognitive factors is attributable to biochemical dysfunction; and show that the biochemical dysfunction creates, rather than results from, the social and cognitive states.

We think that some people are more distressed than others primarily because they are in difficult circumstances which their personal histories have not prepared them to master. The social differences in misery are not just an epiphenomenon of genetics and biochemistry. Certainly, for anything to happen in a human being, there must be a genetic potential realized in biological structure and process. We are social—we think—we feel. These things come from the organism. The basic link between powerlessness and distress probably comes from the organism. But the man out of work, the employed woman wondering if her children are all right, the black facing discrimination, the divorcee alone and uncertain, the old person losing everything, the young family struggling to make ends meet—these come from the world we create for ourselves and each other, from society.

What Can Be Done to Prevent Distress?

Social factors are important explanations of why some people are more distressed than others. They account for at least half of all symptoms, and for the large majority of serious distress. We think the evidence shows that distress, whether moderate or severe, is primarily a normal response to difficult circumstances, rather than a manifestation of unseen flaws in the organism. If we are correct, what does it mean? Is there anything people can do about it? A person cannot stop growing old. A woman cannot become a man. A black cannot become white. The ascribed statuses are given, not chosen. Likewise, if people are miserable because they are poor, what good does it do to tell them they would be happier if they were rich? Chances are they already suspect this is true.

What can be done? Our answer to this question is a judgment: an opinion based on consideration of the evidence and arguments. It is also advice. As researchers, we feel a bit uncomfortable making judgments and giving advice about what to do. Still, it would be false to suggest that we have no opinion. It seems to us that our opinion was formed by the things we learned. Others may feel that our opinion colors the things we learned. In the end, it seems best to say what we think can be done to prevent distress, so you can consider it in making your own judgment.

We think that the informed individual and the informed community can do a great deal to prevent distress. Strategies for preventing distress can be centered on a few simple basics: education, a fulfilling job, a supportive relationship, and a decent living. These are to mental health what exercise, diet, and not smoking are to physical health. Emotional well-being is founded on active, attentive, and effective problem solving. Unpleasant emotions are not themselves the problems; they are signs that problems remain unsolved. Hiding from problems, hoping they will go away on their own, and disowning responsibility for the things that happen in one's life are formulas for failure and distress. Focusing on the distress itself, rather than trying to understand and overcome its cause, is also a formula for continued failure and distress. Drugs do not solve problems, whether they are self-administered or prescribed by a professional. While easing the emotional pain may be humane, may help a person regain sufficient composure to address problems, it is not a solution. Similarly, having someone else solve a person's current problems is not a long-term solution. As with drug-induced relief, it is temporary and counterproductive unless it merely lightens the individual's burdens while he or she is building strength. Emotional well-being is not simply the luck of the draw. It does not come from telling oneself comforting lies, or from being told comforting lies. It does not come from salves and ointments. Emotional well-being comes from facing and solving problems.

Education: The Headwaters of Well-Being

The process of becoming educated is one of encountering and solving problems that are progressively more difficult, complex, and subtle. Even if the things learned had no practical value, the process of learning would build confidence and self-assurance. But the things learned do have practical value.

The most general, and the one of greatest value, is the habit of meeting problems with attention, thought, action, and persistence. Next are the habits and skills of communication: reading, writing, inquiring, discussing, looking things up, asking around, and so on. They are important because they build and provide access to the culture's store of solutions to standard problems, and they enhance the ability to negotiate and coordinate with others toward common ends. The next most general learned items are analytic skills that are used in many different endeavors. These include the traditional mathematical skills, such as algebra, calculus, and statistics; and the newer skills, such as systems analysis, computer modeling, word processing, and the design and management of data bases. Finally, there are the ideas and skills needed to practice a specific occupation, such as chemistry, carpentry, journalism, engineering, printing, agriculture, plumbing, social work, law, nursing, psychology, mechanics, business, geology, and so on. This is where the general means of solving problems are tailored to a specific set of related problems. Education develops the ability to solve problems on all these levels.

Education is available to both the individual and the community as a means toward well-being. Every individual can expand her or his knowledge and improve his or her skills. Many, perhaps most, could arrange additional formal training. It is true that there are large differences in educational opportunity. It is equally true that everyone can exploit the opportunities that are available. We think most would benefit by doing so.

From preschool through postdoctoral training, the community can strive to improve educational quality and broaden educational opportunity for all individuals who want to learn. It is far better to give people the skills they need to solve the problems they encounter than it is to let people become overwhelmed, and become problems for us all. The educated community is a prosperous one. Prosperity improves the emotional well-being of the entire community. When the level or quality of education available to a segment of the community improves, the benefit is enjoyed by all segments.

One important thing a community can do is to treat education as a lifelong process of development. Traditionally, our society has treated education as something like a booster rocket. Some people get a bigger boost than others, but everyone's educational fuel is spent by the mid-20s. Historically it was convenient to organize education this way. These days, it makes less and less sense. Going to school is not just for kids anymore. There is the welfare mother who has decided that dropping out of school wasn't such a good idea after all, the assembly-line worker whose plant has closed, the woman returning to the labor force after years as a housewife, and the 51-year-old chemist facing a company reorganization. If these people want to go to school, it should be possible. Making it possible will require new forms of organization and new support services. Whenever and wherever people realize that they need to learn more, the means should be available.

A Good Job: Adequate Income, A Measure of Autonomy, Accommodation to Family

Education is important to emotional well-being, in part, because of what it leads to, foremost among which is a job. Study after study in the United States finds that employment reduces distress. There is something about having a job, in and of itself, that is good for people. If we compare employed women and housewives with the same levels of family income, the employed women are found to be less distressed. As we have seen, there are conditions that counteract the emotional benefits of having a job, but employment benefits Americans in most circumstances.

Not all jobs are equally beneficial. While it is good to have a job, it is better to have a good job. In terms of its impact on distress, a good job has three major attributes: (1) It pays enough to eliminate the family's economic hardship. Being unable to pay for the food, clothing, shelter, transportation, or health care one's family needs is extremely distressing. (2) A good job allows a measure of autonomy. Jobs that give people a say in what they do and how they do it are much more gratifying than jobs that do not. (3) A good job minimizes conflict between the demands of work and family. Jobs that keep people from ever seeing their families, or make it difficult to manage child care, can be as distressing, and sometimes even more distressing, than unemployment.

Education increases the likelihood of someone's having a good job, helps people to improve their working conditions, and leads to jobs that pay more, and allow greater autonomy, and that provide the flexibility (and sometimes even direct services) that reduce conflicts between work and family. Education also helps people to get more out of the job they have, and to spend their earnings and family income more effectively. At any given level of income, people with higher education have fewer difficulties providing the things their families need. The association between low incomes and a sense of economic hardship is decreased by education. Education also helps people negotiate with their employers or supervisors, allowing greater autonomy and reducing tension between job and family demands. It is not the only way to get a better job, or to make a job better, but it is a good way and an important one.

A Supportive Relationship: Fair and Caring

The final ingredient in well-being is a supportive relationship. Emotionally, it is good to have someone you care about and who cares about you. This appears to be an elementary human need. Supportive relationships reduce distress, whatever the conditions and events of life. To work, the relationship must be balanced and fair, with neither person exploiting the other. Education promotes supportive relationships by increasing the likelihood of employment and the level of pay, and thus reducing economic strains. Poverty makes it very difficult to build and maintain supportive and equitable relationships. Education also helps partners understand and negotiate with each other. Education develops cognitive flexibility, which includes the ability to see more than one side of an issue. Inflexible people respond to differences in preferences, opinions, and goals with anger, indignation, and punishment. Flexible people respond with attempts to understand the other's position and to arrange something that is mutually satisfactory. Flexibility improves the ability to build and maintain a supportive relationship.

"Take Arms Against a Sea of Troubles"

Why are some people more distressed than others? Our answer is that some conditions rob people of control over their own lives. The insidious message of conditions such as joblessness, dependency, alienated labor, and victimization can ingrain a gut sense of futility and powerlessness that demoralizes and distresses. But, however threatening or constricting the situation, it is better to try to understand and solve the problems it poses than to avoid or meekly bear them as the inevitable burden of life. The most destructive situations hide from people in them the fact that everyone has a choice. As Shakespeare's Hamlet put it (Act III, scene i), the choice is to "suffer the slings and arrows of outrageous fortune," or to "take arms against a sea of troubles, and by opposing end them."

Description of Data Sets and Measures

Illinois Survey of Well-Being

The Illinois Survey of Well-Being is a telephone survey of a probability sample of Illinois residents. Data were collected in 1985. Random digit dialing was used in Chicago and surrounding suburbs, and systematic random selection of numbers from current telephone directories was used in other areas of the state. Random digit dialing ensures the inclusion of unlisted numbers (Waksberg, 1978). However, the percentage of unpublished phone numbers outside the Chicago Metropolitan Statistical Area is sufficiently small that random digit dialing was not necessary. For each household, respondents were selected on the criteria of being 18 years or older, and having had the most recent birthday among members of that household (a method for randomly choosing one respondent within the household). The adjusted response rate was 79%, for a total of 809 respondents. Ages range from 18 to 85. We are the principal investigators of this study, which was supported by the Research Board of the University of Illinois. Sampling, pretesting, and interviewing were conducted by the Survey Research Laboratory of the University of Illinois.

Depression levels were measured by a modified form of the Center for Epidemiological Studies' Depression scale (CES-D). Respondents were asked, "How many days during the past week (from 0 to 7) have you . . . (1) felt you just could not get going, (2) felt sad, (3) had trouble getting to sleep or staying asleep, (4) felt that everything was an effort, (5) felt lonely, (6) felt you couldn't shake the blues, (7) had trouble keeping your mind on what you were doing." Responses were summed to produce an index of symptoms of depression. The alpha reliability is .76. This index is correlated .92 with the full CES-D.

Anxiety was measured by a two-item index. Respondents were asked, "How many days during the past week (from 0 to 7) have you . . . (1) felt tense or anxious and (2) worried a lot about little things."

Perceived powerlessness versus control was measured by an eight-item index. Respondents were asked whether they agreed with the following statements, the first four indicating control and the second four indicating lack of control (or powerlessness): (1) "I am responsible for my own successes, (2) I can do just about anything I really set my mind to, (3) My misfortunes are the result of mistakes I have made, (4) I am responsible for my failures, (5) The really good things that happen to me are mostly luck, (6)

There's no sense planning a lot—if something good is going to happen it will, (7) Most of my problems are due to bad breaks, (8) I have little control over the bad things that happen to me." Responses to the first four questions were coded strongly disagree (−2), disagree (−1), neutral (0), agree (+1), strongly agree (+2); responses to the second four questions (5 through 8) were coded in reverse. The final index is the average response to the eight items, which runs from low perceived control (powerlessness) to high perceived control.

Support was measured by the degree of agreement with the following statements: "I have someone I can really talk to," and "I have someone I can turn to for support and understanding when things get rough." Responses were coded strongly disagree (−2), disagree (−1), neutral (0), agree (+1), strongly agree (+2). The items were summed to produce a scale coded from low to high levels of social support.

Women and Work Study

The Women and Work Study is a survey of a representative sample of adults in the United States. Data were collected by telephone in late 1978. Random digit dialing was used to ensure a representative sample, including those with unlisted numbers (Waksberg, 1978). The sample contains 2000 adults between the ages of 18 and 65. It also contains a subsample of married persons in which both spouses were interviewed. After a married respondent was interviewed, the interviewer asked to speak to his or her spouse. There are 680 couples in which both spouses were interviewed. The spouses range in age from 18 to 75. The response rate was 76.5%. Joan Huber was the principal investigator. Data collection was supported by a grant from the National Science Foundation (SOC 78-18015). Sampling, pretesting, and interviewing were conducted by the Survey Research Laboratory of the University of Illinois. Our focus in the study was on psychological well-being and distress. For a focus on women and work, see the book by Joan Huber and Glenna Spitze, *Sex Stratification: Children, Housework, and Jobs* (1983).

Depression levels were measured by a modified form of the Center for Epidemiological Studies' Depression scale (CES-D). Respondents were asked, "On how many days during the past week [from 0 (never) to 7 (every day)] . . . (1) did you feel that you could not shake off the blues? (2) did you have trouble keeping your mind on what you were doing? (3) did you feel that everything was an effort? (4) did you feel sad? (5) did you feel you could not get going? (6) did you not feel like eating? (7) did you have trouble falling asleep or staying asleep? (8) did you feel lonely? (9) were you bothered by things that don't usually bother you? (10) did you think your life had been a failure?" Items 1 through 10 were summed to calculate the total number of symptoms of depression. The alpha reliability of the depression index is .83.

This modified form of the CES-D is correlated .93 with the modified form of the CES-D used in the Illinois Survey of Well-Being.

Family income was measured in thousands of dollars and translated into 1983 dollars. Education was measured in number of years of formal education completed.

Husband's help with the housework is an index composed of the average response to questions on the five most time-consuming household chores: "Who prepares meals on a daily basis?" "Who shops for food?" "Who does the daily chores?" "Who cleans up after meals?" If the couple had children living at home they were also asked, "Who takes care of the children?" Responses were coded, the wife always (1), the wife usually (2), husband and wife share equally (3), the husband usually (4), the husband always (5). Only two husbands usually did the housework and none always did. Thus responses greater than or equal to three were coded as shared.

The husband's and wife's preferences for her employment were measured in the following ways: Husbands were asked, "How do you (or would you) feel about your wife's working?" Responses were coded on a five-point scale from strongly opposed to strongly in favor. Wives were asked whether they preferred homemaking or employment.

Marital power was measured by an index composed of four questions: "Who decides what house or apartment to live in, where to go on vacation, whether the wife should have a job, and whether to move if the husband gets a job offer in another city?" These are comparatively infrequent decisions which affect the entire household, and which a powerful spouse is unlikely to delegate. The response categories are, the wife always (coded 1), the wife usually (2), both equally (3), the husband usually (4), the husband always (5). The answers are averaged so that 1 indicates the wife's dominance, 5 indicates the husband's, and 3 indicates equality in making major decisions.

Health Behavior Study

The Health Behavior Study is a survey of a representative sample of 401 Illinois residents. In 1984, a telephone survey was conducted by the Survey Research Laboratory and by participants in a survey research methods course taught by Joe Spaeth, Guenther Lueschen, and William Cockerham at the University of Illinois at Urbana-Champaign. It was supported by the Research Board and the Department of Sociology. Two methods were used to choose a representative sample: random digit dialing and random selection from telephone directories. Random digit dialing was used for Chicago and surrounding suburbs to ensure the inclusion of unlisted numbers. Systematic selection of numbers from telephone directories was used for the remainder of the state, because the percentage of unpublished numbers outside the Chicago metropolitan area is sufficiently small. A respondent was selected from within the household on the criteria of being 18 years or older and having had the most recent birthday of members of that household. The latter is a method for randomly choosing a respondent within the household (O'Rourke and Blair 1983). The response rate was 70%. The ages of the respondents range from 18 to 83. Our focus was on psychological well-being and distress. For a focus on health behavior, see the article by William Cockerham, Gerhard Kunz, Guenther Lueschen, and Joe Spaeth, "Social Stratification and Self-Management of Health" (1986).

Psychological distress was measured by an index composed of eight items from the Langner index (1962). Respondents were asked, "In the past twelve months, how often have you . . . (1) wondered if anything is worthwhile, (2) been in low spirits? (3) had trouble sleeping? (4) had periods of time when you could not get going? (5) felt that things never turn out right? (6) had trouble remembering things? (7) felt irritable, fidgety or tense? (8) felt restless?" Responses were coded never (0), seldom (1), sometimes (2), often (3). The eight items were summed to produce an index of distress whose alpha reliability is .77. Items one through six are measures of depression; items seven and eight are measures of anxiety.

Overweight was based on the person's self-reported weight relative to height (weight divided by height^2), also called the Quetelet index. Exercise was measured by asking people if they participated in any physical activities, exercise, or sports. If they answered yes, they were asked to list all activities in which they participated, including basketball, bicycle riding, bowling, calisthenics or aerobics, canoeing or sailing, dancing, fishing or hunting, football, gardening, golf, hiking, or climbing, hockey, jogging or running, racquetball or squash, skating, skiing, soccer, softball or baseball, swimming, tennis, volleyball, walking, and weight lifting or circuit training. Activities were summed. Subjective physical health was measured by asking respondents, "Would you say your health is bad (1), not so good (2), satisfactory (3), good (4), or very good (5)." Poor health includes codes 1 and 2.

Life Stress and Illness Project

The Life Stress and Illness Project is a cross-cultural survey. Data were collected by means of a survey questionnaire administered in face-to-face home interviews in 1975 in El Paso, Texas, and Juarez, Mexico, companion cities on opposite sides of the border separating Mexico and the United States. The survey was a comparative study of adults of Mexican and Anglo heritage. Blacks, Asians, American Indians, Jews, and persons not raised in the United States or Mexico were excluded. In El Paso, dwellings were randomly selected from the city directory, and one adult between the ages of 18 and 65 was then randomly selected from each household. The response rate was 73%. In Juarez, a multistage area sample based on aerial photographs was used because of the absence of accurate information on which to base a sampling frame. The response rate was 75%. The total number of cases was 463. The questionnaire was administered in Spanish or English, depending on the respondent's preference. Note that a sample based on telephones produces a representative sample in the United States, where over 95% of the population has a telephone, but would have produced a biased sample in Mexico, so that face-to-face home interviews were necessary. The principal investigators on the project were Richard Hough and Dianne Timbers. Data collection was funded by the National Institute of Mental Health (NIMH-CER RO1-MH16108), the Hogg Foundation for Mental Health, and the University of Texas at El Paso. The 91 symptoms in this data set are listed in Appendix B to Chapter 2. For a focus on cross-cultural comparisons, see the article by Audrey Burnam, Dianne Timbers, and Richard Hough, "Two measures of psychological distress among Mexican Americans, Mexicans and Anglos" (1984).

Bibliography

Alloy, Lauren B., Christopher Peterson, Lyn Y. Abramson and Martin E.P. Seligman, "Attributional Style and the Generality of Learned Helplessness." *Journal of Personality and Social Psychology* 46(3):681–7, 1984.

Alves, Wayne M. and Peter H. Rossi. "Who Should Get What? Fairness Judgments of the Distribution of Earnings." *American Journal of Sociology* 84:541–564, 1978.

Alwin, Duane. "From Obedience to Autonomy: Changing Aspects of Religious Behavior and Orientation in American Society." Changing Societal Institutions Conference, Notre Dame, IN, 1988.

Alwin, Duane F., Philip E., Converse and S. S. Martin. Living Arrangements, Social Integration and Psychological Well-Being. Presented at the *Midwest Sociological Association* annual meeting. Chicago, IL, 1984.

American Psychiatric Association. *Diagnostic and Statistical Manual of Mental Disorders III*. Washington: American Psychiatric Association, 1980.

Aneshensel, Carol S., Ralph R. Frerichs and Virginia A. Clark. "Family Roles and Sex Differences in Depression." *Journal of Health and Social Behavior* 22:379–393, 1981.

Aneshensel, Carol S., Ralph R. Frerichs and George J. Huba. "Depression and Physical Illness: A Multiwave, Nonrecursive Causal Model." *Journal of Health and Social Behavior* 25:350–371, 1984.

Baldessarini, Ross J. *Biomedical Aspects of Depression and Its Treatment*. Washington, D.C.: American Psychiatric Press, 1983.

Becker, Gary. *The Economic Approach to Human Behavior*. Chicago, IL: University of Chicago Press, 1976.

Belle, Deborah. *Lives in Stress. Women and Depression*. Beverly Hills, CA: Sage, 1982.

Blehar, Mary C., Myrna M. Weissman, Elliot S. Gershon and Robert M. A. Hirschfeld. "Family and Genetic Studies of Affective Disorders." *Archives of General Psychiatry* 45(Mar):289–92, 1988.

Block, Jack. "Advancing the Psychology of Personality: Paradigmatic Shift or Improving the Quality of Research?" In *"Personality at the Crossroads: Current Issues in Interactional Psychology,"* D. Magnusson and N.S. Endler, eds., pp. 37–63. Hillsdale, NJ: Erlbaum, 1977.

Booth, Alan. "Wife's Employment and Husband's Stress: A Replication and Refutation." *Journal of Marriage and the Family* 39:645–650, 1976.

Boyd, Jeffrey H., Myrna M. Weissman, Douglas Thompson and Jerome K. Myers. "Screening for Depression in a Community Sample: Understanding the Discrepancies between Depression Symptom and Diagnostic Scales." *Archives of General Psychiatry* 39:1195–1200, 1982.

Bradburn, Norman M. *The Structure of Psychological Well-Being.* Chicago, IL: Aldine, 1969.

Brown, George W. and Tirril Harris. *Social Origins of Depression.* New York: Free Press, 1978.

Burnam, M. Audrey, Dianne M. Timbers and Richard L. Hough. "Two Measures of Psychological Distress among Mexican Americans, Mexicans, and Anglos." *Journal of Health and Social Behavior* 25:24–33, 1984.

Campbell, Angus, Philip E. Converse and Willard L. Rodgers. *The Quality of American Life.* New York: Russell Sage, 1976.

Carroll, Bernard J., Michael Feinberg, John F. Greden, Janet Tarika, A. Ariav Albala, Roger F. Hasket, Norman McI. James, Ziad Kronfol, Naomi Lohr, Meir Steiner, Jean Paul de Vigne and Elizabeth Young. "A Specific Laboratory Test for the Diagnosis of Melancholia: Standardization, Validation, and Clinical Utility." *Archives of General Psychiatry* 38(Jan):15–22, 1981.

Cleary, Paul D. and David Mechanic. "Sex Differences in Psychological Distress Among Married People." *Journal of Health and Social Behavior* 24:111–121, 1983.

Cockerham, William C., Gerhard Kunz, Guenther Lueschen and Joe L. Spaeth. "Social Stratification and Self-Management of Health." *Journal of Health and Social Behavior* 27:1–14, 1986.

Cole, Stephen. *The Sociological Method.* Chicago: Markham, 1972.

Cooley, Charles, H. *Human Nature and the Social Order.* NY: Schocken, 1964 (orig. 1902).

Crisp, A. H. and B. McGuiness. "Jolly Fat: Relation Between Obesity and Psychoneurosis in General Population." *British Medical Journal* 1:7–9, 1976.

Davis, James A. *The Logic of Causal Order.* Beverly Hills: Sage, 1985.

DeJong, William. "The Stigma of Obesity: The Consequences of Naive Assumptions Concerning the Causes of Physical Deviance." *Journal of Health and Social Behavior* 21:75–87, 1980.

DeLongis, Anita, James C. Coyne, Gayle Dakof, Susan Folkman and Richard S. Lazarus. "Relationship of Daily Hassles, Uplifts, and Major Life Events to Health Status." *Health Psychology* 1:119–136, 1982.

Dohrenwend, Barbara S. "Life Events as Stressors: A Methodological Inquiry." *Journal of Health and Social Behavior* 14:167–175, 1973.

Dohrenwend, Bruce P. and Barbara S. Dohrenwend. *Social Status and Psychological Disorder: A Causal Inquiry.* New York: Wiley, 1969.

Dohrenwend, Bruce P. and Patrick E. Shrout. "Hassels in the Conceptualization and Measurement of Life Stress Variables." *American Psychologist* 40:780–785, 1985.

Dohrenwend, Bruce P., Patrick E. Shrout, Gladys G. Egri and Frederick S. Mendelson. "Nonspecific Psychological Distress and Other Dimensions of Psychopathology." *Archives of General Psychiatry* 37:1229–1236, 1980.

Dwyer, Johanna T., Jacob J. Feldman and Jean Mayer. "The Social Psychology of Dieting." *Journal of Health and Social Behavior* 11:269–287, 1970.

Eaton, William W. and Larry G. Kessler. "Rates of Symptoms of Depression in a National Sample." *American Journal of Epidemiology* 114:528–538, 1981.

Eaton, William W., Darrel A. Regier, Ben Z. Locke, and Carl A. Taube. "The NIMH Epidemiologic Catchment Area Program." In *Community Surveys of Psychiatric Disorders*, Myrna M. Weissman, Jerome K. Myers, and Catherine E. Ross, eds., pp. 209–219. New Brunswick, NJ: Rutgers University Press, 1986.

Endicott, Jean and Robert L. Spitzer. "Use of the Research Diagnostic Criteria and Schedule for Affective Disorders and Schizophrenia to Study Affective Disorders." *American Journal of Psychiatry* 136:52–56, 1979.

Feighner, J.P., Eli Robins, S. B. Guze, R. A. Woodruff, G. Winokur, and R. Munoz. "Diagnostic Criteria for Use in Psychiatric Research." *Archives of General Psychiatry* 26:57–63, 1972.

Feinson, Marjorie Chary. "Aging and Mental Health." *Research on Aging* 7:155–174, 1985.

Frerichs, Ralph R., Carol S. Aneshensel and Virginia A. Clark. "Prevalence of Depression in Los Angeles County." *American Journal of Epidemiology* 113:691–699, 1981.

Gabennesch, Howard. "Authoritarianism as World View." *American Journal of Sociology* 77:857–875, 1972.

Gersten, Joanne C., Thomas S. Langner, Jeanne G. Eisenberg and Lida Orzek. "Child Behavior and Life Events: Undesirable Change or Change Per Se?" In *Stressful Life Events*, Barbara S. Dohrenwend and Bruce P. Dohrenwend, eds., pp. 159–170. New York: Wiley, 1974.

Glenn, Norval and Charles Weaver. "A Multivariate, Multisurvey Study of Marital Happiness." *Journal of Marriage and the Family* 40:269–282, 1978.

Goffman, Erving. *Stigma*. Englewood Cliffs, NJ: Prentice-Hall, 1963.

Gold, Philip, Frederick K. Goodwin and George P. Chrousos. "Clinical and Biochemical Manifestations of Depression: Relation to the Neurobiology of Stress (first of two parts)." *New England Journal of Medicine* 319(6,Aug 11):348–53, 1988a.

Gold, Philip W., Frederick K. Goodwin and George P. Chrousos. "Clinical and Biochemical Manifestations of Depression: Relation to the Neurobiology of Stress (second of two parts)." *New England Journal of Medicine* 319(7,Aug 18):413–20, 1988b.

Gore, Susan and Thomas W. Mangione. "Social Roles, Sex Roles, and Psychological Distress." *Journal of Health and Social Behavior* 24:330–312, 1983.

Gove, Walter R. and Michael R. Geerken. "Response Bias in Surveys of Mental Health: An Empirical Investigation. *American Journal of Sociology* 82:1289–317, 1977a.

Gove, Walter R. and Michael R. Geerken. "The Effect of Children and Employment on the Mental Health of Married Men and Women." *Social Forces* 56:66–76, 1977b.

Gove, Walter R. and Jeannette F. Tudor. "Adult Sex Roles and Mental Illness." *American Journal of Sociology* 78:812–835, 1973.

Gove, Walter R., James McCorkel, Terry Fain and Michael D. Hughes. "Response Bias in Community Surveys of Mental Health: Systematic Bias or Random Noise?" *Social Science and Medicine* 10:497–502, 1976.

Gove, Walter R., Michael M. Hughes and Carolyn B. Style. "Does Marriage Have Positive Effects on the Psychological Well-Being of the Individual?" *Journal of Health and Social Behavior* 24:122–131, 1983.

Greden, John F., Robert Gardner, Doug King, Leon Grunhaus, Bernard Carroll and Ziad Kronfol. "Dexamethasone Suppression Tests in Antidepressant Treatment of Melancholia: The Process of Normalization and Test-retest Reproducibility." *Archives of General Psychiatry* 40(May): 493–500, 1983.

Greenley, James R. "Familial Expectations, Posthospital Adjustment, and the Societal Reaction Perspective on Mental Illness." *Journal of Health and Social Behavior* 20:217–227, 1979.

Gurin, Gerald G., Joseph Veroff and Sheila Feld. *Americans View Their Mental Health*. New York: Basic Books, 1960.

Hadaway, Christopher Kirk and Wade Clark Roof. "Those Who Stay Religious Nones and Those Who Don't." *Journal for the Scientific Study of Religion* 18:194–200, 1979.

Hayes, Diane and Catherine E. Ross. "Body and Mind: The Effect of Exercise, Overweight, and Physical Health on Psychological Well-Being." *Journal of Health and Social Behavior* 27:387–400, 1986.

Herberg, Will. *Protestant, Catholic, Jew*. Rev. ed. New York: Doubleday, 1960.

Hiday, Virginia A. "View from the Front Line: Diagnosis and Treatment of Mental Health Problems Among Primary Care Physicians." *Social Psychiatry* 15:131–136, 1980.

Hiroto, Donald S. "Locus of Control and Learned Helplessness." *Journal of Experimental Psychology* 102(2):187–93, 1974.

Hirschi, Travis and Hanan C. Selvin. *Principles of Survey Analysis*. New York: Free Press, 1967.

Hodgkinson, Stephen, Robin Sherrington, Hugh Gurling, Roger Marchbanks, Stephen Reeders, Jacques Mallet, Melvin McInnis, Hannes Petursson and Jon Brynjolfsson. "Molecular Genetic Evidence for Heterogeneity in Manic Depression." *Nature* 325(Feb 26): 805–6, 1987.

Hogan, Dennis P. "The Variable Order of Events in the Life Course." *American Sociological Review* 43:573–586, 1978.

Holland, Jimmie, Joseph Masling and Donald Copley. "Mental Illness in Lower Class Normal, Obese, and Hyperobese Women." *Psychosomatic Medicine* 32:351–357, 1970.

Hollingshead, August B. and Fredrick C. Redlich. *Social Class and Mental Illness: A Community Study*. New York: Wiley, 1958.

Holmes, Thomas H. and Minoru Masuda. "Life Change and Illness Susceptibility." In *Stressful Life Events*, Barbara S. Dohrenwend and Bruce P.
Dohrenwend, eds., pp. 45–71. New York: Wiley, 1974.

Holmes, Thomas H. and Richard H. Rahe. "The Social Readjustment Rating
Scale." *Journal of Psychosomatic Research* 11:213–218, 1967.

Homans, George. *Social Behavior: It's Elementary Forms*. New York:
Harcourt Brace, 1961.

Hough, Richard L., Dianne Timbers Fairbank and A. M. Garcia. "Problems
in the Ratio Measurement of Life Stress." *Journal of Health and Social
Behavior* 17:70–82, 1976.

Hout, Michael and Andrew M. Greeley. "The Center Doesn't Hold: Church
Attendance in the United States, 1940–1984." *American Sociological
Review* 52:325–345, 1987.

Huber, Joan and Glenna Spitze. *Sex Stratification: Children, Housework,
and Jobs*. New York: Academic Press, 1983.

Hughes, Michael M. and Walter R. Gove. "Living Alone, Social Integration,
and Mental Health." *American Journal of Sociology* 87:48–74, 1981.

James, William. *The Varieties of Religious Experience*. Garden City, NY:
Doubleday, 1978.

Jasso, Guillermina and Peter H. Rossi. "Distributive Justice and Earned
Income." *American Sociological Review* 42:639–651, 1977.

Johnson, David Richard and Richard L. Meile. "Does Dimensionality Bias in
Langner's 22-Item Index Affect the Validity of Social Status Comparisons?" *Journal of Health and Social Behavior* 22:415–433, 1981.

Kamerman, Sheila B. and Alfred J. Kahn. "The Day Care Debate: A Wider
View." *The Public Interest* 54:76–93, 1979.

Kandel, Denise B., Mark Davies and Victoria H. Raveis. "The Stressfulness
of Daily Social Roles for Women: Marital, Occupational, and Household
Roles." *Journal of Health and Social Behavior* 26:64–78, 1985.

Kaplan, Howard B., Cynthia Robbins and Steven S. Martin. "Antecedents of
Psychological Distress in Young Adults: Self-rejection, Deprivation of
Social Support and Life Events." *Journal of Health and Social Behavior*
24:230–244, 1983.

Kessler, Ronald C. "A Disaggregation of the Relationship Between Socioeconomic Status and Psychological Distress." *American Sociological Review*
47:752–764, 1982.

Kessler, Ronald C. and Paul D. Cleary. "Social Class and Psychological
Distress." *American Sociological Review* 45:463–478, 1980.

Kessler, Ronald C. and Jane D. McLeod. "Sex Differences in Vulnerability to
Undesirable Life Events." *American Sociological Review* 49:620–631,
1984.

Kessler, Ronald C. and Jane D. McLeod. "Social Support and Mental Health
in Community Samples." In *Social Support and Health*, Sheldon Cohen
and S. Leonard Syme, eds. New York: Academic Press, 1985.

Kessler, Ronald C. and James A. McRae. "The Effect of Wives' Employment on the Mental Health of Married Men and Women." *American Sociological Review* 47:216–227, 1982.

Kessler, Ronald C. and Harold W. Neighbors. "A New Perspective on the Relationships Among Race, Social Class, and Psychological Distress." *Journal of Health and Social Behavior* 27:107–115, 1986.

Kittel, F., R. M. Rustin, M. Dramaix, G. DeBacker and M. Kornitzer. "Psycho-Socio-Biological Correlates of Moderate Overweight in an Industrial Population." *Journal of Psychosomatic Research* 22:145–158, 1978.

Kluckhohn, Florence Rockwood and Fred L. Stodtbeck. *Variations in Value Orientations.* Westport, CT: Greenwood, 1961.

Kluegel, James R. and Eliot R. Smith. *Beliefs About Inequality.* New York: Aldine de Gruyter, 1986.

Kobasa, Suzanne C., Salvatore R. Maddi and Sheila Courington. "Personality and Constitution as Mediators in the Stress-Illness Relationship." *Journal of Health and Social Behavior* 22:368–378, 1981.

Kohn, Melvin. "Class, Family and Schizophrenia." *Social Forces* 50:295–302, 1972.

Kohn, Melvin. "Occupational Structure and Alienation." *American Journal of Sociology* 82:111–130, 1976.

Kohn, Melvin and Carmi Schooler. "Job Conditions and Personality: A Longitudinal Assessment of Their Reciprocal Effects." *American Journal of Sociology* 87:1257–1286, 1982.

Krause, Neal and Kyriakos S. Markides. "Employment and Psychological Well-Being in Mexican American Women." *Journal of Health and Social Behavior* 26:15–26, 1985.

Kruskal, Joseph B. and Myron Wish. *Multidimensional Scaling.* Beverly Hills, CA: Sage, 1978.

Langner, Thomas S. "A Twenty-two item Screening Score of Psychiatric Symptoms Indicating Impairment." *Journal of Health and Human Behavior* 3:269–276, 1962.

LaRocco, James M., James S. House and John R. P. French. "Social Support, Occupational Stress, and Health." *Journal of Health and Social Behavior* 3:202–218, 1980.

Lazarus, Richard S. and Susan Folkman. *Stress, Appraisal, and Coping.* New York: Springer, 1984.

Leighton, D. C., J. S. Harding, D. B. Macklin, A. M. MacMillan and A. H. Leighton. *The Character of Danger: Stirling County Study,* Vol. 3. New York: Basic Books, 1963.

Lennon, Mary Clare. "The Psychological Consequences of Menopause: The Importance of Timing of a Life Stage Event." *Journal of Health and Social Behavior* 23:353–366, 1982.

Lindenthal, Jacob J., Jerome K. Myers, Max P. Pepper and Maxine S. Stern.

"Mental Status and Religious Behavior." *Journal for the Scientific Study of Religion* 22:15–37, 1970.

Link, Bruce G., Bruce P. Dohrenwend and Andrew E. Skodol. "Socioeconomic Status and Schizophrenia: Noisome Occupational Characteristics as a Risk Factor." *American Sociological Review* 51(April):242–58, 1986.

Locke, Ben A. and E. A. Gardner. "Psychiatric Disorders Among the Patients of General Practioners and Internists." *Public Health Reports* 84:167–173, 1969.

Lovell-Troy, Lawrence. "Anomia Among Employed Wives and Housewives." *Journal of Marriage and the Family* May:301–310, 1983.

McFarlane, Allan H., Geoffrey R. Norman, David L. Streiner and Ranjan G. Roy. "The Process of Social Stress: Stable, Reciprocal, and Mediating Relationships." *Journal of Health and Social Behavior* 24:160–173, 1983.

McLanahan, Sara and Julia Adams. "Parenthood and Psychological Well-Being." In *Annual Review of Sociology*, Vol. 13, W. Richard Scott and James F. Short, eds., pp. 237–257. Palo Alto, CA: Annual Reviews, 1987.

Maddox, George L., Kurt W. Back and Veronica R. Liederman. "Overweight as Social Deviance and Disability." *Journal of Health and Social Behavior* 9:287–298, 1968.

Madsen, William. *The Mexican Americans of South Texas*, 2nd ed. New York: Holt, Rinehart and Winston, 1973.

Martin, David J., Lyn Y. Abramson and Lauren B. Alloy. "Illusion of Control for Self and Others in Depressed and Nondepressed College Students." *Journal of Personality and Social Psychology* 46:125–136, 1984.

Mausner, Judith S. and Anita K. Bahn. *Epidemiology. An Introductory Text*. Philadelphia: W. B. Saunders, 1974.

Meissner, W.W. *The Paranoid Process*. New York: Jason Aronson, 1978.

Mills, C. Wright. *The Sociological Imagination*. New York: Oxford University Press, 1959.

Mirowsky, John. "Depression and Marital Power: An Equity Model." *American Journal of Sociology* 91:557–592, 1985.

Mirowsky, John. "The Psycho-Economics of Feeling Underpaid: Distributive Justice and the Earnings of Husbands and Wives." *American Journal of Sociology* 92:1404–1434, 1987.

Mirowsky, John and Catherine E. Ross. "Minority Status, Ethnic Culture, and Distress: A Comparison of Blacks, Whites, Mexicans, and Mexican-Americans." *American Journal of Sociology* 86:479–495, 1980.

Mirowsky, John and Catherine E. Ross. "Paranoia and the Structure of Powerlessness." *American Sociological Review* 48:228–239, 1983a.

Mirowsky, John and Catherine E. Ross. "The Multidimensionality of Psychopathology in a Community Sample." *American Journal of Community Psychology* 11:573–591, 1983b.

Mirowsky, John and Catherine E. Ross. "Mexican Culture and Its Emotional Contradictions." *Journal of Health and Social Behavior* 25:2–13, 1984.

Moore, Mary E., Albert J. Stunkard and Leo Srole. "Obesity, Social Class, and Mental Illness." *Journal of the American Medical Association* 181:138–142, 1962.

Mueller, D.D., W. Edwards and R. M. Yarvis. "Stressful Life Events and Psychiatric Symptomatology: Change or Undesirability?" *Journal of Health and Social Behavior* 18:307–316, 1977.

Murphy, H. B. M. "The Meaning of Symptom-Checklist Scores in Mental Health Surveys: A Testing of Multiple Hypotheses." *Social Science and Medicine* 12:67–75, 1978.

Mutran, Elizabeth and Donald G. Reitzes. "Intergenerational Support Activities and Well-Being Among the Elderly: A Convergence of Exchange and Symbolic-Interaction Perspectives." *American Sociological Review* 49: 117–130, 1984.

Myers, Jerome K., Jacob J. Lindenthal and Max P. Pepper. "Life Events and Psychiatric Impairment." *Journal of Nervous and Mental Disease* 152:149–157, 1971.

Myers, Jerome K., Jacob J. Lindenthal and Max P. Pepper. "Social Class, Life Events, and Psychiatric Symptoms: A Longitudinal Study." In *Stressful Life Events*, Bruce P. Dohrenwend and Barbara S. Dohrenwend, eds., pp. 191–205. New York: Wiley, 1974.

Myers, Jerome K., Jacob J. Lindenthal and Max P. Pepper. "Life Events, Social Integration and Psychiatric Symptomatology." *Journal of Health and Social Behavior* 16:421–427, 1975.

O'Rourke, Diane and Johnny Blair. "Improving Random Selection in Telephone Surveys." *Journal of Marketing Research* 20:428–432, 1983.

Oppenheimer, Valerie Kincade. "Demographic Influence on Female Employment and the Status of Women." In *Changing Women in a Changing Society*, Joan Huber, ed., pp. 184–199. Chicago: University of Chicago Press, 1973.

Oppenheimer, Valerie Kincade. *Work and Family: A Study in Social Demography*. New York: Academic Press, 1982.

Paykel, Eugene S. "Life Stress and Psychiatric Disorder: Applications of the Clinical Approach." In *Stressful Life Events: Their Nature and Effects*, Barbara S. Dohrenwend and Bruce P. Dohrenwend, eds., pp. 135–50. New York: Wiley, 1974.

Parsons, Talcott. "The Social Structure of the Family." In *The Family: Its Function and Destiny*, Ruth Anshen, ed., pp. 173–201. New York: Harper, 1949.

Pearlin, Leonard I. "Sex Roles and Depression." In *Life Span Developmental Psychology: Normative Life Crisis*, Nancy Datan and Leon H. Ginsberg, eds., pp. 191–208. New York: Academic Press, 1975a.

Pearlin, Leonard I. "Status Inequality and Stress in Marriage." *American Sociological Review* 40:344–357, 1975b.

Pearlin, Leonard I. and Morton A. Lieberman. "Social Sources of Emotional

Distress." In *Research in Community and Mental Health*, Vol. 1, Roberta G. Simmons, ed., pp. 217–248. Greenwich, Conn.: JAI, 1979.

Pearlin, Leonard I. and Carmi Schooler. "The Structure of Coping." *Journal of Health and Social Behavior* 19:2–21, 1978.

Pearlin, Leonard I., Morton A. Lieberman, Elizabeth G. Menaghan and Joseph T. Mullan. "The Stress Process." *Journal of Health and Social Behavior* 22:337–356, 1981.

Pedhazur, Elazar J. *Multiple Regression in Behavioral Research*, 2nd ed. New York: Holt, Rinehart, and Winston, 1982.

Peterson, Christopher. "Uncontrollability and Self-Blame in Depression: Investigation of the Paradox in a College Population." *Journal of Abnormal Psychology*, 88:620–624, 1979.

Peterson, Christopher and Martin E. P. Seligman. "Causal Explanations as a Risk Factor for Depression: Theory and Evidence." *Psychological Review* 91:347–374, 1984.

Peterson, Christopher, Stanley M. Schwartz and Martin E. P. Seligman. "Self-Blame and Depressive Symptoms." *Journal of Personality and Social Psychology* 41:253–259, 1981.

Pleck, Joseph. "Husbands' Paid Work and Family Roles: Current Research Issues." In *Research in the Interweave of Social Roles 3: Families and Jobs*, Helena Lopata and Joseph Pleck, eds., pp. 251–333. Greenwich, CT: JAI, 1983.

Preston, Samuel H. "Children and the Elderly in the U.S." *Scientific American* 251:44–49, 1984.

Prosen, Mel, David C. Clark, Martin Harrow and Jan Fawcett. "Guilt and Conscience in Major Depressive Disorders." *American Journal of Psychiatry* 140:839–844, 1983.

Radloff, Lenore. "Sex Differences in Depression: The Effects of Occupational and Marital Status." *Sex Roles* 1:249–265, 1975.

Radloff, Lenore. "The CES-D Scale: "A Self-report Depression Scale for Research in the General Population." *Applied Psychological Measurement* 1:385–401, 1977.

Renne, Karen. "Correlates of Dissatisfaction in Marriage." *Journal of Marriage and the Family* 32: 54–67, 1970.

Richardson, Stephen A. "Age and Sex Differences in Values Toward Physical Handicaps." *Journal of Health and Social Behavior* 11:207–214, 1970.

Richman, Judith. Women's Changing Work Roles and Psychological-Psychophysiological Distress. Presented at the American Sociological Association annual meeting. Boston, 1979.

Roberts, Robert E. and Stephen J. O'Keefe. "Sex Differences in Depression Reexamined." *Journal of Health and Social Behavior* 22:394–400, 1981.

Robins, Lee N., John E. Helzer, Jack L. Croughan, Janet B. W. Williams, and Robert L. Spitzer. The NIMH Diagnostic Interview Schedule (DIS). Washington, D.C., National Institute of Mental Health, 1979.

Robins, Lee N. "The Development and Characteristics of the NIMH Diagnostic Interview Schedule." In *Community Surveys of Psychiatric Disorders*, Myrna M. Weissman, Jerome K. Myers, and Catherine E. Ross, eds., pp. 403–427. New Brunswick, NJ: Rutgers University Press, 1986.

Robinson, John P. "Housework Technology and Household Work." In *Women and Household Labor*, Sarah Fenstermaker Berk, ed., pp. 53–67. Beverly Hills, CA: Sage, 1980.

Robinson, Robert V. and Wendell Bell. "Equality, Success, and Social Justice in England and the United States." *American Sociological Review* 43:125–143, 1978.

Rollins, Boyd and Harold Feldman. "Marital Satisfaction Over the Family Life Cycle." *Journal of Marriage and the Family* 32:11–28, 1970.

Rosenfield, Sarah. "Sex Differences in Depression: Do Women Always Have Higher Rates?" *Journal of Health and Social Behavior* 21:33–42, 1980.

Ross, Catherine E. and Joan Huber. "Hardship and Depression." *Journal of Health and Social Behavior* 26:312–27, 1985.

Ross, Catherine E. and Janet Lauritsen. "Public Opinion About Doctors' Pay." *American Journal of Public Health* 75:668–670, 1985.

Ross, Catherine E. and John Mirowsky. "A Comparison of Life Event Weighting Schemes: Change, Undesirability, and Effect-Proportional Indices." *Journal of Health and Social Behavior* 20:166–177, 1979.

Ross, Catherine E. and John Mirowsky. "Components of Depressed Mood in Married Men and Women: The Center for Epidemiologic Studies' Depression Scale." *American Journal of Epidemiology* 119:997–1004, 1984a.

Ross, Catherine E. and John Mirowsky. "Socially-Desirable Response and Acquiescence in a Cross-Cultural Survey of Mental Health." *Journal of Health and Social Behavior* 25:189–197, 1984b.

Ross, Catherine E. and John Mirowsky. "Normlessness, Powerlessness, and Trouble with the Law." *Criminology* 25:257–278, 1987.

Ross, Catherine E., and John Mirowsky. "Explaining the Social Patterns of Depression: Control and Problem-Solving or Support and Talking." *Journal of Health and Social Behavior* 30, 1989.

Ross, Catherine E., John Mirowsky and William C. Cockerham. "Social Class, Mexican Culture, and Fatalism: Their Effects on Psychological Distress." *American Journal of Community Psychology* 11:383–399, 1983a.

Ross, Catherine E., John Mirowsky and Joan Huber. "Dividing Work, Sharing Work, and In-Between: Marriage Patterns and Depression." *American Sociological Review* 48:809–823, 1983b.

Ross, Catherine E., John Mirowsky and Patricia Ulbrich. "Distress and the Traditional Female Role: A Comparison of Mexicans and Anglos." *American Journal of Sociology* 89:670–682, 1983c.

Rotter, Julian B. "Generalized Expectancies for Internal vs. External Control of Reinforcements." *Psychological Monographs* 80:1–28, 1966.

Rotter, Julian B. "Interpersonal Trust, Trustworthiness, and Gullibility." *American Psychologist* 35:1–7, 1980.

Ruch, Libby O. "A Multidimensional Analysis of the Concept of Life Change." *Journal of Health and Social Behavior* 18:71–83, 1977.

Russell, Dan and Edward McAuley. "Causal Attributions, Causal Dimensions, and Affective Reactions to Success and Failure." *Journal of Personality and Social Psychology* 50:1174–1185, 1986.

Schafer, Robert B. and Patricia M. Keith. "Equity and Depression Among Married Couples." *Social Psychology Quarterly* 43:430–435, 1980.

Schiffman, S.S., M. L. Reynolds and F. W. Young. *Introduction to Multidimensional Scaling: Theory, Methods, and Applications*. New York: Academic Press, 1981.

Schooler, Carmi "Social Antecedents of Adult Psychological Functioning." *American Journal of Sociology* 78:299–323, 1972.

Seeman, Melvin. "On the Meaning of Alienation." *American Sociological Review* 24:783–791, 1959.

Seeman, Melvin. "Social Learning and the Theory of Mass Society." In *Applications of a Social Learning Theory of Personality*, Julian B. Rotter, June Chance, and E. Jerry Phares, eds., pp. 395–404. New York: Holt, Rinehart, and Winston, 1972.

Seeman, Melvin. "Alienation Motifs in Contemporary Theorizing: The Hidden Continuity of Classic Themes." *Social Psychology Quarterly* 46:171–184, 1983.

Seligman, Martin E. P. *Helplessness*. San Francisco: Freeman, 1975.

Selye, Hans. *The Stress of Life*, rev. ed. New York: McGraw-Hill, 1976.

Shepelak, Norma J. and Duane F. Alwin. "Beliefs about Inequality and Perceptions of Distributive Justice." *American Sociological Review* 51:30–46, 1986.

Silverstone, Trevor J. and Thomas Solomon. "Psychiatric and Somatic Factors in the Treatment of Obesity." *Journal of Psychosomatic Research* 9:249, 1966.

Smith Tom W. A Compendium of Trends on General Social Survey Questions. National Opinion Research Center Report No. 129. Chicago: NORC, 1980.

Snider, J. G. and Charles E. Osgood, eds. *Semantic Differential Technique*. Chicago: Aldine, 1969.

Spitzer, Robert L. and Jean Endicott. *Schedule for Affective Disorders and Schizophrenia*. NY: Biometric Research Division, Evaluation Section, New York Psychiatric Institute, 1978.

Srole, Leo and Anita Kassen Fischer. "To the Editor." *Archives of General Psychiatry* 37:1424–1426, 1980.

Srole, Leo, Thomas S. Langner, S. T. Michael, M. D. Opler and T. C. Rennie. *Mental Health in the Metropolis: The Midtown Manhattan Study*, Vol. 1. New York: McGraw-Hill, 1962.

Stunkard, Albert J. and John Rush. "Dieting and Depression Reexamined." *Annals of Internal Medicine* 81:526–533, 1974.

Susser, Mervyn. *Causal Thinking in the Health Sciences: Concepts and Strategies of Epidemiology.* New York: Oxford University Press, 1973.

Tausig, Mark. "Measuring Life Events." *Journal of Health and Social Behavior* 23:52–64, 1982.

Thoits, Peggy A. "Undesirable Life Events and Psychological Distress: A Problem of Operational Confounding." *American Sociological Review* 46:97–109, 1981.

Thoits, Peggy A. "Conceptual, Methodological, and Theoretical Problems in Studying Social Support as a Buffer Against Life Stress." *Journal of Health and Social Behavior* 23:145–159, 1982.

Thoits, Peggy A. "Multiple Identities and Psychological Well-Being: A Reformulation and Test of the Social Isolation Hypothesis." *American Sociological Review* 48:174–187, 1983.

Tilly, Louise. The World Turned Upside Down: Age and Gender in Europe, 1750–1950. Presented at the American Sociological Association annual meeting. Detroit, 1983.

Tufte, Edward R. *Data Analysis for Politics and Policy.* Englewood Cliffs, NJ: Prentice-Hall, 1974.

Turner, R. Jay and Samuel Noh. "Class and Psychological Vulnerability Among Women: The Significance of Social Support and Personal Control." *Journal of Health and Social Behavior* 24:2–15, 1983.

Veroff, Joseph, Elizabeth Douvan and Richard Kulka. *The Inner American: A Self-Portrait from 1957 to 1976.* New York: Basic Books, 1981.

Vinokur, A. and M. Selzer. "Desirable versus Undesirable Life Events: Their Relationship to Stress and Mental Distress." *Journal of Personality and Social Psychology* 32:329–337, 1975.

Vonnegut, Mark. *The Eden Express.* New York: Bantam, 1975.

Waite, Linda J. "Working Wives: 1940–1960." *American Sociological Review* 41:65–80, 1976.

Waksberg, Joseph. "Sampling Methods for Random Digit Dialing." *Journal of the American Statistical Association* 73:40–46, 1978.

Walster, Elaine, G. William Walster and Ellen Berscheid. *Equity: Theory and Research.* Boston, MA: Allyn and Bacon, 1978.

Warheit, George J., Charles Holzer and John J. Schwab. "An Analysis of Social Class and Racial Differences in Depressive Symptomatology: A Community Study." *Journal of Health and Social Behavior* 4:291–299, 1973.

Weissman, Myrna M. "Advances in Psychiatric Epidemiology: Rates and Risks for Major Depression." *American Journal of Public Health* 77:445–451, 1987.

Weissman, Myrna M. and Gerald L. Klerman. "In Reply." *Archives of General Psychiatry* 37:1423–1424, 1980.

Weissman, Myrna M. and Eugene S. Paykel. *The Depressed Woman.* Chicago: University of Chicago Press, 1974.

Weissman, Myrna M. and Jerome K. Myers. "Affective Disorders in a U.S. Urban Community: The Use of Research Diagnostic Criteria in an Epidemiological Survey." *Archives of General Psychiatry* 35:1304–1311, 1978.

Weissman, Myrna M., Kenneth K. Kidd and Brigitte A. Prusoff. "Variability in Rates of Affective Disorders in Relatives of Depressed and Normal Probands." *Archives of General Psychiatry* 39(Dec):1397–1403, 1982.

Weissman, Myrna M., Elliot S. Gershon, Kenneth K. Kidd, Brigitte A. Prusoff, James F. Leckman, Eleanor Dibble, Joel Hamovit, W. Douglas Thompson, David L. Pauls and Juliet J. Guroff. "Psychiatric Disorders in the Relatives of Probands with Affective Disorders." *Archives of General Psychiatry* 41(Jan):13–21, 1984.

Wethington, Elaine and Ronald C. Kessler. "Perceived Support, Received Support, and Adjustment to Stressful Life Events." *Journal of Health and Social Behavior* 27:78–89, 1986.

Wheaton, Blair. "The Sociogenesis of Psychological Disorder: An Attributional Theory." *Journal of Health and Social Behavior* 21:100–124, 1980.

Wheaton, Blair. "Uses and Abuses of the Langner Index: A Reexamination of Findings on Psychological and Psychophysiological Distress." In *Psychosocial Epidemiology: Symptoms, Illness Behavior and Help-Seeking*, David Mechanic, ed., pp. 25–53. New Brunswick, N.J.: Rutgers University Press, 1982.

Wheaton, Blair. "Stress, Personal Coping Resources, and Psychiatric Symptoms: An Investigation of Interactive Models." *Journal of Health and Social Behavior* 24:208–229, 1983.

Wheaton, Blair. "Models for the Stress-Buffering Functions of Coping Resources." *Journal of Health and Social Behavior* 26:352–364, 1985a.

Wheaton, Blair. "Personal Resources and Mental Health." In *Research in Community and Mental Health*, James R. Greenley, ed., pp. 139–184. Greenwich, Conn.: JAI, 1985b.

Williams, Ann W., John E. Ware and Cathy A. Donald. "A Model of Mental Health, Life Events, and Social Supports Applicable to General Populations." *Journal of Health and Social Behavior* 22:324–336, 1981.

Winokur, George. *Depression: The Facts.* New York: Oxford University Press, 1981.

Young, Laura M. and Brian Powell. "The Effects of Obesity on the Clinical Judgments of Mental Health Professionals." *Journal of Health and Social Behavior* 26:233–246, 1985.

Author Index*

---

*Numbers in italics indicate page where complete reference is given.

Subject Index